THREE COUNTRIES, THREE LIVES

THREE COUNTRIES, THREE LIVES

A Doctor's Story

Lindy Rajan Cartner

ALEPH

ALEPH BOOK COMPANY
An independent publishing firm
promoted by *Rupa Publications India*.

Published in 2014 by Radcliffe Press as *And the Twain
Shall Meet: Three Countries and Three Generations, a
Doctor's Story*.

Published in India in 2023
by Aleph Book Company
7/16 Ansari Road, Daryaganj
New Delhi 110 002

ISBN: 978-93-95853-94-1

1 3 5 7 9 10 8 6 4 2

For the grandchildren
Dominic, Sebastian, India, Anika, Rhea
and
in memory of my mother,
Alice Rajan.

The only constant in life is change.

Heraclitus c. 500 BCE

CONTENTS

Part I

....

Burma

Chapter 1

A MAGICIAN'S TRICKS

Very much an unwanted child, I was born into an arranged marriage which had started to crumble from its inception. My father's parents had died when he was four and he was brought up by his three older brothers and close relatives, all living in Madras, South India. When he reached his mid-twenties, they sought a suitable bride for him. They approached my mother's parents and made what was called an offer. Her pedigree was thought to be above average. She belonged to a family which was educated and reasonably wealthy. Her father was a doctor. The skeletons in the cupboard had not produced any noteworthy scandals. So she was in considerable demand, especially as she was pleasant to look at and had a fair complexion—fair, that is, by Tamil standards, Tamils on the whole being very dark skinned. Other less important credentials were also considered, and deemed desirable. She was of adequate height, five feet two inches, buxom with good hips—necessary for childbearing—and well educated, but not so well educated as to make her husband feel threatened; my father, too, had a university degree.

It was customary for the proposal to come from the bridegroom's family. My mother was nineteen and in her second year at Judson College, Rangoon University, reading English, Logic and Geography. She had excelled in English since she was a small child and read voraciously. She had already had several offers of marriage, unbeknown to her, which her parents had turned down. It was usual for all negotiations between the parties to be carried out behind the backs of the bride and groom, and only when a firm decision was agreed would the couple be informed or, if they were lucky, be consulted. My grandmother, having returned to Burma from an unusually long trip to Madras, told my mother that a suitable groom had been found for her, and that the marriage would take place the following year when she was twenty. She was horrified. Nothing was further from her mind than marriage.

She knew that her parents were very traditional. They would not let her become a doctor because she was a woman, and when she wanted to learn to swim with her brothers, she was told this was an unhealthy activity for a girl. But she never dreamt they would foist marriage on her at such an inappropriate time, and at such an early age. Besides, her older sister Biggy's arranged marriage, eight years earlier, was a disaster.

My mother flatly refused to be married. For years, she had immersed herself in English literature, where women for the most part experienced romance and love, and chose their husbands. She considered this to be the civilised way to conduct one's affairs. Besides, she disliked Indian men intensely, Tamil men in particular. Those she had come across, mainly relatives and vicars, she found pompous, overbearing and condescending towards women. Their wives were docile, and pandered to their husbands' selfish ways. Her father and brothers were exceptional in that they were kind, unassuming and considerate, as I was to discover as I got older.

⌇

Thatha, as I called my mother's father, means 'grandfather' in Tamil. He was born in 1870 to a Hindu family in the small village of Kanandivillai on the outskirts of Tuticorin, a minor port on the south-east coast of India known to have been trading with Europe since the sixth century CE. Named Esakymuthu Gnanamuthu Viswasam, he was given a small black tattoo on his forehead to ward off evil spirits. His father was a self-taught doctor of native medicine, also famous for his tricks and spells but mainly for something else: making sterile women fertile. He was well known and admired in several of the surrounding villages.

Thatha was the eldest of four children: three boys and a girl. They went to the local Tamil school, and learned to read and write on sand before moving on to a slate, and then to a notebook. He was serious and studious, and hoped one day to become a school teacher. One of his brothers, Ponnsamy, embarrassed the family by running away from home in his teens and joining a touring circus. He became their strongman. He would lie on a bed of nails, wearing only a pair of short sheepskin pants. A board would be placed on the front of his body for an elephant to walk over. He would then stand up and show his back to the audience. There would be nail marks on his skin, but not a drop of blood. He became famous when his circus toured Europe and he claimed he performed for King Edward VII in England. He called himself Professor Ponn, and had many ladies in his life. He was an embarrassment to his family, and Thatha preferred not to talk about him.

When Thatha was sixteen, his life changed dramatically. His father wanted Thatha to follow him in his profession and go with him on his tours. When Thatha discovered how his father made sterile women fertile, and was expected to do likewise, he was shocked and filled with disgust. He ran away to a neighbouring village. Homeless and penniless, he was taken in by a poor pastor and his wife, who adopted him as their son. So moved was he by the message of the New Testament, expressed in the simple, generous and honest life of the pastor, that without any pressure on him, he asked to be baptised. After Thatha's father died he was reunited with his family, who together with several others in his home village of Kanandivillai embraced Christianity. For them, however, apart from attending church every Sunday, praying together as a family and studying the Bible, life continued as before, with their superstitions and caste prejudices.

Thatha passed the matriculation examinations and became a middle-school teacher. He discovered that he had a flair for art and drawing and was appointed as the school's art master. He was interested in organ music in church and was taught music by a missionary. Within a few years he became the church organist.

Thatha's secret wish as a boy was to become a doctor, but he knew this was not possible. His parents did not have the means to fund a university education in Madras, and the pastor he subsequently lived with was poor. Moreover, his command of English was not adequate. But as he gained confidence as a teacher, he developed a special interest in science, and his English improved as he moved among missionaries from the West. He had a glimmer of hope that his dreams might materialise. He lived frugally and saved all he could.

Madras University had been established by the British in 1857. One of the oldest universities in India, it was organised on the model of London University. The diploma course in medicine was open to Indians, and led to the licentiate in medical practice. It was a shortened version of the MBBS, the latter not being available to Indians such as he. But there was a problem. The maximum age allowed at entry was twenty-five and he would be twenty-six at enrolment. Even then a man of great integrity, he was faced with a dilemma. Should he state his year of birth as 1871 and not 1870, so as to appear a year younger? Or should he give up any idea of becoming a doctor? Encouraged by his friends and family, who said many Indians did not really know their exact date of birth, and besides, no one really cared, he stated his year of birth as 1871, and was accepted to study medicine. From then on, his date of birth on all documents was stated as 1871. We came to know this only after his death, from one of his sons: Samson, the only one he had confided in. A devout Christian, Thatha carried this burden of guilt all his life.

When Thatha was in medical school, his mother wished him to be married. His pastor found him a suitable bride, a Christian girl barely fifteen years old, the daughter of a catechist. She was finishing high school, and was called Annie Bakkiam. He saw her for the first time at the altar. It was to be the happiest of marriages and lasted forty-one years, until her death in 1938. Ten children were born to them in seventeen years, the first a stillborn daughter and lastly, twin boys: six sons and four daughters in all. Eight survived into adulthood.

When Thatha qualified, just before the turn of the century, India and Burma were administered together by the British. He applied to work for the British government, and volunteered to go to the northern states of Burma where plague was endemic. It was difficult to get doctors of any nationality to work there. The area was rich in minerals and precious stones and the government was keen to open up the area for prospectors, but the presence of plague inhibited them.

Before Thatha left India, he was asked to change his

surname to one which his British superiors would find more pronounceable. He readily agreed. So Viswasam was anglicised to Wason, pronounced 'Wahson'. This was the name by which his children would be known permanently. He reverted to his original name on retirement.

Thatha and Paati (Tamil for grandmother) arrived in Rangoon by steamer from Madras in the year 1900 and proceeded to Myinmu, their destination, by boat and then by palanquin and on horseback. Four men were hired to carry Paati and the luggage in a palanquin, while Thatha rode ahead on horseback, to make arrangements for accommodation and food in the villages along the way. On one exceptionally hot day, while passing a stream, Paati asked the palanquin bearers to put her down for a drink. The banks were muddy and slippery and, wondering how to get to the water, she saw a partly submerged log and stepped on to it to get to the water's edge. She stooped to get a handful of water, and the log started to move. She realised she was standing on an enormous python. Terrified, she stepped off it and struggled through the mud, shouting for the palanquin bearers. When they saw the python, they fled and were never seen again. The python slowly slithered away and showed no interest in her. She picked up some of her belongings and kept walking on the dirt track towards the next village. After a few hours, she saw her husband riding towards her. As the palanquin had not arrived, he had become worried and had come in search of her. New bearers were found and sent to retrieve the palanquin and luggage. The following day they continued on their journey.

Paati was a small, serious, fairly plain, and placid woman. At seventeen, she gave birth to a stillborn daughter. A year later she had another girl who survived, as did the following eight children, all of whom were given English first names: royal, biblical, or literary, perhaps out of deference to the ruling race. Their second names would be Indian. This was common practice among Indian Christians. My mother was called Alice Navamani (nine jewels). My aunts and uncles were Rosalind, Davis, Edward, Samson, Jessica, Thomas, Alfred, and Henry. The last two were twins. Henry died in infancy, and my mother always maintained that it was due to neglect. Paati was so exhausted and fed up with having so many children, that the less robust of the twins was allowed to fade away.

The children had a strict Christian upbringing along Victorian lines, and photographs taken at that time show them in Western dress. The girls changed to saris in their mid-teens; these were considered to be more modest as the legs were covered. The children obeyed their parents and were loyal to them, but were not particularly close to them. Arguments were between the children, and never with their parents. Teenage and menopausal tantrums were not part of Indian culture. As a young girl, my mother was quiet and reserved. Being a middle child, she was hardly noticed and was always immersed in her books. She was a voracious reader and devoured anything she could lay her hands on. Her school encouraged her to read Dickens, Austen, and Scott. George Eliot was a favourite and later John Galsworthy; she identified herself with Irene in *The Forsyte Saga*. Virginia Woolf and the Bloomsbury set were discovered later and much admired. Her explosive temper, which manifested in her early thirties, was surprisingly quiescent during her youth. She was deeply religious. No one would have believed that she would one day declare that she had been an atheist for most of her life.

Chapter 2

A PROTEST IN VAIN

Thatha was a poor man when he went to Burma, and his title was Sub-assistant Surgeon. He was required to work within his competence, which meant he had to deal with everything that came his way: duties as a general practitioner, assisting the local midwives with difficult births and carrying out minor surgery—sometimes not so minor—using chloroform. A considerable part of his time was spent going to the outlying areas, to inoculate the population against plague, which was endemic in the region. He was often away for several days at a time, and his wife and children saw little of him. He was an able rider and would go on horseback with an assistant.

Thatha was attached to a small hospital. He was required to be on call twenty-four hours a day and was given a house near the hospital. His salary was modest, but he was allowed unlimited private practice. Most of his patients were very poor, and he rarely charged them. He was a serious man, fierce in appearance, with an impressive moustache, but he was a kind man, very conscientious and hardworking, and considerate of women. Grateful patients would bring him sacks of rice and wheat, eggs, fish, prawns, chickens, vegetables, even a goat. The better-off ones would try to pay sometimes with imported foods, such as tinned butter or jam, which were readily available in the bigger towns. These were regarded as great luxuries. My mother remembers one room in the house filled to the roof with unopened tins of Huntley and Palmer biscuits. They seldom had to buy food, even though the family was ever enlarging. At Christmas, local grandees would present them with land, horses, even firearms. This was considered normal practice.

Until the age of eight or nine, the children had little formal education. Then they were sent to Christian boarding schools in nearby towns. Born on a train between Prome and Rangoon, my mother went to St Michael's School in Maymyo, a flourishing hill station. By the time she left for school her parents were quite affluent, but extremely frugal. The school had four categories of boarders: first, second, third and Parlour, the latter enjoying the best food and lifestyle and comprising the children of Europeans or of the local rich. Third-class boarders were at the bottom of the heap and were invariably poor or of mixed race, such as Anglo-Burmese orphans. My mother was a second-class boarder, not because her father could not afford anything better but because he regarded anything other than mere necessities to be a waste of money. 'Mere waste of money' was a phrase I was to hear over and over again from him, with 'mere' pronounced 'MEERR'!

The children were fluent in three languages: English, Tamil and Burmese. Prayers were said in Tamil before every meal and at bedtime. Relays of servants were imported from Thatha's village near Tuticorin. Though my mother and her siblings were born and brought up in Burma, and lived there even as adults, their parents ensured that they regarded India as home. Visits to India were frequent. It was just as well, as there was much hostility towards Indians from the Burmese. My grandmother, who could speak only Tamil when she arrived in Burma, soon became fluent in English and Burmese but spoke them with a strong Tamil accent. From time to time, she and Thatha would encounter visiting British folk: civil servants, missionaries, and medical officers.

Of these it was the British officers of the Indian Civil Service who most impressed Thatha. They were men of the highest calibre, often very young. They were educated in the best schools in Britain, and well prepared before they left for India. They were admired for their diligence and hard work, their competence and impartiality in settling local disputes, and their ability to withstand the harsh environment they encountered. It was a matter of much pride to Thatha, that his wife could converse with them, and as her confidence grew she was able to entertain them to a meal. Paati later became interested in small business ventures and by the time Thatha retired she was trading successfully in several commodities, from fowls to firearms and haricot beans to horses. In this way she steadily added to the family coffers. By the time they retired to Madras nearly thirty years later, they were very wealthy.

My parents were married in May 1928 in Madras, May being a favourite month for marriages despite the temperature hovering around 110°F. My father's name was Daniel Swamidas Thyagarajan, called Thyagu by family and friends, including my mother, but she disliked his surname and insisted that it be shortened to Rajan. And thus it was. He was twenty-seven, seven years older than my mother, who was still at university in Rangoon. Of reasonable appearance, slight in build, and as light skinned as she was, he was a history graduate from Madras University, and had become an accountant. My mother neither liked nor disliked him, but she did find him irritating. Her objection to both marriage and my father was overruled. Her parents knew what was best for her, and should she refuse altogether, they made it clear to her, they would cease to support her financially at university. They said it was normal for young women to be apprehensive about marriage and to postpone it for as long as was possible, but they were certain that she would develop affection for my father and be contented. For it was contentment which was regarded as more important than happiness.

Once he had seen my mother, my father was very keen to marry her and told her he had developed a great attraction and affection for her and that she would come to reciprocate his feelings. But it did not happen. Emotionally, they could not connect. My sister and I did not ever feel able to ask my mother why she asked my father to leave after fifteen years of marriage. Incompatibility is not uncommon in arranged marriages, but the two parties somehow come to terms with it, and remain with each other. Divorce was unheard of, and living apart was considered shameful for the entire family. Decades later, I asked Aunt Jessie, my mother's younger sister to whom I had become very close, why my parents' marriage had failed. She smiled and said, 'Your mother simply would not adjust. Your father was a good man.' That was the important word. Adjust. How many times have I heard this word, in relation to arranged marriages? 'You adjust a little here, and you adjust a little there, and he does the same and you get to like each other, and if you are lucky, you may even fall in love and love each other till death.' As Mark Tully, the

English broadcaster and journalist states, in India, unlike in the West, love and sex come after marriage, not before. And perhaps that is why so many of them are successful. My own view is that Indian women do most of the adjusting and compromising, and their tolerance and forbearance is formidable.

My mother's abhorrence of an arranged marriage was, to a large extent, influenced by the plight of her older sister Biggy, who was very different to her. My mother was closer to Biggy than anyone else in her family. Jolly and an extrovert, Biggy was not interested in further education. Given to reading romantic novels of the *Mills and Boon* variety, she longed to be married, even at eighteen. She was plump, buxom and bonny, and even fairer than my mother. Offers for her hand were numerous, and my grandparents finally accepted a tall, dark, handsome, and extremely charming and clever headmaster of a boys' school in Rangoon. He was not Tamil, but came from the neighbouring state of Kerala. Malayalam was his mother tongue, but he was fluent in Tamil. He was a Christian, and though not from Tamil Nadu, was chosen as he was considered to be superior to the other suitors. And he was persistent in asking for Biggy's hand. Biggy was ecstatic. This was her golden prince, but not for long. He turned out to be a dreadful man, a drunkard, and an adulterer; he subjected his wife to terrifying violence, and when he broke a stone rolling pin on Biggy's head, my grandfather took matters in hand and started divorce proceedings, much to Biggy's dismay as she was steadfastly loyal to her husband. She then announced she was expecting her fifth child. Her husband wept and pleaded with Thatha to call off the proceedings, promising he would mend his ways. Thatha reluctantly agreed. The baby was a girl and Thatha asked that she be named Irene, which means peace. Another son was born two years later. Peace came to Biggy only when she died at the age of forty-one. She bled to death during a hysterectomy at Rangoon's General Hospital. I was five at the time, and I remember the funeral well because it was the only time I saw my mother weep. I also remember nineteen-year-old Denis, Biggy's eldest son, at the graveside, sobbing and begging for the coffin to be opened, for one last look at his mother, to whom he was utterly devoted as she was to him. Denis loathed his father and a few years later permanently severed all connections with him and stopped using his surname.

Like the other houses in the street, Biggy's rented house had very little front garden. The comings and goings of the neighbours were common knowledge. In the house opposite there lived a lodger, a Mr Naidu, a Telegu and a single man. Tall and well built, he was gentle and kindly, fond of children. Biggy's other boys, Willie, Bertie and Michael, were a wild bunch and played in the street, much to their mother's dismay. They soon made friends with Mr Naidu. When we visited Biggy, Anne and I used to be taken by our cousins to see him. We had to climb up some very steep steps to his flat, with me usually sitting on Denis's shoulders. He always had sweets and little gifts for us. He had become friends with Biggy and her husband, and later with my parents. He was generous to a fault, bringing with him chocolates, fruit and gifts for the adults. He asked us to call him Cheena, as that was what his two brothers called him. His parents were dead. He worked as a timber passer in Burma's teak industry and was wealthy. One day he told us he was no longer Mr Naidu but Mr P. R. Stanislaus, P and R standing for Philip and Raymond. He had converted to Catholicism, and these names had been chosen by his priest. Cheena was aware of my mother's and Biggy's unhappy marriages. A few years later when Jessie, their youngest sister, reached marriageable age, it was hoped she would marry Cheena, even though he was a Catholic. Thatha and Paati approached him but he declined.

Biggy's death and the war changed our lives and we lost track of Cheena, but he was to come back into our lives some years later.

After her marriage, my mother returned to Judson College to continue her studies. A year later she graduated and joined my father, who was working as an auditor in a small firm in Rangoon. He was often away on tour.

Thatha retired from government service in 1922 and after a few years retired to Madras and lived in rented accommodation. At his retirement, he had been awarded a 'Certificate of Good Service' and a gold watch by the Lieutenant Governor of Burma, in recognition of his work and in particular of his efforts to contain and eradicate plague. This certificate was framed and hung in their drawing room. It now hangs in mine.

Thatha had made detailed plans to build two houses on a substantial plot of land he had bought in a sparsely populated suburb of Madras, called Mambalam, part of a larger area called T'Nagar, which was dominated by Brahmins. This was a brave move by him, a non-Brahmin, as Brahmins had their own form of apartheid. He built a street off the wide main road named after Sir Mohammed Usman, a Muslim philanthropist. The local council named this street Wason Street, after my grandfather. Subsequently two adjacent streets were built and called after Gandhi and Nehru. The first two houses built on Wason Street belonged to Thatha: one palatial, called Annie Lodge, after Paati, and the other smaller, called Neik Bahn ('Heaven on Earth' in Burmese). Both were in the same compound. They chose to live in the larger house; the smaller was rented to a dysfunctional Brahmin family. Using a water diviner, a well was sunk between the two houses, providing an abundant supply of clear water. Electricity was brought to the area, though gas was unknown. Cooking was done by servants in the kitchen, on a range built with mud and using firewood. My grandmother always maintained that food cooked over firewood tasted better than that cooked using kerosene oil, the alternative. Over the next fifteen years more houses, no two of them alike, were built on the street, all by Brahmins. They were prepared to live near us because my grandfather was a doctor and wealthy. Until his death in 1960, they used him as their family doctor. He never charged them, and they never offered to pay.

⌣

Two years after her marriage, my mother decided to get a licentiate in teaching. She did the one-year course in Madras, and lived with her parents. One night when her parents thought she was sleeping she overheard her mother say to her father, 'It was a *mahathapoo*, a grave mistake, when we got Alice married.' My grandfather did not reply. That there was no sign of a baby was something else which worried them.

My mother returned to Burma having obtained a teaching

qualification, and joined my father in Mogok, in northern Burma. A year later, in May 1932, my grandparents received a telegram: 'Alice had a baby girl on 18 May. Both well.' They were astonished and delighted. They did not even know she was pregnant. Paati took the first boat to Rangoon, and then went by train to Mogok. Boats plied three times a week between Madras and Rangoon, and reservations were not required. It was similar to getting a bus, if one was prepared to rough it out on the deck. Thatha thought booking a berth in a cabin was a mere waste of money.

It was and still is usual practice for an Indian woman to go to her parent's house to have her baby. My mother was roundly reprimanded for breaking with tradition. She was urged to return to Madras a few weeks later with Paati and the bright-eyed lively baby. My mother agreed. My father was probably disappointed the baby was not a son. She was given a single name: Anne.

My mother was very relieved to leave the rented house in Mogok. It was a large dilapidated wooden structure, in a spacious unkempt garden. She was neither nervous nor superstitious, but said it was the only time in her life that she felt a house was haunted. Doors and windows would shut of their own accord, and she and my father would hear heavy breathing, even though they were the only occupants. She felt conscious of being surrounded by something evil. My father was even more terrified than my mother. When she told her midwife that she experienced these feelings, the midwife said she too had felt uneasy, and suggested they leave the house as soon as possible. She added that the house used to stand empty for long periods; tenants would not stay, as they too had had similar experiences.

The journey across the Bay of Bengal was always a trial, because the crossing was invariably rough and seasickness was a problem. My grandparents doted on the baby. The foundations of the two houses had been laid, and a hut was constructed on the premises, so that my grandparents, my mother and the baby could spend occasional days at the building site. It was always very hot, and Anne would lie naked on a piece of coconut thatch while my mother read.

Anne was an exceptionally bright child. She was light skinned like her parents and resembled her father. Milestones came early.

She walked at nine months, and spoke fluent Tamil and English by eighteen months: Tamil to her grandparents and the ayah; English English to her parents.

The marriage, however, did not improve.

On her return to Rangoon and my father, my mother was appointed to Girls' High School, Kemmendine, to teach English as a foreign language to high school students. It was the beginning of an interest in, and a love of, the teaching of English. The school had been founded by American Baptist missionaries. The head was an American, but most of the teachers were either Burmese or Karen Christians. My mother was one of two Indians. Most of the pupils were Burmese and Buddhists.

My mother was a gifted teacher. Anyone who has taught English to children or adults for whom it is not their mother tongue will know only too well what a challenge and frustration it is. Spellings, pronunciation, idioms—all defy defy logic. Nevertheless, she thoroughly enjoyed her work and had great rapport with her pupils, and it helped that she could speak Burmese fluently. Leaving her baby with a Karen nanny was an accepted norm, and Biggy would arrive unannounced to ensure that her niece was well looked after.

My mother was fascinated by her little daughter and got much pleasure from her. A daughter was what she had wanted, not a son. Her wish for a daughter surprised her family and friends, and even my father, as in India it is a boy that is desired, especially as a firstborn. This is particularly so among Hindus, because it is the duty of the son to look after his parents in their old age and to light his father's funeral pyre. Furthermore, it is he who brings in the dowry at his marriage. This is used to fund his sisters' dowries and help to sustain his parents in old age. They feel more comfortable living in their sons' houses, not their daughters'.

Disillusionment in her marriage led to my mother's declining interest in her faith and religion. And to my grandmother's alarm, Anne had not been baptised. To make matters worse, Anne's ears had not been pierced, the mandatory custom before a girl's first birthday.

'It is barbaric,' my mother announced, 'to make holes in a child's body to string ornaments.' Anne's ears were never pierced.

Anne had started to read in English after her second birthday. There were no Tamil books in the house and my mother, an Anglophile, taught her English nursery rhymes and introduced her to books, poems and characters that middle-class English children were familiar with. Pooh Bear, Humpty Dumpty, and Peter Rabbit became household names. Anne had little in common with her Tamil cousins, but they did share Bible stories. My grandparents, who visited my parents often, were much taken with Anne's great curiosity and progress, and declared she was by far the cleverest of their grandchildren. They doted on her.

When Anne was nearly three, my mother, much to her dismay, became pregnant again. She admitted that Anne was a good thing and had brought her much happiness. Anne's vitality was a great joy to her, but she definitely did not want another child. She was not sure the marriage would survive.

My father became increasingly perplexed by my mother's attitude towards him. He provided adequately for her and was pleasant and kind to her, even though she spent too much time reading English books, leaving household chores and cooking to the servants. He could not understand what else was required to lift her mood. He did smoke a little and drink an odd tot of toddy, which she disapproved of, but these were minor matters. He was away from our home in Rangoon often, on auditing assignments. Perhaps this absence more than anything else held the marriage together and free from rancour and overt disharmony.

Chapter 3

AN AVIATOR'S NAME

I was born on 16 October 1935 in the Dufferin Hospital, Rangoon. Darker skinned than my sister and healthy, I was still considered 'fair' by Tamil standards. Relatives said I was vellai (white), but Anne was *poothu* (new). Indians are obsessed by skin colour; it was more desirable to be new. My mother was greatly relieved that her baby was another girl. No one this time commiserated with her, as it was now well known that she had a strong preference for girls. My mother called me Lindy after the American aviator Charles Lindbergh, whom she greatly admired. Throughout her life, my mother had heroes and heroines of all nationalities and in all walks of life, usually Europeans. Dag Hammarskjöld, one time secretary-general of the United Nations, was another such hero.

When I was four months old, she went back to work. Teaching fulfilled her more than anything else. It also gave her an interest outside the house and brought her new and lasting friendships. Anne went to nursery school and I was looked after by an Indian ayah, called Annathai, barely thirteen years old. There was also a maid, a cook, and a gardener. The maid was required to supervise my ayah, who did not last long as I sustained a cut on my forehead while she was bathing me in a zinc tub. A Karen nanny was then employed, and this time the Tamil cook was dismissed because he was taking an unhealthy interest in her. Biggy continued her frequent visits to our house and did not approve of my mother going to work.

When I was fourteen months old my grandparents visited us and managed to persuade my mother to have Anne and me christened. This was arranged at Holy Trinity Cathedral, Rangoon, which we regularly attended. We both walked to the font during the service, causing much amusement to the congregation as children are usually christened as small babies, long before they can walk. A proper name had to be found for me. My mother decided on

Rosalind. It was long for Lindy and was also Biggy's name.

'What about second and third names?' said Paati.

'They are unnecessary,' said my mother. My father agreed.

In our teens, Anne and I complained to our mother that we would have preferred to have had Indian names.

'Don't be so silly,' she said. 'English names are so much nicer. Look at Thatha's dreadful names.'

My mother had developed a lifelong interest in photography. She bought a second-hand Rolleicord camera and had much pleasure in taking pictures of us and other small children. She had her camera with her wherever she went, usually in her shan bag, a cloth bag worn slung over the shoulder.

When I was two my mother became seriously ill, and a few days later, Anne also developed a fever. Both were admitted to hospital and nursed in adjoining beds. Typhoid was diagnosed, and neither of them was expected to survive. But as my mother improved, Anne became steadily worse and was in a coma for several days. This was the pre-antibiotic era, and the sulpha group of drugs was not always effective. Anne did recover, but had lost the ability to walk and talk. She could recognise her parents and relate to them but that was all. After much perseverance on my mother's part, she learned to walk and talk again, and eventually relearned to read and write, but the sparkle had gone out of her and her intelligence had declined significantly. She had been the star of our extended family, but she no longer occupied centre stage. This now passed to me. 'Isn't Lindy clever,' they would say. Clever I was, but I would often be reminded by my mother that I was not as clever as Anne had been. The change in her greatly affected my mother. She would try to be patient, but she would also become frustrated and angry. Her rages and violence in the form of shouting, throwing things, and hitting us had begun.

Some months later a telegram arrived to say that Paati, my grandmother, was seriously ill. Four years earlier she had been confirmed as diabetic. My grandfather had made the diagnosis when he noticed that when she used their squatting style lavatory, it was visited by a line of large black ants suggesting that there was sugar in her urine. Her urine was examined and this was confirmed. It was the pre-insulin era, and she was inadequately controlled with diet. She developed a tooth abscess which led to blood poisoning. She went into a coma. So her children were summoned by telegram. My mother arranged to leave Rangoon on the next boat for Madras, but another telegram came to say Paati had died and was being buried the same day, as was the custom in Madras, because of the heat and poor mortuary facilities. My grandfather was inconsolable. Twelve years older than her, he had not expected to become a widower and besides, especially since retirement, he had come to rely on her more and more. They still had four unmarried children. Eddie, the eldest son and a doctor, had had a successful arranged marriage to a beautiful girl from Tuticorin and was the father of three sons. Samson, the next son, had returned from Germany after his studies and continued to live in Annie Lodge. Thomas, younger than my mother and older than Jessie, was going seriously mad. Refusing to study after school, he had become interested in the cult of black magic and would lock himself up in his room 'doing experiments'. Alfred, the youngest son and favourite uncle, also a doctor, would have to be found a wife. Jessie, a teacher, lived with my grandparents. She would now take over the running of the household, but a suitable boy had to be found for her. My grandfather felt completely out of his depth.

After a few months, relatives of his generation who visited him urged him to remarry. Such suggestions were rebuffed with disgust and anger. Remarriage of Indian widowers is the norm, and usually takes place after the first year. A younger wife is chosen, but often one who has been left on the shelf. This is because she is ugly or dark-skinned, or cannot command a dowry. Sometimes, it is because she has been abandoned by her husband.

For my grandfather, there was never any question of remarriage.

*

Over the next year, Thatha became increasingly concerned about Jessie's single state. He made a few visits to Tuticorin, where he originally came from, to find suitable Christian men. He did not find any. He asked Biggy to come from Rangoon and join in the search. A very personable, handsome man was recommended from Chingleput, a town thirty-five miles from Madras. Thatha and

Biggy went to see him and considered him suitable. He came to meet Jessie. They agreed to marry and the wedding date was fixed. Biggy returned to Rangoon and gave my mother the news. The bridegroom was called Simpson Rajarathnam, a schoolteacher in a Christian school on a modest salary. My grandfather did not pay a dowry for any of his daughters nor did he take one for any of his sons. This was contrary to usual practice in our community.

Anne and I were asked to be bridesmaids, or flower girls as they are called in India. I was four and Anne, eight. With Biggy and her two daughters, Daisy and Irene, we sailed for Madras two weeks before the wedding. My mother made some excuse and did not go with us. She had developed a distaste for weddings, a most un-Indian characteristic. This later extended to funerals as well, almost certainly because she did not want to meet any relatives, most of whom she loathed—especially the men, whom she regarded as arch gossips.

Annie Lodge had been completed several years earlier and the house and garden were a child's delight. The trees had all matured and were fruiting heavily: coconuts, guavas, pomegranates, mangoes, papayas, bananas, gooseberries, and a host of others. The house was huge, with terraces and verandahs everywhere. As Alice's children, we were cosseted and spoilt.

Anne and I were measured by the family tailor for white, low-waisted, short-sleeved satin dresses and matching hair bands with rosettes. White satin shoes, imported from England, had already been bought in Rangoon where they were readily available. My mother insisted we wore shoes made in England.

Jessie Aunty (in Indian languages the name comes first, and even when we spoke in English we often used this form) wore a white and gold silk sari with a white net veil. She kept her eyes down and looked sad throughout the wedding, as Indian brides do. But secretly she was very pleased with the choice of husband. Simpson Uncle, in a Western-style suit and tie, looked exceedingly handsome. Theirs was a long and happy marriage but blighted by poverty as schoolteachers were very poorly paid. Three daughters were born to them. Simpson Uncle would have liked a son, but felt very blessed by his girls: Padmini, Vatsala, and Indra. They grew up into lovely women and married fine young men.

Young as I was at the time of the wedding, an impression that remained with me was how cruelly even the best of people could treat their servants and that it happened in my own family. I saw my grandfather hitting one of the male servants, a middle-aged man, for not carrying out an instruction. Indian servants were generally regarded as part of the family, and as physical chastisement was often meted out to children, it was regarded as quite proper to do the same to servants. But it upset me, and I would often think about it.

Samson Uncle continued to live in Annie Lodge, but that was no consolation as he remained unemployed and unmarried and spent a lot of time doing errands for the Holy Fathers at Loyola College, a Catholic institution nearby. It was the servants who catered to Thatha's needs. A new servant had been imported from Tuticorin, a friendly, cheerful boy called Velu. Pleasant to look at, fair skinned, and confident, he wasn't quite like a servant. Only about thirteen years old, he was made the deputy cook.

Chapter 4

THE WAR ARRIVES

War was declared shortly before my fourth birthday. I was vaguely aware of it because the adults spoke openly about it in front of the children, and my mother spent even more time listening to the radio. She had acquired her faultless, nearly accentless English from listening to the BBC for hours, day after day. She said we were on the side of the British, and she expected Indians to make a substantial contribution to the war effort, as they had done in the First World War. We had already heard about Germany, because Samson Uncle had spent a year there as a postgraduate student studying engineering. He had told us many stories, all complimentary, about that country. Now it was the enemy. He had spent three years before that at Manchester University. He was the brightest of his siblings, with a flair for mathematics and his father did something unheard of in the family: he sent him to study in England, a country we were in awe of, and among Englishmen of whom we were in even greater awe. That Thatha, this once poor schoolteacher who learned to read and write on the sand and on a slate, should actually have the money and courage to do this would at one time have been unthinkable.

The entry of Japan into the war changed our lives forever.

Since I was three I had been attending Lady Paw Tun's Kindergarten School and Anne was at the Rangoon Diocesan School for Girls. It was anticipated that sooner rather than later Rangoon would be a target, and in late 1941, the schools had started closing. My mother arranged for Anne, me, and Biggy's two youngest children, Irene and Michael, to go and stay in Pyapon, a nearby town, where her brother Eddie, a family doctor, lived with his family. Biggy had died in July that year and the children lived with their father. He wanted his youngest children to be shielded from the bombing likely to happen any day. I could not bear to be parted from my mother and begged her not to send us away.

She said it was for our safety, and it would be for a short time only, but I would not be consoled. Early in December my mother took the four of us to Pyapon, and left us there indefinitely. Eddie Uncle was a kind, warmhearted man, quite different from his wife Violet, who was reserved and did not show her feelings. But she was considered to be the perfect wife all the same. Beautiful, quiet, and demure, she had produced three sons. Eddie Uncle adored her. She treated her three boys, Edwin, Tom, and Ernest, differently from us, especially when it came to food, always giving them the tidbits and extras in between meal times. The seven of us fought with each other all the time, and she would always take the side of her boys. Two weeks later, my mother came to visit us for the day. I refused to talk to her, sat on the outside verandah, and cried all day. But she left us behind and returned to Rangoon.

On 23 December 1941, Rangoon was heavily bombed by the Japanese and then again on Christmas Day. There were many casualties, dead and wounded. The servants, Alfred Uncle (now a newly qualified doctor), male cousins and my father set about building an air-raid shelter on a *maidan*, across the road from 99 Garden Street, Kemmendine, where we lived. Supervised by my mother, they excavated a slightly curved ditch about fifteen feet long, six feet wide and five feet deep. There was an entrance and an exit with steps cut into the mud. Thatch mats were placed on the floor, with dhurries, cushions and rugs. Boxes with a small supply of food and water were placed in the trench. Wooden planks were laid across to make a roof and camouflaged with mud, branches, and plants.

Rangoon was being bombed night and day, and my parents were worried that it would be cut off from Pyapon, perhaps for years—a fate worse than Anne and me being exposed to the bombing. We were delirious with happiness when we were brought back to Rangoon.

Eddie and his family, when they tried to leave Burma two months later, found it was too late. They stayed in Pyapon throughout the Japanese occupation and we did not see them again for four years. When the Japanese arrived in Pyapon, Eddie was summoned by the army's commanding officer and asked where his loyalty lay. He told them he was a doctor, was neutral and would continue to treat patients regardless of who they were. This was acceptable to the CO but on one condition: Eddie was to witness public executions and certify death.

He found this extremely difficult, but agreed as this was the only way he and his family would stay together and survive.

To Anne and me, the trench in Kemmendine was a novelty and an adventure. We would drag the reluctant nanny into it to play with us. When we heard the siren, we were the first to rush into the trench. We were not afraid. On one occasion, my mother was sitting at the entrance to the trench looking out, and she saw a plane in the sky. It had been shot, had caught fire, and was rapidly spiralling downwards. She ran out of the trench, towards the house, screaming, 'Camera, camera.' My father was shouting, 'Get back, get back.' By the time she got back from the house with her camera, the plane had crashed onto the far side of the *maidan*.

When Anne and I returned to Rangoon in January 1942, we were perplexed at my mother's disappearance for long periods during the day. We knew she was not at school. The schools had all closed and some had disappeared altogether, such as my school, which was now a heap of rubble. Telling us to be good, she would drive away cheerfully in the little second-hand soft-top Fiat she had bought the previous year when my father was on one of his auditing tours. He strongly disapproved of it and of her driving it. He was embarrassed. Indian women did not drive cars. When my father was away, she would drive Anne and me along the Kokine lake on moonlit nights.

My mother had become a despatch rider, working for the British government, taking messages from department to department. Some of these were highly confidential and urgent, and she never discussed this even after the war. My father strongly disapproved, but as usual she took no notice of his views. On a few occasions, she had been stopped in the middle of an air raid and reprimanded by a warden for not taking refuge in a public air-raid shelter. Friends and relatives thought she was irresponsible doing this type of dangerous work when she had two young children.

The fall of Singapore to the Japanese on 11 February 1942 made it inevitable that Rangoon would follow. My parents were advised to leave and go to India. From confidential information, to which my mother had access, she was aware that the Bay of Bengal, which ships had to cross to get to Madras, was now a dangerous area. She did not consider the land route an option. She was confident that very soon reinforcements would arrive, and the British would throw the Japanese out of Burma. She had no wish to live in India. She would often say that Burma was her country, not India. My father's view on the matter was quite different. He wanted us to leave for India.

As the sense of panic in Rangoon grew, my parents decided to move up the Irrawaddy river to a town called Pakkoku, and live there till the war was over. A house was found for us to rent. There would be seven of us: our family of four and Biggy's three youngest children. Her three eldest sons remained with their father; the four of them eventually trekked to India and survived. Several trunks were hastily packed with clothes, books, and cooking utensils. Anne and I were allowed a doll each, and I was allowed to take my yellow Sunday School bonnet provided I wore it or carried it myself lest it got squashed. Everything else in the house was given to the servants. The Fiat fetched almost nothing.

We were required to be at the jetty before dark, and our ship was to slip away during the darkness. That night the jetty was bombed and several ships were sunk, but our ship was unscathed and left quietly after the air raid. It was a slow journey, and after a few days we disembarked at a muddy jetty in Pakkoku. My bonnet fell off onto the ground and inadvertently a barefoot coolie stepped on it and squashed it. I was inconsolable. It was not usual for Indian children to wear bonnets or hats, but my mother had pandered to my vanity when we were in the 'English' shop one day buying shoes.

In Pakkoku we had rented a large shabby wooden house, sparsely furnished but adequate in the circumstances. We children slept on mats on the floor. The Burmese neighbours were accepting and friendly, and a maid who cleaned and cooked was hired. The medium of instruction in the local schools was Burmese, so we did not go to school. My mother insisted that we did some reading every day, but otherwise our time was spent roaming about on bicycles and climbing trees. Life was very enjoyable. But it was not to last. Early in March, Rangoon fell to the Japanese and it was anticipated that they would start moving up the Irrawaddy. My parents decided to leave Pakkoku for Mandalay, a much larger town, again by steamer. The journey was in a very overcrowded boat and took nearly two days. There was only seating accommodation, and young children like myself slept on our parents' laps. There were several Chinese on board, and I was fascinated by the tiny bound feet of their women.

In Mandalay we were met by a young lad of about eighteen, a contact of our neighbours in Pakkoku, and taken to a house in a row of six. He and his family owned some of these, and they were happy to rent us one. It was even more basic than the previous house in Pakkoku. It had a small bathroom, and an outside lavatory. At the far end of the compound was a deep, well-built air-raid shelter with one entrance. The roof had wooden beams, reinforced with corrugated tin and covered with earth. It had not been used by the previous tenants, as there had not been a need.

As in Pakkoku, it was easy to find servants, and a maid had been hired to clean the house and look after the younger children. Not a great cook, my mother did some basic cooking using firewood, but in the nearby market delicious freshly cooked food was plentiful and cheap. Our favourite was a fish curry called *mohinga*, eaten with rice vermicelli, fried and raw onions, and hard-boiled eggs and garnished with fresh coriander leaves.

⌣

The morning of Good Friday, 3 April 1942, started like any other day. The maid was in the midst of getting me dressed. I had on a vest and knickers and my leather flip-flops; the latter, or noisy wooden slippers with a leather bar across the top, were standard footwear in Burma for all ages. I was dawdling and the maid was getting irritated. Suddenly, there was a whistling noise, and then a loud thud. The house started to shudder. The sky became overcast with hundreds of planes, all Japanese. Bombs were exploding everywhere; there had been no siren warning. 'Run,' my mother yelled. 'Quickly, everyone, run to the trench as fast as you can.'

The maid and I ran and jumped into the trench. There were no steps cut into it, as there were in our Rangoon trench. Everyone else was in the trench already, terrified. We wondered when the roof would cave in. Bombs continued to thunder around us and debris from the roof was falling. We were showered with mud. 'Put your fingers in your ears and say *Aah, Aah,*' shouted my mother. This was to stop our eardrums from shattering. My father looked out of the trench. Everything was ablaze, and there was a strong smell of burning. Just then the house took a direct hit and caught fire. My mother leapt out of the shelter and shouted to all of us to run as fast as we could. My father hurled Anne and me out, and I just ran and ran and ran, anywhere where it wasn't burning.

There was devastation everywhere. Fires were raging. Huge green trees were burning fiercely and crashing down. The heat was overpowering. Suddenly, I realised I was alone. I had lost my mother. And everyone else. But I kept running and running to avoid the heat and falling branches. There were huge craters in the ground, and dead bodies and limbs and heads and blood everywhere. I just picked my way through them. I do not remember any sense of revulsion or panic. But I do remember being concerned that I had lost one of my flip-flops, and that my mother would scold me. I was certain I would be found by her, and that from somewhere she would turn up, as she always did. It never occurred to me that she might be dead. She had always been my security, not my father, who was often away touring and when we went to him for something or the other he would say, 'Go and ask your mother.'

I came across a man, half-naked, with just a loin cloth, sitting on his haunches. He grinned and asked me in Burmese if I was lost. I stopped and talked to him. I then noticed that he had only one leg. The other was severed at mid-thigh. It had clearly happened some days ago. There was no dressing, and large black sutures were visible. I do not know why I remember this man and his black sutures, but I can still see him. He kept on grinning at me. I felt uneasy and moved away from him, and sat on a large flat stone under a tree which was not burning. The crows were making an awful noise.

People were running in all directions, shouting and screaming and sobbing. Some were calling out loved ones' names. Others were beating their breasts. After a time, I cannot recall how long—perhaps it was only a few minutes, perhaps it was some hours—a distressed woman in a crumpled pale sari, with dishevelled loose hair strewn about her shoulders and down to her waist, walked quickly past me muttering to herself. I thought she was a mad woman. And then, I suddenly recognised her.

'Mummy, Mummy,' I screamed, running after her. She stopped and turned around and said, 'It's you, Lindy. Where are the rest?' She expressed no emotion, neither surprise, nor delight, nor relief. She took my hand and we walked away from the furnace. Her forearms were covered in soot and later, I saw the hairs on them were singed. We were hungry and thirsty, but there was no safe water to be found. We walked about aimlessly and then my mother said, 'I think Anne must be dead or kidnapped.' She was aware that there were predatory men roaming about on their bikes. Hours later, just as the sun was setting, a young man on a bike rode towards us, put his hand up, and stopped. It was the lad, our neighbour, who had met our boat at Mandalay.

'They are safe,' he said, 'all of them, and they are in a compound nearby. I will take you to them.' Anne, my father, and my cousins had managed to stay together when they fled from the trench.

Mandalay was full of people in our situation, strangers and homeless. My parents thought of going back to the house to see if anything could be salvaged, but the lad on the bike told us that all six houses were reduced to rubble and burnt out and only one or two outdoor lavatories could be identified. He also told us that there was a hastily assembled camp on the outskirts of Mandalay, from where homeless persons were being taken by trucks to refugee camps in Myitkyina, nearly 500 miles away. There were rumours that from there, there were still flights across the Indian border into Dibrugarh, a town on the Brahmaputra river in Upper Assam. If this was true, it was likely to be mainly Indians and Anglo-Burmese who were trying to get on to these flights to India.

By now my mother too had been convinced that we had to do everything possible to get to India and then to Madras. Four days later we had arrived at camps in Myitkyina, run by English women. Food was scarce, but horse meat and beans were plentiful. My mother declined the horse meat, so we lived on beans. We were also inoculated against plague. That night I developed a reaction, and my temperature soared to what my mother thought was at least 105°F. I was delirious, and my mother was certain I would die. She said to my father, 'Where will we bury Lindy?' He was very attached to me and sat by me all night and wept. But I recovered quickly.

We were in the queue for flights to Dibrugarh, but did not know when our turn would come. It could be days or weeks or never. The flights were restricted to women, children, and older men. No one knew anyone's ages, and it was not specified who were children or older men. My father, at forty-two, was completely grey and looked much older. Attempts were made to keep families together. Names would be called, and we would be herded to the runway, and the unlucky ones would be herded back for another day. One day our luck held, and all seven of us managed to get on board. I don't think my mother approved of my father coming with us, as she did not consider him old at forty-two. Her respect for him took another knock. The plane was a Royal Air Force Dakota, with all the seats removed to maximise capacity. We were packed in, to sit on the floor. My only recollection of the flight was feeling my mother's vomit running over my face.

There were not many flights after we left. The last flight made a quick stop to take officials. The previous two flights were machine gunned by the Japanese, just before take-off. The British then bombed the runway, so it could not be used by the Japanese.

At Dibrugarh we were given a place on the crowded deck of a boat going to Calcutta. We were at the rear-end of the boat where the canvas roof fell short. It was very warm, and when it rained on the first day we were drenched. Still in my vest and panties since the day of the bombing, but now also wearing an oversized dress given to me by one of the ladies in the camp, I was the only one in our party allowed to strip completely. My clothes were wrung out and tied to a pole on deck, and the breeze dried them rapidly. It was considered too immodest for the others to strip, so they stayed in their clothes which dried on them. My other flip-flop had fallen off while my mother dragged me around Mandalay, and I had been barefoot ever since.

On arriving in Calcutta, officials took us to the railway station and gave us tickets to Madras. There was one train a day and it took us nearly two days, sitting on hard wooden seats in a third-class (the cheapest) compartment, to reach Madras. The journey was an adventure for us children. Every station on the way was a bazaar, with hawkers selling cheap food; puri-potato was our favourite. The train came to a sudden stop as we were going through a forest and my father went to investigate. An albino elephant was standing on the track, amid much commotion. Some of the Hindu passengers regarded an albino as a divine intervention and started praying and chanting to the elephant. It was finally persuaded to move and we were on our way again, pulled by the steam engine.

Arriving at Central Station, Madras, we were astonished to see a smiling Samson Uncle on the platform. 'But how did you know we were on this train?' we asked excitedly. It was common knowledge in Madras that trains were arriving every day from Calcutta, bringing refugees and news from Burma. Every day for a month he had met this train, only to return disappointed to Annie Lodge. Thatha would be standing in the porch, waiting for him.

Gathering our belongings from the train, we crossed the road to the bus stop and caught the No. 11 bus to Mambalam. From there it was a fifteen-minute walk to Annie Lodge. We had arrived home.

Thatha wept. It was a long time before he could bring himself to speak. All he could say was, 'What about Eddie?' We could give him no news. The servants, also weeping, assembled in the drawing room, and choking, Thatha said a short prayer of thanksgiving for our return.

Part II
....
India

Chapter 5

THE MYSTERY ROOM

Annie Lodge, where we could get completely lost from the adults, was a haven for children. A handsome house with seven bedrooms, many verandahs, terraces, and top terraces, it was set in an acre of land which it shared with a smaller house, rented by Thatha to a Brahmin family. The wide front steps of the house led to a porch, supported by two fluted columns. On either side of the verandah at the front were two rooms. One was my grandfather's consulting room with a couch, desk and chair, and a glass-fronted cupboard with pills, powders, lotions, and a balance. The other room was always locked. I would occasionally see one of the male servants going into it, and then carefully locking it when he came out. Both rooms had windows looking on to the garden, at the side of the house. The porch led to the living room, sparsely and simply furnished. In one corner was a five-octave organ, and above the door leading into the dining room was a Thomas Seth grandfather clock. On one wall was a framed picture of Jesus, looking like an Englishman with long, light-brown hair, blue eyes, and a beard. There were two built-in book cases with glass doors, and in one was my grandmother's silver betel nut box. A bead curtain separated the living and dining rooms. The latter had a table and six stools. As I was by far the smallest, a high stool was hastily made for me. As there were nine of us, there had to be two sittings for meals. Thatha insisted that I sit next to him. It is Indian custom for the men and boys to be fed first; if the food was finished, it was accepted that the women and girls would have to do without. This rarely happened in our house, as the servants had to be fed after us. The rice they ate was of an inferior quality, and cooked separately, but the other dishes they ate were what we had just eaten. Servants in our house were well fed: my mother saw to that. They were the envy of other servants in the neighbourhood.

Thatha's room was next to the dining room and had an attached bathroom. A similar room and bathroom on the other side of the dining room was used by Samson Uncle. Both bathrooms had doors leading into the garden, which were used by the gardeners to fill the large brass urns with cold and hot water, for baths and washing. There was no running water. In each bathroom there were two commodes; the sweeper came in three times a day to empty them. The kitchen was off a corridor from the dining room to the store room. The cooking range was built with clay, and only firewood was used as fuel. Velu, the young deputy cook, and another male servant did the washing-up, sitting on their haunches in a corner of the kitchen, using water from a large aluminium urn. Outside, there was another washing-up area for pots and pans. Water was kept in a large barrel, which the children would try to overturn when it was nearly empty. It was a cool hiding place for small snakes. There also were two outside lavatories and bathrooms for the servants.

Upstairs, there was a central living room opening on to four bedrooms, and a covered verandah, which was often used as a bedroom. A door from the rear of the living room opened on to a very large terrace and bathroom. There were steps from either end of this terrace going up to two side terraces, and from each of these were more steps going to a large central top terrace. It was quite a spectacular house. One servant spent all day, every day except Sundays, cleaning it.

A well with a trough was the boundary between the two houses and determined which fruit trees were for the Brahmin neighbours. We could pluck the fruit from their side, but they were forbidden to pluck from ours. Their three daughters were well into their teens and saris, so there was no temptation for them to climb trees. Anne, our cousin Michael, a year older, and I soon learned to climb like monkeys, expertly taught by Velu, who was often in trouble with the head cook for neglecting his duties and spending time with us. In the afternoons, when the adults and older servants were having their siesta, we would roam about the garden with Velu. He would willingly provide a shoulder for us to climb on to a higher branch to get a guava or a plum. He could spot a ripe papaya before a crow got a peck at it first. When we were naughty, he would gently reprimand us. We loved the stories about his village in Tuticorin, where crabs were so large that they could slice off a man's thumb.

Apart from chores in the kitchen, Velu was required to see to Thatha's needs. He cleaned and tidied his room, ensured his bath water was at the right temperature every morning, put out his clean clothes every day, gave the *dhoby* the dirty clothes every week, arranged for the barber to shave Thatha's face twice a week and filled his snuff box. He also massaged his legs every night and slept on a mat on the floor by his bed. Thatha would scold him for all kinds of trivial matters, but he also had a great affection for him and would occasionally give him a hug. He was clearly the favourite servant.

One day when we were playing in the garden, Velu blurted out to Anne: 'I am your cousin-brother.' In India, every male is a cousin brother to someone, and it can mean something or nothing. 'Don't be silly,' said Anne, and told us what Velu had said. He looked dejected, while we raced off to ask my mother if this was true, half hoping it was, as we adored him.

'Yes,' said my mother. 'He is your second cousin.'

'Then why is he treated like a servant?' we remonstrated. 'Why does he work in the kitchen? Why does he not eat with us? Why does he sleep on the floor?'

And then this extraordinary story came out. Velu's grandmother was Thatha's younger and only sister. She had the misfortune to be born with blue-green eyes, called *poona-kunnu* (cat's eyes) in Tamil. This was very rare among those of Dravidian lineage, as we were. They were considered unlucky. Tamils have dark brown or black eyes. No one would marry this unfortunate girl. Eventually a man from a lower caste agreed to marry her, for a sizeable dowry. She was abandoned by her husband after giving birth to a daughter, who grew up, married, and bore Velu. Both his parents died when he was an infant, and he was raised by his grandmother. He had never been to school and was illiterate. She committed suicide when Velu was about thirteen, and he was sent to live with Thatha. It was common practice among Indians to adopt the children of destitute relatives and use them as servants and send their wages to their families. My mother abhorred this practice. She would have sent Velu to school, but it was now too late. But she did patiently teach him to write his name in English and Tamil.

Velu's one ambition in life was to own what was called a *bunk* shop. These were small shops, often not more than a shack, selling bidis, cigarettes, sweets, soft drinks, and biscuits. When he was nineteen, he asked if he could set up a shop in the now unused garage, in the garden at the rear of the house. Samson Uncle's soft-topped car had long since disintegrated, through neglect. Velu was certain that Thatha would refuse because it would be considered to be in poor taste to set up a shop on the premises. He was right. Thatha did refuse; but my mother managed to persuade him to agree eventually. She reminded Thatha that we had an obligation to advance Velu from being a mere deputy cook, to a position where he could support himself.

Velu enthusiastically set up his shop in the garage, with help from all of us. He sat on a stool with his goods neatly around him. Best of all, during school holidays, he let me sit next to him and sell to customers. I could deal better with the change than he could. The neighbours were horrified there was a bunk shop in their street and being visited by their young children, but even worse, they complained to Thatha that a child of the house, me, was sitting in it and selling to strangers. He agreed with them, but my mother said, 'Oh, let Lindy be. She's not causing any harm.' So I continued to be Velu's assistant.

The shop broke even and then made a small profit, but it was not a success and was closed after two years. About this time, Alfred Uncle, my mother's youngest brother, a doctor and unmarried, needed someone to run his house and Velu seemed to be a suitable person. Later Alfred Uncle returned to Burma and joined Burma Railways, and Velu went with him. I saw him only once after that, a confident, happy young man and as amiable as ever. He was thinking of asking Jessie Aunty to find him a suitable bride. But a few months later we had a telegram from Alfred to say Velu had contracted pneumonic plague and died. Seldom have I felt such a deep sadness.

By the age of seven, I realised that we were different from the rest of the people living on our street, which was named for my grandfather. They were all Brahmins and we were Christians. They belonged to the highest caste; we were below the midpoint of the caste system. They seldom employed servants; the domestic work was done by their women folk, usually the daughters-in-law. We had several servants, some of them Harijans or untouchables who were outside the caste system. There was little doubt that the person most respected and admired in our street was my grandfather, but that was because he was a doctor, wealthy and elderly. His opinion and advice over many matters were frequently sought. But every single Brahmin in that street felt superior to us, by virtue of birth.

Most Indian Christians belonged to the lower castes and the untouchables, and had been converted by foreign missionaries, not because of conviction but for some benefit; or, in the case of Harijans, they thought they would altogether escape caste prejudices. For these reasons, Christians were generally despised by Hindus. Missionaries made the situation worse by treating upper-caste and Brahmin converts preferentially. Unfortunately, over the decades Christians have continued to practise caste discrimination, especially in marriage.

Some months after we came to live in Annie Lodge, I noticed that the house opposite had a handwritten *To Let* sign on the gate, and under it was written in capital letters '*For Brahmins Only*'. Incensed, I got a large piece of cardboard, wrote on it in capitals *For Christians Only* and tied it to our front gate. The gardener, who was illiterate, was puzzled when he saw it, and brought it to my mother's attention. She told him to take it down.

'Don't be so foolish, Lindy,' she said. 'Why do you want to be like them? They don't know any better.'

'But they think they are superior to us,' I said. 'How can they think like that?'

My mother replied, 'They are the only people who think they are superior. No one else does. Besides, there are good people among them. Who can be better than Dr Rangachari and his wife?'

Dr Rangachari was a young Brahmin doctor who had recently bought a house on our street. Handsome, charming, and friendly, he and his wife had called on us to pay their respects to Thatha. We had adopted him as our family doctor. Ever obliging and competent, he never charged us. My mother reminded me that the worst and best existed in every community.

Our neighbours consulted Thatha frequently for minor ailments when I often would be with him. They did not seem to mind. He would show me how to weigh various powders on the balance, place them on a rectangular piece of paper and carefully fold it, tuck the edges in, and label it. I became a dab hand at dispensing for Thatha.

Occasionally, one of the Brahmin women would shriek, 'Don't touch me. I've just had a bath.' This would usually be on a Friday, when Brahmin's have special ceremonial baths, and my grandfather being a non-Brahmin was deemed to be unclean. They would come to us for all kinds of favours and advice, but each would make sure the other did not know. Often a face would come up after dark at the kitchen window: 'Can I please have some of your curds to ferment my milk.' They knew it would be clean. Or they would come, again at night, for advice on endless matrimonial problems. They were middle class and affluent, and most of the men were university educated.

Our immediate neighbour was a retired inspector of police. He and my grandfather exchanged newspapers every day. He took the *Indian Express* and my grandfather, *The Hindu*. Both were quality English papers, but dull. The inspector was a tall, thin, quiet man with grey hair. His wife was short, fat, and belligerent, and terrorised her exquisitely beautiful daughter-in-law, Sita. We could hear her shouting at her all day. Her son Mani, an accountant, suffered from severe depression and seldom went to work, staying in his room. He and Sita had had an arranged marriage, had four children and they all lived together in a joint family system. When my mother was in the garden, Sita would come discreetly to the fence and pour out her woes to her. My mother was a great source of wisdom and advice to many of the Brahmin women in the street. She understood their orthodox culture, and did not foist her liberal views on them. When Sita was twenty-nine, she developed breast cancer. She was not allowed to go to hospital in case she was seen by male doctors. My mother repeatedly asked her husband and in-laws to take her to hospital, and volunteered to take her herself. But they declined. I went once with my mother to see her. She was lying on a dirty mat on the floor of the living room, emaciated and gaunt. She died soon after. Within six months Mani had remarried, this time to a short plump girl, barely into her teens. She quickly produced two infants. The cycle of misery continued.

ᔑ

The room opposite the medicine room kept me wondering. I had seen Velu go in and out, sometimes with another servant. I thought perhaps they were stealing and hiding things. They always locked the room when they left. I was becoming uneasy about it.

One day I said to Anne, 'What do you think is in there?' But she wasn't interested. She and my mother often called me a 'nosey parker' because I was very curious. Samson Uncle said I was inquisitive. I didn't quite know what that meant, but I had a fair idea. My cousins, Daisy, Irene, and Michael, had by this time gone to live with their father and brothers in another suburb of Madras.

One very hot afternoon, while the adults and servants napped and Anne was nowhere to be seen, I was doing my usual barefoot exploration of this fascinating garden. It was so hot, even the lizards and chameleons were hiding. I noticed that there was on the outside wall of the house a ledge, about an inch wide, running around it. It was two feet above the ground. The open window of the mystery room with its vertical iron bars, a usual feature of ground-floor windows, was another three feet above it.

If I took a running leap and got my big toe on the ledge, I could grab a bar momentarily before I fell back. I might possibly catch a glimpse of what was in the room. I thought I would give it a try, and I did. I was transfixed with horror. Lying on the bed was a huge naked black man, but worst of all, our eyes met. I fell back onto the ground and ran as fast as I could to wake my sleeping mother, and tell her what I had seen. I knew she would be furious with me and I would be smacked, which was a frequent occurrence, but I didn't care. I was shaking with fright. She was not angry with me. She said, 'We were wrong not to have told you children about your Thomas Uncle, my brother. We should have realised the truth would have come out sooner or later.' So this was Thomas Uncle. Mad Thomas Uncle, who we thought had disappeared forever, years ago.

When Thomas Uncle was about sixteen, he showed an abnormal interest in the occult and black magic. His parents thought this was a teenage fad and would pass. But he became more and more withdrawn, and started to show definite signs of what we would now call schizophrenia. Thatha took him to the Madras Mental Hospital, then called the Lunatic Asylum, but to no avail. He deteriorated and stopped talking altogether, except for occasional loud laughs and swearing. He would disappear for months at a time, then reappear dishevelled and dirty, with a long beard. What was left of his clothes would be in shreds. It would be the prodigal son returning. My grandfather would be filled with joy and hope; the servants would rejoice and hug him. He would allow himself to be bathed and shaved and would have his hair cut. Clean clothes would be found for him. He would eat ravenously, but his only reply to every question put to him was 'Hmm', and he would then retire to his room, the mystery room. It would be left unlocked during the day, and he would take himself to the lavatory. At meal times after every one had eaten, a servant would call him to eat. He would eat sitting cross-legged on the floor of the corridor, between the dining room and kitchen, using his fingers, in an almost non-stop action of putting the food to his mouth and chewing fast. There would always be a servant with him, usually Velu. He refused to sit at the dining table. He spent the rest of the time lying on his bed staring at the ceiling. Occasionally he would shout army commands, which suggested that he had been living rough near army camps.

Thomas Uncle had reappeared shortly before we arrived in Madras, after a particularly long absence. It was decided by Thatha, Samson Uncle and my mother, that we children should be shielded from him. His room was kept locked. His daily baths, in the servant's bathroom near the well, only took place when we had gone out, or had gone to bed. A commode had been placed in his room and was emptied by the sweeper three times a day, again when we were not around. All his meals were taken to him. The adults were relieved that the secret was out as they had been living under a great strain, worrying when the lid would blow open. The old routine was re-established.

Anne and I would talk to him. 'Is the food nice, Thomas Uncle? Why don't you talk to us? Shall we go for a walk in the garden?' The only reply each time was 'Hmm'. Thomas Uncle was generally docile, but had occasionally become violent and once hit Simpson Uncle. He had his likes and dislikes. Biggy had been his favourite, and now it was Velu. One day when he had just finished his meal, I climbed into his lap and sat for a little while. Thomas Uncle thought it funny, and laughed loudly. Just then my mother came along and became very angry with Velu and me. She told me I was never to do that again. The adults were aware that violence could erupt at any time. Thomas Uncle was a big man, over six feet tall, and there was something menacing about him. He was always kept locked up and did not protest.

One day a relative who lived in Vepery came in a big hurry to see Thatha. A Christian faith healer from America had come to Madras and was reputed to heal sick people, including mad ones, at a *maidan* near his house. Thatha and my mother were very sceptical, but Thatha felt that no opportunity to cure Thomas should be missed. He and two servants took Thomas to Vepery by bus, but by the time they got there the healer had gone.

My parents, my father in particular, were becoming increasingly uneasy about us young children sharing a house with a mad and unpredictable man. I think my father was frightened of Thomas. My mother and Thatha decided to have him permanently admitted to the mental hospital. They would visit him three or four times a year, but he never showed any recognition of them and resorted to 'Hmm' when he was spoken to. They would take him a box of assorted cakes and he would eat them all, one after the other. He became thin and grey. The doctors said that very occasionally he would make a rational remark. On one occasion a conversation was overheard by a warder. An inmate accused Thomas Uncle of stealing his soap and he retorted, 'Why would I want to steal your Sunlight soap [used by the poor]? In my house we use Pears soap.' Visits to him became more and more infrequent; Thatha was finding the bus journey to the hospital difficult. One day Thatha went to see him, and he was taken aback when the warder brought a small and shrivelled man to him.

'Here is your son Thomas,' he said.

'This is not my son,' Thatha replied. 'This is someone else. I know my son.'

The identity disc on the wrist stated Thomas Wason.

'There has been a mistake,' said Thatha. 'Take me to see the superintendent.'

A helpful man, the superintendent agreed that there could have been a mistake, and he suggested an identity parade. Thatha and the servant with him, who had known Thomas for many years, scrutinised every inmate. But Thomas was not among them and was never found. Somewhere, he lies in a grave with another man's name on his headstone.

⁓

I had my seventh birthday in Annie Lodge. My mother always made a fuss of our birthdays and had wonderful cakes made. But we were given only one present, and that would be a hard-backed book. I had learned to read before I was four, and when we arrived from Burma I was six. Every night I had to read to Thatha from his large, well-thumbed King James Bible. The dates of births, marriages and deaths of his children and grandchildren were recorded in his hand on the blank pages at the back of the Bible.

Before I was three I could speak Tamil, Burmese, and English fluently: Tamil to Biggy and the cook, Burmese to the nanny, and English to my parents. Reading and writing were learned only in English. Reading to young children is not an Indian habit. Children are taught to read very young, so that they can read to themselves, including at bedtime. By the time I was seven, we had been in India for six months, and still had not been sent to school. My mother taught us English and my father concentrated on teaching us maths. He used to enjoy playing number games with us. Anne was slow, and very soon I caught up with her.

There was a Catholic school with European nuns a couple of miles away. It was called Church Park Convent, and we were sent there by rickshaw. My only memory of it was being taught something called moral science. This consisted of questions and answers such as 'Who made you?', 'God made me', and so on.

After some time, it became apparent that there was some form of apartheid in operation. Non-Brahmin Indian children were treated less favourably than Brahmin, Anglo-Indian, and European children, and there was segregation. My mother was indignant, withdrew us and sent us to Doveton Corrie School in Vepery. A Church of England School, it treated all its pupils equally. Travelling to school now required two rickshaw journeys and a ten-minute ride in an electric train. Anne was told to look after me.

The headmistress was an Englishwoman, a Miss Falloon. Single, middle-aged, blonde, and skeletal, she lacked in warmth; but the school flourished under her. Most of the pupils were Anglo-Indian or European. There were a few Indians from educated middle-class families. My teacher, Miss Pharaoh, was a genial Anglo-Indian. My first morning started with mental arithmetic. We were required to write our answers, all numbers, rapidly in our notebook, as Miss Pharaoh walked quickly up and down between our ink-welled desks shouting, 'Nine sevens are..., write two hundred thousand and seventeen..., what is ninety-seven minus thirteen?' and so on at a tremendous speed without a pause. There were usually twenty questions. I was totally lost and got about four right. Miss Pharaoh said to me, after classes were over, 'You are a year younger than the other children. You are in this class because you are supposed to be clever. I can see no evidence for this. You had better tell your mother you cannot keep up with the other children in maths, and ask her to come to see Miss Falloon.' My mother and Miss Pharaoh agreed that if I did not improve in a month, I would go down.

At interview before admission I had been required to do a short test, and Miss Falloon had said that despite my having had very little schooling, I was well above average. She was putting me in an older class, to which my mother agreed. I was therefore quite unabashed and determined to improve. My mother encouraged me to catch up rather than be put down to the lower class. Already, my reading and writing were excellent.

Every day after school, when we got home, Anne and I would be ravenous. We would each be given a heavily buttered fresh bun from the local bakery. It had lashings of condensed milk and we would be dreaming about it in the rickshaw, all the way to

Annie Lodge. I would then get on with my homework, and when my father got home from work we would get down to mental arithmetic. In less than a month, much to Miss Pharaoh's surprise and delight, I was achieving full marks. Within three months, I was ranked first in the class.

In India it is not just the three R's that young children have to learn. There is a fourth: remembering. A well-trained memory is essential for success in education, as a lot is learned parrot-fashion. Understanding comes later. It is not unusual for six-year-olds to reel off their thirteen times table: it does them no harm. We also had to learn a lot of poetry, and my mother would make us recite poems over and over again in front of her until we were word perfect. Then she would teach us to recite with expression. Anne would often be shy, but I revelled in this. Some of these poems I have never again encountered, but they were great fun. One about a cannibal started thus:

> Okey-pokey Crack-Me-Crown,
> King of the island of Gulp-em-Down,
> Oka-poka Chinga-Ma-Ring,
> Eighteenth wife of this mighty king.

My mother made us learn some of her favourites, by Christina Rossetti and others from *A Child's Garden of Verses*. After Sunday School at St George's Cathedral, Thatha insisted each week that we learned a psalm by heart.

⌒

We were destitute when we arrived in Madras from Burma and we were supported by my grandfather. My father worked most days as a temporary auditor. He could not find a permanent post. This situation exacerbated the unhappiness and tension between my parents, something I had not noticed before now. More and more I could hear arguments between them, especially at nights when they thought we were asleep. My mother became very irritable and would fly into irrational rages. She would constantly find fault with Anne and me. I was high-spirited and argumentative and hardly a day would pass without my being beaten, but I never cried. I knew my father disapproved, but he said nothing.

Samson Uncle was another source of irritation to my mother. Sitting on his bed in his room, propped up by pillows, and always in white socks usually with holes, he would smoke and read nearly all day. In the evenings, he would meet friends and sometimes give physics tuition to students of the prestigious engineering college in Guindy, a suburb of Madras. He would not charge them. He would appear at meal times, meddling in the running of the house and giving unwanted advice. Thatha supported him financially. Samson was generally a genial person and liked children. I would visit him in his room. He and I would have long conversations, and he would test me in my tables. He would buy me books, beads, ribbons, and tennis balls. One day, he and my mother were arguing. She called him a parasite. He locked himself in his room and refused to come out.

My mother persuaded her father that it was time that he stopped pampering Samson. He had been living in Annie Lodge since his return from Germany in 1929. His return then was anticipated with great excitement, and marriage offers from parents of young Christian girls came pouring in. Paati had great pleasure in sifting through them and arguing with Thatha as to which girl would be most suitable. Samson could have had the pick of them. He was fair, tall, handsome and of a pleasant disposition, and after a Western education had a glittering career ahead of him. But a great shock awaited his parents. He refused to work. He refused to marry. And worst of all, he had converted to Catholicism in Germany. Night after night Paati wept. When she died in 1938, nothing had changed.

Thatha knocked on Samson's door, went in, and after a time, came out. Samson had agreed to find work, and would start to contribute to the household expenses. He joined us for meals again. He looked crestfallen. We felt sorry for him as we had a great affection for him.

Samson Uncle became self-employed as a sanitary engineer, which is what plumbers were called in India. Everyone was curious as to what exactly he did. I said to him one day, 'But what do you do, Samson Uncle?' Without any hesitation he said, 'I install *Bumbai cuckoos*,' which was what water closets were called, a great novelty at that time only enjoyed by the rich. He was much in demand, but my mother and Thatha were shocked that this was all that this well-educated engineer could rise to. He soon acquired two workmen who were devoted to him. They would set off for work, early every morning, but after a few months his customers were arriving at Annie Lodge to complain of unfinished and shoddy work. We were embarrassed. Not long after, he redeemed himself somewhat by obtaining a lectureship in physics at the engineering college in Guindy. He also gave private tuition in physics to students from Loyola College, where he was very friendly with the Catholic priests. He never married.

My eighth birthday was approaching, and at last my father had found a permanent job in Deolali, near Poona. Deolali, pronounced 'Doolally' by the British, is a well-known term referring to someone who is mentally unstable. British soldiers unable to cope with the rigours of their posting were sent to Deolali to recuperate. I asked my father to stay for my birthday, which he did, and the following morning he left. I never saw him again.

Chapter 6

NEC DEXTRORSUM NEC SINISTRORSUM

Anne and I were well settled in Doveton Corrie School. My mother looked for part-time work, but there were no openings in the local schools. She had a distant relative called Kapurthala who lived in Madras city. He had wide contacts and said he knew the right job for her. He knew someone, who knew someone else, who knew someone in what was known as the 'Censor's Office' in the city, and though they employed only Europeans and Eurasians they would consider an Indian, provided she was well educated and fluent in English. My mother was interviewed by a male English Army officer, and given the job on the spot. She was told the work was confidential and not to tell anyone where she worked. If asked, she was to say she worked for the Women's Auxiliary Corps (India). The latter was set up by Lady Moncton in India in 1942. Consisting mainly of Europeans and Eurasians, but also Indians, the corps were required to do the so-called soft jobs, so as to release forces personnel to fight the war.

My mother was required to wear khaki uniform. She had not worn Western clothing since she was a little girl and refused to wear what the European women wore. An exception was made for her; she was told to get her own khaki sari and blouse the latter to have one stripe on the shoulders. Where was she going to get this uniform, she wondered? The ever-resourceful Kapurthala asked her for six white saris and blouses, and had them dyed khaki. The office was on Mount Road, the main road in Madras, where there were offices and shops well served by the No. 11 bus, but she preferred to go by a hand-pulled rickshaw, so as to be discreet.

My mother, when she was not in a rage, screaming at servants, her children and husband, was very charming and personable. She had a disarming smile. For the most part, she found her European colleagues very congenial and helpful; a few resented an Indian working alongside them. At first, she was a curiosity, but it soon became apparent that she was far better educated than they were, and both her spoken and written English were better than theirs, which to their credit they quickly and readily acknowledged. It could not have been easy for them as the only Indians most of them knew were servants.

The ladies in the Censor's Office were mostly wives of men who were in middle-grade administration or trade. These memsahibs had not got beyond high school, if that. A few had had secretarial training. They lived in fine houses away from Indians, were chauffeur driven, had numerous servants, and their children were in good schools in hill stations. Their lives revolved around the Gymkhana Club, which for the most part was off limits to Indians. It was not as bad as a White's Only Club in Bombay, where we knew of a mixed-race woman who was allowed membership but not her brother as his skin was not deemed fair enough.

The role of the censor's office, as its name implied, was to censor letters and publications which might inadvertently adversely affect the war effort. They came from the post office, offices, publishers, and bookshops. Because of the volume of material, most of the material was cursorily examined. This was a struggle for some of the women, who were barely literate. The Scots and Europeans seemed better educated than the English. On one occasion when my mother was working in the books section, she came into a room and found several women poring over large books entitled *War and Peace*. She laughed and said, 'You can pass that book.' They had never heard of Leo Tolstoy.

My mother got her two stripes after a few months. She was given more and more responsibility and was soon a supervisor. Supervisors were promoted to three stripes, but hers were not forthcoming. More than a year passed and she still was not given three stripes. Her colleagues were becoming very embarrassed as it seemed obvious to them that this was flagrant racial discrimination. They approached the officer in charge and told him of their concern. He did not take any notice, but she did eventually get her three stripes. To celebrate, her friends in the office went to Higginbothams, the nearby bookshop, and bought her a book. In it they inscribed: 'For dear Alice—Mrs Three Stripes (much delayed).' My mother said to Anne and me, 'You see, the worst of people may be British, but the best are also British.' Two Englishwomen in the office, Margaret Cooper and Audrey Forret, became very special lifelong friends.

Discussing our schooling with her friends in the Censor's Office, my mother became convinced that Anne and I should go to boarding school in Bangalore, a semi-hill station at an altitude of 3,000 feet.

Though Doveton Corrie was a very satisfactory school, travelling back and forth by hand-pulled rickshaw, train, and again by hand-pulled rickshaw was not. Besides, Anne complained incessantly about my behaviour on the journey. She objected to my conversations with the rickshaw-wallahs and strangers on the train and my tendency to run off to a different compartment from hers. During the rainy season the roads would flood and the trains were unreliable.

The thought of going away from my mother was quite unbearable for me. Despite her strict ways, smacks, and rages, she was warm, funny, and affectionate. She was very interested in everything we did and embraced my high-spiritedness with humour. I adored her. She gave me a total sense of security. We wrote to my father and received letters from him occasionally, but he had always been a somewhat remote figure. My mother encouraged us to write to him. His letters would end: 'Your affectionate Father, D.S.T. Rajan.'

No matter how much I disliked the idea of going to boarding school, I did not express any objections. My mother's word was always law. Ever since I could think and speak, I was brainwashed into believing that I would be a doctor one day, just like Thatha. I admired him more than anyone else and going to boarding school was one more step on the way.

⁀

On the recommendation of her friends in the Censor's Office, my mother decided that we should go to Bishop Cotton Girls' School, usually referred to as 'Cottons' or 'Bishop Cottons'. It was situated in Bangalore in South India and was very highly regarded. Founded in 1865, it was originally called Westward Ho and linked to the Church of England to provide sound Christian education for the sons and daughters of British and Eurasians in India. The former were mainly from the lower middle and working classes. There were also some missionary children, but like those from the middle and upper classes they were sent to boarding school in England or Scotland. A few places were given to the children of wealthy and well-educated Indians, and it was mainly these children who contributed to the high academic standard of the school.

George Cotton, after whom the school was named, had been assistant master at Rugby School, and in 1852 was appointed Headmaster of Marlborough. Six years later, he was personally requested by Queen Victoria to become bishop of Calcutta, a position he accepted after some hesitation. He developed a scheme of education for several schools in India, including the famous Cathedral School in Bombay. His life was tragically cut short at the age of fifty-three when, following the consecration of a cemetery, he slipped from a plank leading from the bank to a steamer and fell into the Ganges. He was never seen again. The motto of the school was *Nec Dextrorsum Nec Sinistrorsum*—Neither to the Left nor to the Right. This was the family motto of an English missionary, Dr G.U. Pope, who was much involved with the school. He was a distinguished Tamil scholar, whose memory is enshrined in a statue of him in Madras. In keeping with the motto, the first verse of the school song ran thus:

> *On straight on*
> *On Cottonians on*
> *Muster on the side of right*
> *March like warriors to the fight*
> *Mark the foe and strike with might*
> *Nec Dexstorsum Nec Sinistrorsum*

The school, one of several boarding schools in Bangalore, was in the Cantonment area of the city. Inhabited by many retired second-and third-generation British, it was also home to an abundance of Eurasian families, a minority of whom were university educated and had held senior positions in public services, such as the post and telegraphs. Like the railways, these jobs were reserved for them, and well paid. Bangalore was a clean and ordered city largely due to the British, and was known for its colonial-style houses with colourful gardens, interesting parks, and wide roads. It was 200 miles—a night's journey—from Madras.

Our relatives, including Jessie Aunty and Simpson Uncle, who visited us frequently with their small daughters, disapproved of our being educated and living with European children. Thatha was equally unhappy and said his children had attended similar schools only because there was nowhere else to educate them. My father had little say in the matter. He was working in Poona.

Europeans and Eurasians looked down on Indians, and would have been surprised to know that this feeling was reciprocated.

'Learn their good qualities like discipline and time keeping, but do not grow up like their women, who dress immodestly and have loose morals,' Thatha used to say to Anne and me. This was unfair to my mother's European friends, who were thoroughly decent people.

Anne and I had to be got ready for an English-type boarding school. We had to be comfortable eating with a knife and fork. Indians eat with their fingers and always with the right hand. It was strange to put food into one's mouth with a fork with the left hand. This is totally unacceptable to Indians, who regard the left hand as the dirty hand, as it is used to wash one's bottom. We learned to use lavatory paper, again frowned upon by Indians. These white people, they would say. They don't even wash their bottoms.

An inventory was taken of all the things we were required to take to school, and our clothes had to be labelled. Two sturdy tin trunks were bought, together with what were called holdalls. This was an ingenious invention. A holdall was just over six feet long and made from sturdy canvas. It had two sleeves on either side and took a full-size single mattress, tucked into both ends, with pillows and bed linen and anything else we wished to stuff into it, such as towels and shoes. It was then rolled up and secured with two leather straps around it and secured with a leather handle. It was an elegant piece of luggage and survived being thrown around by the coolies. It must have been invented by the British. Indians travel with their bedding rolled up in a thin dhurry tied with a rope.

In January 1945, three months after my ninth birthday, my mother took us to Bangalore to start the new school year. The luggage—two trunks, two holdalls, and a leather suitcase—was taken by wooden cart to Central Station in Madras, some three miles from Annie Lodge. We had no car, and taxis were not in existence. My mother, Samson Uncle, Anne, and I went by bus to the station. Before we left the house, Thatha said some prayers but could not finish as he started to sob.

At the station we were reunited with the luggage and met the school party of six girls, all European, and a mother, a very friendly lady who was accompanying us. Compartments were reserved for us in second class. The berths were upholstered in leather and we each had one. The holdalls were placed on them and opened by the coolies so that we could have our own bedding. There was a clean bathroom attached to each compartment. It was a nine-hour overnight journey, and we alighted at Bangalore Cantonment, the train terminating at the next stop. We were met by the school bus.

We were welcomed by Miss Watt, the acting headmistress. Miss Waller, the head, also an Englishwoman, was in England on furlough. I was to be in Standard Four and Anne in Standard Six. The school had a kindergarten and nine standards in the main school. Two examinations were taken at the end of the year in the ninth standard: the Bangalore European High School Examination and the Cambridge examination, referred to as 'Senior Cambridge'. The latter had equivalence with O levels/London Matric/GCSEs. Question papers were set in England and sent to India. Answer papers were sent to England for marking. We had to wait five months for our results. Everything went back and forth by ship. The curriculum for both our examinations was deliberately similar, the Indian one being adapted to the English. The English exam, naturally, was given more kudos, but standards were higher in maths and English in the Indian exam.

There were 50 boarders in the school total of 300, but only three of the boarders were Indian, including Anne and myself. The third girl was in the ninth standard and a prefect. We looked to her for protection but she completely ignored us.

The other boarders were English, Scottish, Irish, and Anglo-

Indian. The meaning of the term 'Anglo-Indian' had altered since it was first introduced to describe the British who went to India. They either settled there or were committed to the country, being mainly traders or those who were in the administrative service. The term now included those who were wholly British in ancestry, sometimes going as far back as the East India Company; those who were of mixed race, European, and Indian, often not knowing when the mixing occurred; and some who were wholly Indian, usually Harijans (untouchables) who had worked for European employers as butlers, maids, or cooks and had adopted their masters' names, religion, and dress. Some Goans of mixed Indian/Portuguese ancestry also called themselves Anglo-Indians, as the latter were considered to be higher up in the pecking order of mixed-race people. The Anglo-Indian could therefore be of any appearance, from a white-skinned blue-eyed blond to a black-skinned, black-haired, dark-eyed person. Within the Anglo-Indian community the fairer ones considered themselves superior to the darker ones. It was not uncommon for siblings in a family to look so different from each other that they appeared not to belong to the same race.

The British looked down on Indians and Anglo-Indians, the Anglo-Indians looked down on Indians, and the Indians looked down on both. Anglo-Indians tried to pass themselves off as Europeans if they could. It was an unnecessarily complex and unpleasant situation. It caused considerable suffering, and a sense of inferiority and unworthiness. Most of the Anglo-Indians in my school, teachers and pupils, were pale skinned. We had two teachers who were sisters, Joan and Margaret, with the surname Brown, but their skin colours were different. They were referred to as Light Brown and Dark Brown. Each of the three groups spoke English differently, with a different accent and intonation, though there was some overlap.

To her great relief, Anne and I were in different dormitories: she was in St Catherine's and I was in St Margaret's. As we were shown to our respective named beds, lockers, and cupboards, we were the objects of much curiosity. We were not just new girls, but Indians. The other girls in my dormitory kept walking up and down past me, clutching their dolls and soft toys. This was something new to me, as Indian children rarely play with dolls and never with soft toys. Anne and I did have beautiful porcelain dolls with pale pink skins and blue eyes which opened and shut. They had been imported from England, but we had left them at home.

The bathing arrangements in the school were not acceptable to my mother, an exceptionally fastidious lady. For each dormitory, the cleaning of teeth and washing of hands and faces was communal, not in hand basins, but in a long trough with taps. For bathing, each child was allotted a named cubicle, shared with another girl. There was a row of cubicles with metal doors and six-foot-high partitions. Each had a portable zinc bath tub with handles. Every evening except Sunday, at five thirty, a *mali* filled the tub with warm water up to a height of about four inches, but baths were only taken on alternate days. My mother insisted that we bathe daily, except for Sundays which was the mali's day off. She pointed out that it was unhygienic not to have daily baths in the tropics. She was firmly told by the matron that this was the norm in public schools in Britain and reminded that this school was modelled along those lines. My mother also told the matron that she considered it dirty to sit in a tub and wash in one's own dirty water and that she wanted us to sluice ourselves with water from the tub and wash ourselves in the Indian style, sitting on a stool or standing outside the tub. This was agreed, and we were provided with tin mugs with handles. This deviation from normal practice caused us much distress, as we became the objects of ridicule. I, in particular was subjected to all kinds of taunts. While I was bathing, girls would climb on to the walls of my cubicle and peer at me. 'Isn't her skin a funny colour? Just like a monkey's!' Another would say, 'She is an Indian so she must be dirty. That's why she has to have a bath every day.'

My mother stayed for a week in Bangalore to see us settle in. She was allowed to visit us every evening but we did not complain about anything. We remained silent and miserable. I wept quietly into my pillow every night for weeks, not because of the misery but because I wanted my mother. Anne was of no comfort to me whatever. She, no doubt had her own demons. She seldom spoke to me, except to reprimand me for my sins: tie not straight, shoes unlaced and not polished, tops of socks not matching and so on. I was a constant source of embarrassment to her.

It was difficult to know whether the matron, Rhoda Payne, responsible for the junior dormitories, was European or Anglo-Indian. Unattractive and sour, with dark shoulder-length frizzy hair, she was a spinster in her fifties. She did not smile or laugh. Her cheeks were sallow, and one was disfigured by a collection of purple warts, which the nastier girls used to refer to as Rhoda's bunch of grapes. Walking up and down the dormitory, she would scold us for all kinds of minor misdemeanours. Most of all, she did not like chatter. 'Keep qui-ett, keep qui-ett,' she would repeat. Her constant complaint was that we were uncivilised: 'They don't behave like this at Home. Remember you are Europeans [pronounced 'Uu-ropeans'].' I was obviously irrelevant. She did eventually leave Cottons to go Home, though I doubt if Home came up to expectations.

Anglo-Indians would always refer to Britain as Home, even if they, their parents or even their grandparents had never been there. After Indian Independence in 1947, many of them did go to the promised land. It was a rude shock. The climate was dreadful, there was rationing, they were poor, but worst of all, they were not welcome. Some stayed on and made good, but several went on to Australia, mainly Perth, and were successful and contented.

⁀

Because of her gentle nature and not being given to controversy, and also because she was older and more mature, Anne made friends easily in her dormitory and among the day girls in her class. Though I had a more extrovert nature than her, this was not so with me. I soon realised that I was two years below the average age for my class, and the girl closest in age to me was almost a year older. I was also small and thin, with spindly legs, being only four feet two inches in height, the smallest girl in my class. I must have stood out like a runt. I finally found friends among the day girls, in particular a girl called Elizabeth Josephs, an Anglo-Indian. A year older, she was quiet and clever and friendly. We decided we would become doctors one day. It was the beginning of a lifelong friendship. Among the boarders, there was Maureen Bowell from

Madras, exceedingly pretty, doted on and spoilt by her parents and grandmother who lived in Bangalore. Somewhat aloof, she had a following and the largest tuck box in the dormitory; perhaps the two were connected, as we were always hungry. Her best friend, Leonie Whitlock, also from Madras, was very popular and without guile. Both girls were English, middle class, and lived near the harbour, in style, in large houses with numerous servants. This was one of the few areas in Madras where the Europeans lived. There was no obvious segregation or apartheid as such, but there were defined areas where they lived, where a few wealthy Indians also lived. On the whole, Europeans would not have entertained the thought of living where I lived, any more than my family, Thatha in particular, would have wished to live among them. My mother's friends, the Coopers and the Forrets, lived in the same area, the Coopers living on Springhaven Road, where the Whitlocks also lived. Leonie's mother Margaret, a delightful woman, was a qualified nurse but did not work. Her husband, Leonard, was a harbour pilot. Maureen Bowell and her parents returned to England after Indian Independence in 1947, and we made contact again as adults When I was ten, I remember going to a birthday party she held at her home. Behind her house there were some less salubrious houses, lived in by Anglo-Indians, and I remember some of them peering through the fence at us. One little boy invited to the party was Arnold Dorsey, later called Gerry Dorsey, who eventually metamorphosed into the pop star Engelbert Humperdinck. As for Leonie, we never lost touch and became firm friends as we grew up. She lacked prejudice; she and her mother even took me to swim at the Gymkhana Club, when Indians were not welcome.

In India there is not the same obsession with age as there is in Britain, where children of a similar age are lumped together in the same class. In India, children are placed in a class according to ability and at the end of each academic year are assessed as to whether they have progressed sufficiently to move to the next class. Invariably, about 10 per cent are kept behind. There is much to be said for and against such a system. I got used to being called a brat by my classmates, and often being excluded, but this was more because I was Indian than because I lacked maturity.

The curriculum was that of an English school. Some of it went over my head. When our strict English music teacher made us sing a spring song which began 'Oh! *What a commotion under the ground...*' I was merely perplexed.

I excelled in all subjects, in particular in English and maths. Despite being small, I was good at sports and could outrun nearly everyone in my class. I could read and recite well, and was often asked to do so from the front of the class. I enjoyed Dramatics, but because of my appearance was given small, unimportant parts. Heroes and heroines were chosen from among the fair skinned.

After two months we had tests in all subjects and I scored 96 per cent in maths, the highest in the class. I overheard one of the girls say, 'The WOG has done it again. She's top in maths.' This word WOG I had not heard before, and thought it was slang for someone who excelled in maths. It was some years later that I learned it was a derogatory word used by the British for people east of Suez. It started off as a term meaning Westernised Oriental Gentleman, but over time descended into an insult. I was frequently the butt of racist jokes in my dormitory, the classroom and at table. I do not think the teachers and matrons were aware of this, as it was never done in their hearing. They were kind to Anne and me, but I could never be sure that I would have their sympathy were I to bring this to their attention.

The arrival of a new headmistress at the beginning of the next term transformed the school. Miss Waller's health did not improve sufficiently and she retired. The new head, an Englishwoman called Elizabeth Margaret Hardy, was an Oxford University graduate and in her fifties. She had been headmistress of the Diocesan Girls' School in Rangoon, when Anne had been there very briefly. Rumour had it that Miss Hardy was involved in the war effort in Burma, and as a result had become 'shell shocked', whatever that meant, and had been sent back to Britain. This accounted for her insomnia. She used to be seen striding around the school compound in the early hours of the morning. Her strange manner of walking earned her the nickname 'Strider'. Miss Hardy was colour blind. We were neither white nor brown nor in between. We were her 'gels' as she called us, in her upper-class accent. She had been a senior mistress at a girls' public school in the south of England and was clearly taken aback by some of the poor standards in Cottons. She set about changing them. She took over the teaching of English in the four senior classes. Weekly essays were set; compulsory elocution lessons were introduced; English girls who said 'Soonday' and 'ih' instead of 'Sunday' and 'it' were taught to talk properly; we were required to attend weekly music appreciation classes; the playing of pop music, which Miss Hardy called 'noise', on school pianos was banned; the idle standing and looking down the long school drive, to see if Cottons' boys were passing by, was stopped; boarders had to run once round the hockey field before breakfast; dormitories were locked during the day so they remained tidy at all times; senior boarders were each given a small plot of land to cultivate; house points were given for memorising and reciting to Miss Hardy the General Thanksgiving and Confession; and Psalms and Latin were introduced in the sixth standard. These changes produced much rage among the older boarders, many of whom enjoyed doing nothing out of class hours. Miss Hardy could not tolerate older girls hanging around idly and talking. She knew the main topic of conversation was boys, and this she considered a thoroughly bad thing.

My mother used to write to Anne and me, at least once a week, long interesting letters in her beautiful hand, separate letters to each of us as she had different things to say to us. There would be news of Annie Lodge, but there were also her views on topical subjects, including politics. There was no dearth of advice and wisdom. She never said so in so many words, but we knew what she meant, and her deep affection and concern for us shone through in every letter. Anne and I rarely shared our letters. Every Sunday afternoon, every boarder was required to write home. Our letters were not censored. I would write long descriptive letters to my mother. She wanted to know everything I was thinking and doing. There were girls who would complain that they had to write to their parents, and wrote only one or two sentences. These were girls who had poor relationships with their parents, having been sent to boarding school at a very young age, sometimes at four. It was a shock to me that there were girls who did not love their mothers, as I did.

After Miss Hardy's arrival, I wrote and complained to my mother that I was being repeatedly bullied by some girls because I was Indian. One of them forced me to eat Lux (white) soap to make my skin paler. My mother immediately came to Bangalore and asked to see Miss Hardy, who was horrified that this was happening in her school. She called these girls 'guttersnipes', and said, had they been living in Britain, they would not have had access to a school such as Cottons. At morning assembly the following day, Miss Hardy spoke very forcibly to pupils and staff. She said she would not tolerate any form of racism, and would expel any girl who taunted Indians in any way. After this I was not subjected to any physical or verbal abuse, but until I left Cottons six years later, snide remarks and jokes persisted. What is of interest is that it was those girls who had been born in India, or came to the country when very young, who were infected with racist feelings, not the newly arrived.

In my first term Anne and I started piano lessons. After the first month she refused to carry on, something she regretted later. My mother considered her to be emotionally fragile, and allowed her to have her own way. Edgar Fewkes was my piano teacher. He and the other piano teacher, Miss Heysham, were both English. Mr Fewkes, though very strict and exacting, had a twinkle in his eye. I felt very intimidated by Englishmen, as most Indians did, but he soon put me at my ease. He was squat in appearance with a stiff brown moustache and no neck. At the middle of the back of his head, where his neck had once been, was a round lump about an inch across. He would frequently comb his hair over the lump, taking a little white comb from his trouser pocket. The lump was referred to as 'the carbuncle' by his pupils. Many of them disliked him because he would scold them for not practising enough, and not showing sufficient interest. They were the source of a rumour that Mr Fewkes would drop dead if his carbuncle was poked with a pin. They were forever plotting to do this, but no one volunteered.

Mr Fewkes's wife Marion, also a musician, taught in Baldwins School, our rival and run by the American Methodist Mission.

She towered over her husband and was of a peculiar shape, and was rudely referred to as 'six feet high, six feet wide'. She wore sack-like dresses down to her ankles. They were a devoted childless couple. He told me he composed his best music when he was engaged to her.

Mr Fewkes took an instant liking to me, and we had an excellent relationship for the next five years. I was a very enthusiastic pupil and learned quickly. It was he who started my love of Western classical music. When I was ten, he entered me for the Grade One examination of the Associated Board of the Royal Schools of Music. Every November, examiners would come from England to examine candidates in India. I was terrified when I learned that an Englishman from England was to be my examiner. When the day of the exam arrived, it was a cold crisp December morning. My fingers felt stiff and I was very nervous. I walked into the music room, and the middle-aged examiner smiled and asked me if my hands were cold. I said, 'Yes,' and he said, 'Put them in mine,' and he held them in his until they warmed. I passed with a merit and his comments were: 'Should develop well.' I got as far as Grade Five, always doing well, but I never got a distinction.

Mr Fewkes used to tease me and say I was too serious, like a little old woman. He started to call me 'Granny'. At the end of every term he would slip a five-rupee note into my hand. 'For the bean feast,' he would say. He knew we had midnight feasts on the last night of term, when we would get the day girls to bring in delicious *masala dosais* and *bondas* from Indian cafés. This was strictly prohibited, but it was what we did once we were promoted to the more senior dormitories, and the matrons turned a blind eye.

Mr Fewkes used to compose little pieces for me to play and write on them 'For Granny'. In my last year in school, I stopped lessons as he became ill, and he and his wife returned to England. I did not see him again. I hope he knew how much I loved him.

From Standard Five onwards, when girls were twelve, we went once a month, on Saturdays to Bishop Cotton Boys' School, a short distance across the road, for Whist Drives and Socials. Boys and girls would dance with each other at the latter, but it was the boy who would ask the girl to dance, and never the other way around, which meant that there were always some girls who wished to dance but remained wallflowers. I was only ten when I had to go to these occasions and felt acutely uncomfortable. Fortunately, I was never asked to dance until I was much older. My mother strongly disapproved of these occasions, but was told this was part of Western culture.

The Eurasian and English girls' constant obsession with boys and romantic love was perplexing to Anne and me. Many of the girls had boyfriends among the Cottons boys. Letters were exchanged between them, usually through go-betweens, who were little boarders from the Boys' School but attended kindergarten in the Girls' School. Letters from the older boys and girls would be slipped into the blazer pockets of these little boys, unknown to them. Occasionally they would be intercepted by teachers, and the offending pupils would be punished by being gated. This meant they were either not allowed on school walks at weekends, or missed the next Whist Drive or Social. These relationships would be initiated by the boy, who would write to the girl he fancied, asking her to accept his love, and she would either write back saying she would, in which case they were an item, or just ignore the letter. In the six years I was at Cottons, no Indian girl ever had a boyfriend, though Anne and I did receive such letters, which we ignored. Indians girls just did not go in for this sort of thing. But there were Indian boys from Cottons boys who did and found willing partners among the European and Eurasian girls. Some of these boys were princes from minor Indian states and were very wealthy. Romantic love was generally frowned upon by Indians and regarded as lust. The cultural divide between Indians and the rest was wide.

The number of Indian boarders increased slightly while I was at Cottons. There would have been more, including several from minor Indian royal families, but apart from making concessions, such as their not having to eat beef, Miss Hardy would not yield to their other demands, such as having separate rooms or wearing different uniforms which covered their legs. Some even wanted to send their servants to be with the girls.

The school uniform consisted of sleeveless blue tunics, white blouses, black leather belt, and a green and gold tie, the latter being the school colours. We also had green blazers with gold trimmings with the school crest on the upper pocket. For sports, we wore navy shorts with green and gold stripes on the sides. Shoes for school had to be black leather or white canvas, which we also used for games and athletics. I soon discovered that if my belt around my tunic was tight enough, I could shove various things down my front, such as tuck bars and various other small odds and ends. But I did not go as far as some girls, who kept baby squirrels and harmless grass snakes, which would sometimes peep out during class, to the consternation of the teachers. Some older girls, usually the lovesick ones, used to have a constant battle with Miss Hardy about the length of their tunic hems, which were required to be no higher than the knee. 'Kneel, and it must touch the ground' she would say. We would have regular uniform inspections, and no sooner was Miss Hardy's back turned than large safety pins would appear, and the hems would go up.

Boarding school did not improve me. On the contrary, I became more and more wayward. When I lived at home and went to Doveton Corrie School, though high-spirited and talkative, I was industrious, disciplined and well behaved. Homework was always completed to a high standard. I handed in written work, and what had to be memorised, I learned thoroughly. Indian schools, parents and pupils take homework very seriously, and it is started by the age of five. My shoes were polished, my uniform was clean and tidy, my pencils were sharpened, my pen was filled with ink and I took to school what I needed to take. My mother considered me to be very diligent and hardworking.

All this evaporated when I left home. My class teacher, a Mrs Walker, was a tall, skeletal, cranky, middle-aged lady who was permanently in a bad mood. She resembled the archetypal frustrated spinster, except she was married to a very pleasant retired doctor and they had four children. She had a short fuse, and I was a thorn in her flesh. She frequently asked me to leave the class because of bad behaviour. I would be talking out of turn, walking up and down between the desks, arguing with her or having a fit of the giggles. I would have to stand outside the classroom door on the verandah, all the class rooms being around a large, attractive open quadrangle with trees and flowerbeds. After about half an hour, she would send for me, but by then I was in more trouble as I would have wandered off and struck up a conversation with one of the *malis* working in the quadrangle. Talking to servants, apart from ayahs, was forbidden, and talking to them in an Indian language was totally forbidden. I would talk to them in fluent Tamil. They would be very pleased to be having a conversation with me. I was not even allowed to speak to my sister in Tamil. As every Indian child in the school spoke excellent English, usually better than most of the other children, this restriction of our mother tongue was totally unwarranted.

An avid reader, I took to reading story books from the school's well-stocked library during study periods for boarders—which were each of 45 minutes duration, one before breakfast and the other after tea—and before games. So my homework was either not done, or was done haphazardly at the last minute. Regular school reports about me, sent to my mother, would read 'Can do much better' or 'Playful and careless' or worse still 'Disruptive'. Despite this, I was always near the top of the class, and top of the class in some subjects. I did not do well in subjects which required a lot of reading, such as History, Geography and Scripture. These bad learning habits which I picked up in my first year at boarding school, exacerbated by inadequate supervision, I carried with me into adulthood.

Bad behaviour was punished in many ways. Lines had to be written, such as 'I will not be late for chapel', usually one hundred times, or we would be gated. We could also lose House points. I was in Barton House. The other two were Foley and Maiden. On one occasion, having been given (very unusually) a major part in a play, I had it taken away from me. This was the worst punishment I could have been given. Trips to the cinema came to an end after Miss Hardy's arrival. She declared most films to be rubbish, something my mother agreed with. We were, however, allowed to see films such as *Great Expectations* and *Scott of the Antarctic*. Every Sunday morning, we went to church in the Boys' School.

Miss Hardy, forever innovative, abolished all end-of-term and end-of-year exams. Instead, every month, without any prior warning, we had exams in three subjects, lasting all day. There was great panic when it was announced at assembly that it was Exam Day. This was intended to encourage us to study and revise consistently throughout the year, but it made no difference to me.

The end of the first term, in April, was heralded by the enormous cassia tree, near the dormitories, suddenly bursting forth into a huge canopy of pink blossom, a truly wondrous sight. Other large trees, jacaranda and gulmohur, would also be a feast for the eyes, covered in blue and orange-red flowers respectively. Our trunks and holdalls came out of the storerooms and were packed by the matrons and ayahs, and we were accompanied once again by a parent on the overnight train to the fierce summer heat of Madras for our six-week summer holidays.

My mother was standing on the platform at Central Station with the other parents. Our luggage was loaded on to a wooden handcart and taken away by two men. Unlike the others, we had no car. We crossed the road once more to get the number 11 bus. On arrival at Annie Lodge, Thatha, Samson Uncle, and the servants greeted us warmly, and Anne and I reverted once again to our Indian ways: walking barefoot and eating with our fingers. My mother went through our trunks and holdalls to find that many of my things were missing: odd socks, blouses, scissors, toothbrush, and other small things. This sent her into a rage and I was given a good beating for being so careless. These items had mostly been stolen by other girls. This happened every term until I was about twelve, and I swore to myself that if ever, one day, I had children of my own, I would never lay a hand on them.

Michaelmas holidays for two weeks followed in the next term, and in the October I was ten. I received a parcel in the post. It was a birthday present from my mother, a book of course: A *Child's Garden of Verses* by Robert Louis Stevenson. 'What?' said my friends. 'Is that all? Only a book.' But I was thrilled with it. I was, however, indignant when I read the poem 'Foreign Children', which went thus:

Little Indian, Sioux or Crow
Little frosty Eskimo
Little Turk or Japanee
O! Don't you wish that you were me?

And so it went on, comparing the superior life of this English child. I did not dispute that; it was the assumption, that I, an Indian, would want to be English. Of course, the Indian referred to here was what we called 'Red Indian' or 'Native American', as they are called today, but I was not to know that then. On reflection, I can say with certainty that I have never wished to be anything other than Indian, even in times of greatest racial humiliation that were yet to come.

Before we knew it, the school year had come to an end and we were home for the six-week Christmas holiday break. My school report said 'Promoted to Std V'.

On my return to school the next academic year, to Standard Five, there were a few girls who had been left behind in my old class They were deemed to have failed, just as were a number of girls in my new class, some three years older than me, who had failed to get promoted. It did not seem to bother them. Some were a foot taller than I was.

This was the year when algebra and geometry were introduced as separate subjects. I was exhilarated by algebra and consistently got full marks in tests, working rapidly, often to the annoyance of my teacher, Marie Peck, a pretty young Anglo-Indian. I would finish my work and then disrupt others. French was taught by Margaret Allen, a small thin bespectacled English spinster with dull light brown hair. 'Mousey', we called her. She would endlessly make us recite French verbs in unison. Miss Hardy decided that Latin should be taught in Standard Five, and she taught it herself. She was always accompanied, wherever she went, by her little docile white terrier, Peter, who would sit quietly in the classroom. She had a habit when she asked a question of pointing to a student and saying in a very loud voice, 'You there.' Once when I was not paying attention, she yelled, 'You there,' and pointed at me. 'Describe him,' she said, indicating the dog. Startled, I blurted out 'Peter piger est (Peter is lazy)'. She was not pleased. Latin was not at all popular, but I enjoyed it as well as French, and was glad I did not have to study Tamil, a very difficult language. It is the only classical language still in everyday use. We were required to memorise large chunks of Latin from *Caesar's Gallic Wars*, and then recite them to Miss Hardy in her office. She would give us House points if we made no mistakes. House points were also given for memorising and reciting the General Thanksgiving and Confession from the *Book of Common Prayer*. Indians are noted for their phenomenal memories, and I was no exception. Though House points were also deducted for my naughtiness, I used to be a significant contributor to the end-of-term totals.

When I was ten, our Shakespeare text was *A Midsummer Night's Dream*, which we studied line by line, and parts of which we acted at concerts. The other text was Walter Scott's *The Talisman*, which was quite incomprehensible. Miss Hardy would take English classes from time to time, to ensure teaching was up to her expectations. As a class, we decided we could not cope with *The Talisman*, and that we would ask Miss Hardy to substitute something easier in its place. But we were all scared of her. She was very strict and serious, and seldom smiled or laughed. She had no sense of humour. Who was to bell the cat? No one would volunteer, so I did. I knocked on her office door and went in, all four foot four inches of me, thin as a rake, and with spindly legs. I told her we found the book difficult and boring, and wanted another book instead. Her eyes nearly popped out with astonishment and rage.

'How dare you come into my office and tell me what you should and should not be taught,' she thundered. 'Get out of my office at once.'

Terrified, I fled to my classmates, who were eager to know the outcome. A few days later, we were asked to hand in our copies of *The Talisman* and an easier book was substituted.

Chapter 7

THE SUN SETS ON THE RAJ

My father continued to write to us when we went to boarding school, but after some months, the letters stopped. I had asked him in my letters why he did not come home during his leave, but he never answered my question. During one of our holidays at Annie Lodge, my mother said, without any emotion, 'I have asked your father not to come back.' Anne and I said nothing. I had not seen much of my father in my ten years, and did not feel close to him, but it was a bereavement all the same. I was overwhelmed with a dreadful shame, which stayed with me well into adulthood. Shame and honour are embedded in the Indian psyche.

In my community, and for that matter among Indians, divorce was unheard of. It only happened when one of the parties was insane, and even then, the sane one was expected to endure it. My mother told Thatha of her decision. He was not surprised. Her siblings were very distressed when they were told about the separation, but none more so than her youngest brother, Alfred. A doctor, he was single, boyish and handsome, and our favourite uncle. Very generous, he would visit us often, play board games with us, take us to the cinema and the beach, and bring us the best mangoes. He would tease us, and there was a lot of laughter when he was around. He had told Jessie Aunty that what concerned him most was that Anne and I no longer had a father.

Alfred Uncle was thirty and in need of a wife. Acquaintances with eligible daughters were falling over themselves to head the queue for this most suitable young man. Thatha and my mother decided to find a bride and went to Tuticorin, from where brides and grooms were often found for my family. They set off to interview the parents of suitable girls, with photographs and details they had already received. The visit was doomed even before they set off, as my mother and Thatha had different ideas as to who, and what was suitable for Alfred. Thatha was in favour of high school-educated, demure, plump, buxom girls who would be docile and good home makers. My mother preferred well-educated, attractive girls with a sparkle, who would make good companions, and be socially adept. The intention was to make a shortlist of three and let Alfred decide. But they came back empty handed, much to Alfred's disappointment. He had returned to Rangoon and was a medical officer to Burma Railways, and told Jessie Aunty that if a marriage was not arranged soon, he would marry a Burmese woman. This was not acceptable to our family, except to my mother, who said, 'Why not? Let him choose for himself.' But he seemed unable to do so.

In mid-1947 my mother announced that she was returning to Burma, having been asked by the headmistress of the school to come back and teach English. I hated the thought of returning to the country which had left me with so many bad memories, but even more so that of my mother being so far away. She consoled us by saying that we would go to Rangoon for the Christmas holidays, and she would come back to Annie Lodge in summer. That first summer I had asked her to bring me a Burmese cheroot, the type poor middle-aged and elderly women smoked. I was always fascinated by them. They were nearly an inch in diameter and over six inches long. They were made from coarse tobacco leaves. I was surprised that she brought me one, and did not disapprove of my smoking it in private. I kept it and a box of matches between two twigs, high up in the jackfruit tree directly in front of the house. I would climb up in the afternoons and have a few puffs when the adults were asleep. One afternoon, to my horror, just as I took a long puff, I looked down to see Thatha standing in the porch. He happened to look up and saw the glowing end of the cheroot and gasped with shock. And then after a moment he laughed and said, 'I will not tell your mother'. I came down and threw away the cheroot. It had a horrible taste and I had had enough of the bravado.

Reluctantly, we spent the Michaelmas holidays at school.

My mother was finding it increasingly difficult to live in Annie Lodge. Her brother Eddie, his wife Violet, and their three sons, Edwin, Tom, and Ernest, had come back to India after the war, having survived the Japanese occupation. They too regarded Annie

Lodge as home. Two women running a house, especially when there are servants to manage as well, was a recipe for strife, especially if one of these women was my mother. Violet was a gentle, biddable person, but she would inadvertently give instructions to servants that would be in conflict with my mother's orders. This would send my mother into a rage and reduce Violet to tears, increasing the servant's confusion. Eddie returned to his thriving practice in Burma shortly thereafter, and left his family in Annie Lodge. His sons went to local schools, and were considerably behind in their education. The years they spent under occupation had set them back considerably.

*

When my mother arrived in Rangoon in the summer of 1947, she was shocked at the state of this once lovely city. What the Japanese did not destroy, the British did as they abandoned the city. Large areas of the city were cordoned off and were under curfew. Damaged buildings and potholes in roads were to be seen everywhere. There had been no attempt to repair them or even remove the rubble. The country was to become independent of the British the following year, but was in a further state of turmoil following the assassination of its leader Aung San and his cabinet. Lawlessness was rampant. Dacoits, as the thugs and robbers were known, made it unsafe to venture out after dark. My mother's school in Kemmendine, however, was intact, and functioning with practically all of the old staff. She was delighted to be back and immediately felt at home. She was even more pleased when she found that Cheena, Biggy's neighbour, had also returned to Rangoon. We had had no contact with him for the past five years. He had been a timber passer with a large firm, Burma being famous for the quality of its teak, which was exported all over the world. He had left Burma for India during the war, to join his two brothers in Calcutta. His firm had asked him to return to Rangoon and he was happy to do so. Burma had been his home; he was well remunerated and was supplied with a house and servants.

Anne and I were to spend our Christmas holidays in Rangoon that year, and my mother asked Samson Uncle, still living in Annie

Lodge, to arrange our travel there by ship. We spent a couple of days with Thatha, Violet Aunty, and her boys. Tom, the middle one, a year older than me, was tall, charming, and good-looking. He was showing great promise at school, especially in maths and physics. He and I had become good friends, and we enjoyed roaming around on our bikes together.

When we got on to the ship, we were surprised and delighted to find that we were sharing the four-berth cabin with one of our teachers from Bishop Cottons: Gwen Staggs, newly married, and about to join her husband in Rangoon. No sooner had we left the harbour to cross the Bay of Bengal than we sailed into a most ferocious storm. The ship rolled and pitched and was tossed about like a matchstick. All passengers were confined to their cabins for four days. When we looked out of the porthole of the cabin we would see the sky, and then, as the ship rolled, the sea, but both looked similar, just grey. We thought we would die, but even worse, Anne and I were consumed with the most appalling seasickness. We vomited and retched for four days, unable to leave our berths. We survived because we were diligently cared for by our 'cabin boy', a middle-aged Goan man whom we called Dad. He gave us soup and water to drink, cleaned us up, took us to the lavatory, changed our clothes and made our beds, all so cheerfully. On the fifth morning we found the seasickness had suddenly left us. The engine was making a different noise, and when we looked out of the porthole we saw that the water was now brown and there were no waves. We were on the Irrawaddy river, and nearly into Rangoon. I was so weak, I could barely stand. My mother and Cheena were at the harbour to meet us and were allowed to board the ship. My legs recovered rapidly, but the experience has left me with a lifelong aversion to sea travel.

Cheena drove us in his jeep to my mother's house in the school compound. It was newly built, with teak and bamboo, and was on stilts, four feet above the ground. It had a front verandah, sitting room, dining room, two bedrooms with ensuite bathrooms, kitchen and store room, and was extremely comfortable. There were six such houses for senior teachers, my mother being the only married one. When we arrived, several of the teachers rushed out to greet us, hugging and kissing us and saying, 'How you have grown.'

They had known me since I was a baby, and had last seen us in 1941, six years earlier.

Cheena would come to visit us every evening, and often take us to his house for dinner, where his cook would produce delicious Burmese food. Cheena too lived in a house like ours, except the stilts were higher as he lived on the bank of the Hlaing river, a tributary of the Irrawaddy, which would occasionally flood. A pontoon ran from the bank over the river and we would sit on it to see some spectacular sunsets. It became apparent to us that Cheena had become a part of my mother's life in Rangoon and we resented it, Anne particularly, as we always hoped our parents would reconcile one day. Cheena being around could be a hindrance.

I never ever fathomed what my mother's relationship to Cheena was, nor did I ever have reason to believe that it was anything other than a deep platonic friendship. My parents did not reconcile, nor did they ever see each other again. They did not divorce, or have a legal separation. Till his death twenty-two years later, Cheena remained an important part of our family and helped to support us financially. He did not show any inclination to marry, but cherished being part of a family, and was readily accepted and much liked by our friends and the rest of our family. I did not ever regard him as a father figure. I did not need one. My mother was everything to me.

But in Rangoon, Anne was clearly adversely affected by Cheena's presence and his daily visits to see us. She deeply resented him. I became extremely fond of him and ours was an easy relaxed relationship. He was extremely generous and indulgent. I enjoyed our evening jaunts into the city to the ice cream shop, or to Moghul Street restaurants where *parathas* and *kababs* were brought to us to eat in the jeep, after we watched them being made expertly on the roadside. But my mother and Cheena would sometimes have ferocious arguments, largely because of her general intolerance and tendency to erupt. This would upset Anne even more. One evening, after one such eruption, when we came home, she threw herself on her bed and started to sob uncontrollably, but would not say why. My mother was clearly troubled and I had a great sense of unease. At my mother's request, Cheena did not come for several days, but we then carried on as before. Anne and I felt unable to talk about my parents' separation until many years later, when we eventually became very close. Until the end of Anne's school days we remained distant, and I continued to be a source of embarrassment to her, because I was constantly in trouble at school. Anne was made a Senior Prefect in 1947, her penultimate year, and ignored me even more.

The same year and even earlier saw the exodus of most of the British girls and their parents from India. Indian Independence was looming and the date had been set for 15 August 1947. The newly created Muslim nation of Pakistan was to become independent the previous day. India had decided to be a secular country, even though it was overwhelmingly Hindu. This was due to the wisdom of its Hindu and Muslim leaders.

The conversation at school, among the British and Anglo-Indian girls went thus: 'Who would want to stay in India with Indians ruling us? They are so stupid, how can they rule without us. The whole thing will fall apart soon. We can't wait to go Home.'

I listened quietly without saying anything. Inside me there was a rage when I heard this kind of talk, but I was also thrilled about Independence and the departure of the British, particularly the girls who had been unpleasant to me. But my mother felt differently. She hated the thought of her friends leaving, and an India governed by Indians.

On 15 August there was a public holiday. There were massive celebrations throughout the country, but in school it was like a Saturday, except that at chapel that morning Miss Hardy prayed for the new India and government. 'God Save the Queen' was replaced by 'God Bless and Guide the Maharajah the Good', Bangalore being in Mysore State, an independent princely state. The Indian national anthem 'Jana Gana Mana' came later, when India became a republic in 1950.

At the time of Independence, we in Southern India had no idea of the carnage that was taking place in the north of the country, as a result of the partition of India, so as to enable Pakistan to be created. This puzzled my mother, who had a great interest in politics and was constantly glued to the radio. That most of the world only had an inkling of the magnitude of the massacres must be attributed to a deliberate blackout of news to save British embarrassment.

꙳

When I was ten, my mother gave me a small hard-backed book called *Being Born*, and asked me to read it. Simply and matter-of-factly, it explained everything from menstruation to marriage and birth. Not really knowing my own anatomy, and not having encountered anything remotely similar in the book, I was puzzled in a somewhat shocked way, but I seem to have imprinted the facts in my mind, because at moments of serious discussions among my dormitory mates, I would be able to give them facts they did not know, or correct their misinformation. They were able to put me right on anatomy. All this was done with good humour and much laughing and giggling. My friends thought I had a very enlightened mother, as their parents had not broached the subject of sex. Being a couple of years younger than my contemporaries, my delayed adolescence was a source of great mirth. Some of these girls were tall, heavy breasted and already into bras, whereas I was four feet eight inches tall, thin and puny.

My continuing irresponsibility and infringement of minor rules was a thorn in the flesh for Anne, especially now that she was a Senior Prefect and was required to reprimand and report me. However, there were two areas in which I excelled, Dramatics and Sports, and this to some extent redeemed me in her eyes. I had also won the annual school elocution contest with the first prize as a substitute entrant at the last minute, the girl chosen from my year having become ill. I had beaten the girls in the upper classes. Miss Hardy beamed as she presented me with the prize at assembly one morning, a book of plays by John Galsworthy.

I had had a growth spurt in the previous six months, and was now over five feet tall and had started to fill out; even the spindly legs were not so spindly. I was less of a runt. No longer the shortest in the class, there were now five girls shorter than me. During school hours, we were required to do physical exercises for twenty minutes each day, and were supervised by Miss Suares, the PE mistress, a tall athletic Goan. She had boundless, infectious enthusiasm and was a member of the Indian Women's Hockey team. I played basketball, hockey and tennis with much enthusiasm. But it was athletics I loved best, and in which I excelled.

Once a year in September we had Sports Day, for which we trained for six weeks. Excitement would mount as tracks were marked out on the hockey field two weeks before Sports Day. There would be a week of heats before the big day, and what a big day it was. There was no day quite like Sports Day. Marquees would be put up for the spectators, including boys from the Boys' School. A local grandee, usually a politician, would be invited to present the prizes. There were tents for the press, officials, caterers and participants. Competition was between the three Houses. The police band and loudspeakers would be in full force. Flags on tall masts would be flying in the wind, and on the field there would be smaller ones to demarcate areas. It was all very festive and I would get gooseflesh just thinking about it.

We had a very fair system, where we were divided into three groups according to our class and height. Each group had six events and we could compete in as many as we wished. When I was twelve, I was in the group with the shorter girls and came first in every one of the six events. The next day the Deccan Herald, Bangalore's most read English newspaper, ran this headline on its back sports page: 'STURDY RAJAN POTENTIAL CHAMPION SPRINTER.' I was ecstatic, and cut it out and sent it to my mother. She was pleased and amused. Heaping praise on Anne or me, for any achievement, was not her style. The Interschool Sports, with thirteen schools participating, followed the next month. It was a massive affair. I got into some of the finals, but did not come in the first three in any event. My enthusiasm for athletics remained, however, and better things were to come.

⌣

At the end of January 1948, Anne and I returned to Madras from Rangoon. We dreaded the journey but the sea was calm; that is, as calm as the Bay of Bengal can ever be. We were seasick as soon as we left the Irrawaddy behind, but after a couple of days got our sea legs, and were able to spend a lot of time on the deck. We arrived in Madras and spent a night in Annie Lodge, and the following evening set off for Central Station for the train to

Bangalore, this time in a hired car. As we approached Madras city, we noticed large crowds everywhere. The approach to the station was almost impossible to get through. People were beating their chests and shouting. Women were weeping and fainting. Clearly something dreadful had happened. Samson Uncle asked the driver to stop and ask someone what was going on. He came running back crying, 'They have shot him. They have shot Gandhiji.' We were speechless. We got to the station, where fortunately the trains were still running, and we got to Bangalore and school. We were a few days late and arrived on a Saturday. For the next few days the entire country was paralysed. All institutions were closed. Miss Hardy was noticeably moved by Gandhi's death. She admired his Christian values, though he was not a Christian. But the English and Eurasian girls who used to constantly ridicule him were upset only because all the cinemas were closed, and they missed their weekly outing.

'If only he had been shot earlier in the week, the cinemas would be open this Saturday,' they callously complained. I was looking forward more than ever to the departure of these girls from India.

Some of the Anglo-Indians planning to go to Australia were encountering problems, as Australia had a Whites Only policy. Families had to be interviewed before they were allowed in. Many were olive skinned and they used to wear hats and long-sleeved white jackets to avoid sunlight. When a family was required to attend, a darker child would be left at home on the pretext that the child was ill, fearing the whole family would be turned down. Even after Independence, there were Clubs in India who had a Whites Only policy. They would admit a fair-skinned person, but not the sibling who had darker skin.

At the end of that year Anne finished High School, scraping her exams with a third class. More was not expected of her. But the big dilemma for her and my mother was what she was to do next. She definitely did not want to train to be a teacher, even though it only required a one-year course to get a diploma. She was considered too dull to get into Madras University, though with some string-pulling it might have been possible for her to get into one of the less desirable colleges, to read an Arts subject. In India, anyone with a bit of brain did Science. The Arts and Humanities were for those less able.

Anne surprised everyone by declaring that she would do nursing. My relatives were appalled. Nursing was for girls from poor, ill-educated, low-caste families. No one from our family or extended family had ever been a nurse.

'If Anne wants to be a nurse, she will be a nurse,' said my mother flatly.

'But who will marry her?' the relatives whispered. No one was prepared to argue with my mother.

The Christian Medical College in Vellore, a town eighty miles from Madras, had a hospital and School of Nursing famous for its excellence. The Medical College was founded by an American missionary, Ida Scudder, to train Indian women doctors to look after women, especially those who refused to be treated by a male doctor. In 1947 male medical students were also accepted, and the institution grew rapidly to be recognised as the finest in Asia.

My mother and Anne went to see the Dean of Nursing, another American missionary. The Nursing School had a certificate course lasting three years, but was just about to introduce a four-year degree course, based on the American system. The Dean suggested that Anne apply for it, as her English was excellent and she had studied in a very good school. Those entering the certificate course came from vernacular schools, where the medium of instruction was in the State language, and their English was poor and they often struggled. Anne was a bit hesitant, as she was unsure she would cope with the fairly high standard of Physics and Chemistry, which had to be passed at the end of the first year. She was encouraged by the Dean and my mother, and Samson Uncle volunteered to coach her in these subjects.

To everyone's astonishment, Anne never looked back and excelled in every subject from her first year. In the first university exams, taken after two years, she stood first.

'Anne,' I said. 'What has happened to you? We all thought you were stupid.'

She said, 'I became a swot and worked really hard, and for

the first time I enjoyed what I studied. I realised I was at least as good as anyone else. In school between those Anglo-Indian and English girls, not to mention the even snootier Parsis, they made me feel so inferior, because I was Indian. So I didn't even try. Of course, I had some lovely friends such as Elsie Hamilton and Eileen Patton, but many of the others were so abominable. Also I was so unhappy about Mummy and Father, I used to think of little else.'

Anne passed her final exams two years later with a first class and a first rank in the university. Even greater glories lay ahead.

⌁

Returning to school from Rangoon without Anne in January 1949 felt quite different. To some extent I felt liberated, but I also missed her. Though we rarely talked to each other, I knew I had a sister to whom I could turn if I was in any serious trouble, however most of the time when I approached her about something, usually a minor problem, she told me to go away, and would promptly write a letter of complaint to our mother. But once she had left school my relationship with her changed for the better.

The girls in my class had entered puberty and were becoming indisposed once a month. To my great disappointment, nothing like that was happening to me. I was of course younger than they were. As a thirteen-year-old, and in the eighth standard, I was summoned one day to see Miss Hardy in her office. I tried to remember my latest misdemeanour. Very matter-of-factly, she said, 'We have decided to make you a Junior Prefect.' I stared at her in astonishment and disbelief. Prefects were grown up and goody-goodies. Not someone like me, always late, breaking rules, forgetting homework and worst of all answering back. She added, 'Your teachers and I have had many long discussions about you, and though most of them disagree strongly with me, I feel that making you a Prefect will enable you to fulfil the potential I believe you have.' She pinned a cotton green and gold badge on to my tunic. I was embarrassed and dreaded facing my classmates. There were only two other Prefects in my class. I went back to my classroom, and it was a little time before my badge was noticed.

'What!' they gasped. 'She's a Prefect. We don't believe it.' From that day, my behaviour changed completely. No longer did I raid the tuck cupboard, swap food at table, climb prohibited trees, wear socks that did not match, keep live golden giant beetles down my tunic, talk to the servants in Tamil or do all the other things that got me into trouble. Furthermore, my minions, the girls in the lower classes I used to keep company with, were now told by me to behave properly, and behave they did. Within six months I was made a Senior Prefect, and Miss Hardy pinned a silver badge on me at a short ceremony on the stage, after morning assembly. I had become a reliable and responsible girl.

That year, after I had recovered from a mild bout of influenza, I suffered a sharp pain in my chest after a vigorous game of hockey. I reported it to the matron. I had to see the school doctor, a Dr Moon. A stern and sour-faced bicycle riding Anglo-Indian spinster, she declared I had a weak heart, and was not to play games or take part in athletics for a year. My disappointment knew no bounds, especially as I felt so fit. After my success on the sports field the previous year, I was hoping to do even better. I started to protest, and was promptly cut short by Dr Moon. I immediately wrote to my mother in Burma, who was only concerned about my disappointment at not being able to take part in any sports. She wrote to Miss Hardy suggesting a second opinion with a heart specialist.

'Nonsense. Quite unnecessary,' said Dr Moon, who added that I was to take a few drops of a drug called Coramine 'to support the heart'. Miss Hardy said I was to take her advice. I was not allowed to take part in Sports Day that year. I was devastated. During the Christmas holidays my mother took me to see a heart specialist who pronounced my heart to be entirely normal, and with a twinkle in his eye, said he suspected it was always so. My mother wrote a tactful letter to Miss Hardy, expressing her thanks to Dr Moon for helping in my recovery.

Mrs Arklie, the matron, later told me Dr Moon had been furious that I had had a second opinion.

That year, a few months before my fourteenth birthday, I attained puberty, much to my relief, as I was now like the other girls in my dormitory and class. I immediately wrote to my mother to tell her. She wrote back to me and ended the letter: 'One day, Lindy, you will be a beautiful woman.' During the Christmas holidays in Rangoon that year, I overheard her and Anne discussing me in the next room and my mother said, 'It looks as though the duckling is turning into a swan.' Relief engulfed me. I had ceased to be a runt.

I took my studies more seriously at this time and excelled in the subjects I was interested in, such as algebra, English and Physiology.

Our Eurasian teachers were outstanding. As Eurasians they were unusual in that they had all been to university and were very committed teachers. Christine Gaughan was a young, slim, gentle, beautifully groomed lady who taught us maths. When she emigrated to England several years later, and taught in a Secondary Modern School in Essex, she so transformed their maths results that she was quickly headhunted by a private school nearby.

Merlin Martin, another young and brilliant Anglo-Indian, taught Science. She was one of the three resident teachers, and would good-naturedly take us boarders on walks, crocodile-style, at weekends. We would go to Cubbon Park on Saturday afternoons, where in pre-Raj days the bandstand would come to life, a police band playing traditional popular British music. She would also accompany us to the Lalbagh Gardens, to the annual flower show, unsurpassed in the rest of India. It was a three-mile walk from the school. There, we would be allowed to disperse for two hours, to admire the trees and a brilliant display of plants. While most of us would make a beeline for the out-of-bounds South Indian café at the rear of the gardens, to gorge on *bhondas* and *masala dosais*, the senior girls would be meeting their boyfriends behind the bushes. Resident teachers would also accompany us to the Sunday morning Eucharist Service in the Boys' School chapel, Socials and Whist Drives, also held at the Boys' School.

Yvonne Beale was the Deputy Head. Very able, serious and strict, she generously dished out minus House points, and not surprisingly I was at the receiving end frequently. When I was eleven she was my form mistress and often sent me out of the class for disruptive behaviour. Despite this I had a great affection and admiration for her. She taught History and Geography throughout the school. Her grasp of Indian History was impressive, and she was noted for attempting to pronounce Indian names correctly. This would send us into floods of giggles. Eurasians and the British would not and could not pronounce Indian words and names correctly, as it was not the done thing, anyway, to talk like Indians. Mrs Beale was Anglo-Burmese and had trekked from Burma to India during the war, losing two sisters on the way to dysentery and malaria. When I unexpectedly met her in England twenty-five years later, she said to me, 'You were such a naughty little girl, but so bright. We always knew you would bring credit to the school.' No one had ever told me that in those days.

In my penultimate year at Bishop Cottons, my mother had one of her brainwaves. She decided that I should drop French, which I had studied for four years and greatly enjoyed, and learn Hindi instead. After Independence the latter was declared the national language, despite protests from South Indians who wanted the country to have two national languages, English being the other. Hindi and its variants were spoken in the north of India, the home of most of India's leaders. My mother thought it would be an advantage, were I to work in the public sector later on. I did not know any Hindi, but the Hindi teacher assured Miss Hardy that he could bring me up to the required standard in two years. I learned the script quickly, and could read fluently, but I could barely understand what I was reading. By the time of the examination, my vocabulary was enormous but my sentence construction poor and knowledge of gender laughable.

The year moved on quickly, and once again Sports Day was looming. I had been very active in games that year, having been released from Dr Moon's grip. I played hockey, basketball and tennis and was in the house and school teams. Bangalore had several schools, and hardly a week went past when there wasn't an inter-school match. But as always, it was athletics which I enjoyed most. I got up early in the morning, weeks before Sports Day, and started to train, running and jumping. Alfred Uncle had been a champion athlete in his youth, and he took a great interest in how I was performing and sent me Harold Abraham's book on athletics. Trying my very utmost, I won the championship in my section, coming first in the 50 and 100 metres and in both the jumps, and second in the discus throw. Miss Suares, the games mistress, was very surprised that I won the jumps.

'It is that grim determination of yours,' she said, when I broke the record in the high jump, using the scissors style. I could not master the Western roll. The Fosbury Flop had not been invented. Once again, I was in the headlines on the back page of the Deccan Herald, Bangalore's daily. This time it was: 'STAR PERFORMANCE BY ROSALIND RAJAN.' I cut it out and sent it to my mother. My mother had never seen me perform, either at games or athletics or on stage, acting or playing the piano. I preferred it that way. I think I would have been embarrassed to have her watch me.

Within a few weeks of our school Sports Day, we were getting ready for the Bangalore Schools' Athletic Meeting at which hundreds of girls and boys competed. This year it was being held in the new stadium built for the recent Indian Olympics. We were thrilled to run on a cinder track with eight lanes. The march past of the athletes, with a band, was an inspiring sight, but Miss Suares would not let me take part, as she thought it would tire me. I was entered for the sprints—50 and 100 metres—and the 4 × 100 metre relay, running the last leg. For the first time, the 200 metres had been introduced for girls, amid some controversy as it was thought to be too strenuous. Only a few robust girls were entered, so there were no heats, just finals. I did not expect to get into any of the finals, as there were some outstanding state athletes in the other schools, and they used to practise all the year round. I was eliminated in the heats of the 50 metres, and to my surprise came second in the 100 metres. Having finished my events, I was sitting on the stadium steps with the spectators and other athletes, talking and laughing with the other boys and girls. Miss Suares came to me and said she wanted me to run in the 200 metres. The entrant from our school had scratched as she was unwell. I was required to be the substitute. I was horrified. I said I had no idea how to run the race and didn't think I could last the distance.

'Just go and run it,' Miss Suares said, and added, 'You can do it.' Advice and encouragement was being shouted at me from all sides. One said run slowly at first and pick up speed. Another said run fast at the beginning and when your legs give up, you can run slowly. The younger brother of my classmate Joyce Applegate said, 'Here, I'll lend you my spikes.'

'Yes,' said the others. 'Try them, you will run faster.'

I had never run in spikes, but I put on Mickey Applegate's spikes and he showed me how to tie the laces round the instep. Just then the 200-metre race was called, and I carefully went down the steps on to the track. My heart was thumping, and I had pins and needles in my hands. I was on the inside lane. There were seven other girls running.

I warmed up a bit, and then we took up the crouch position. The starter's gun went off and I ran as fast as I could from start to finish. One by one I picked off each girl, to the roar of the spectators, and to my total astonishment breasted the tape first. It was my greatest moment of glory, never to be repeated.

Chapter 8

AN UNSUITABLE GIRL

I had mixed feelings about leaving school. There were friends, teachers and matrons for whom I had the greatest affection, but I could never think of the school without remembering the six years of racism I had encountered. But I did not feel bitter, just perplexed, sad and sometimes angry. There was one person who was special to me, Mrs Arklie, my matron for the last three years. She was a kindly, gentle Anglo-Indian widow in her mid-forties, with sad eyes and I got to know why. Her husband had died suddenly several years before, leaving her with five daughters and a son, Gerald. He had been the apple of her eye, and the man of the house. Though not yet twenty, and despite his mother's pleas to the contrary, he enlisted in the army and was sent to the Far East, where he became a prisoner of war and was killed by the Japanese. One of her daughters, Phyllis, now a twenty-year-old, had been struck down with polio when she was five and confined to a wheelchair, and she lived with her mother on the school premises. Mrs Arklie would let some of us into her room sometimes, to listen to the radio. We were able to listen to Princess Elizabeth's wedding ceremony in November 1947. She also turned a blind eye to many of our misdeeds, even on the occasion when she caught us smoking Players cigarettes.

In my last year at school, a new girl from England joined our class. She had the splendid name of Vera Mary Marjorie Moxey. Her father was a senior officer in the Royal Air Force, and had been loaned to the newly independent Indian Air Force for two years. Tall, sporty and extremely friendly, she was very popular. After she had been in school a few weeks, she said to me, 'Lindy, do you think I could ever become as brown as you? I'd just love to.'

I was quite taken aback. She was so unlike the other girls. She, like Leonie Whitlock and Betty Josephs, has remained a lifelong friend.

On the last day of school we said our tearful goodbyes, and before we got the train to Madras that night, four of us went to the cinema to see an X-rated film for the over-eighteens.

'How old are you?' the man at the ticket office asked.

'Never mind,' we said. 'We have finished school.' He gave us the tickets. I was fifteen years and two months. I cannot recall the name of the American film, but it was about a young unmarried mother about to give birth in prison, having been sentenced for life. It was grim.

I stayed in Annie Lodge for a week until there was a boat going to Rangoon. I went with Samson Uncle to get my entry permit. He went everywhere on his cycle, and suggested that I ride my bike with him to the permit office. We rode on the main road, but whenever he heard a car or bus behind us, he would quickly disappear left on to the next minor road, and then turn around back to the main road. I would then be yards ahead. I found this very trying and reprimanded him. As always, he merely smiled.

Leonie came to see me off. Her father was a friend of Captain Worthington, the ship's captain. He had my cabin upgraded to one which opened on to the deck. The sailing was smooth, and four days later we docked in Rangoon where I was met by my mother and Cheena.

⁓

In India, the European and American schools' year started in January, unlike the Indian schools, colleges and universities, for whom the academic year began in June or July. To go to medical school I had to study for two more years to take the Intermediate Science exam, similar to the International Baccalaureate/A levels. I was determined to do this at Queen Mary's College in Madras, a secular women's college, on the Marina, a beautiful beach road. Nearby was Presidency College, the men's college. But I was certain my mother would put pressure on me to attend Women's Christian College, a twenty-minute bus ride from Annie Lodge, which was rated very highly, but was much more staid. Two of my mother's cousins, both sisters and single women, were lecturers there. The college had a large proportion of Malayalee girls from the state of Kerala. Historically, there has always been unease and friction between the people of Kerala and those of Tamil Nadu, which was my state, and this was reflected in preferment of one over the other in trivial matters, such as the choosing of student officers, depending of course on who was doing the choosing.

My mother abhorred this kind of pettiness, and I soon realised she had very different ideas for me.

I had to make my application in January, and when I mentioned to my mother that I was sending for the appropriate forms, she said the finest college in India was not in Madras, Bombay, Delhi or Calcutta, but in Lucknow, in Northern India, fifteen hundred miles away.

'What!' I exclaimed. 'But that is another country. I'm certainly not going there. Anyway, what is this place called?'

'Isabella Thoburn College (IT),' said my mother. 'And affiliated to Lucknow University.'

I had never heard of it, and I could not understand what was so special about it. My mother had been involved with the YWCA for several years, both in Rangoon and Madras, where she had met women in all walks of life, nationalities and ages.

She added, 'In Madras, I have met so many young women from all over India but only a few have been really impressive: smart, well educated, well groomed, well mannered, cultured and articulate. When I asked them where they studied, they invariably said "Isabella Thoburn College".' She too had not heard of it, but she had made enquiries and found it was a single-sex college run by American Methodists and staffed by Americans and Indians. The Principal was a Sarah Chakko, the most prominent Christian woman in India and one of six Presidents of the World Council of Churches. She was a Malayalee from Travancore State, later called Kerala.

My mother had intended to leave Rangoon for good that summer, and return to Madras and Annie Lodge. Thatha was eighty, and from his letters it was obvious that between Samson Uncle and the servants he was not adequately looked after, though he did not complain. Cheena had decided to resign at the same time from his job in Rangoon. He was being required to pass substandard timber for export. He had acquired a very good post in Sarawak in Borneo. I thought how nice it would have been for me to study

in Madras, and be near my mother for the first time since I was
nine. Teenagers in the West long to get away from their parents,
but it is the opposite for Indians. We like to be near our parents.
But my mother was gently persuasive, and the prospectus from
IT was most attractive and inviting. Reluctantly, I agreed to go
to Lucknow. About a third of the students in the college boarded.
I had an immediate response to my application from the Acting
Principal, Miss Hunt, an American. Sarah Chakko was away on
sabbatical in Geneva. Miss Hunt was delighted that I had chosen
IT in preference to the Madras Colleges, whose high reputation
was well known. Though IT did not take students under sixteen,
Miss Hunt said she was prepared to waive the rule for me. So
that was settled in January 1951. The College year would start
in July of that year and first-year students, freshers as we were
called, would arrive a fortnight early for initiation. I had passed
the Bangalore High School exam, just scraping in Hindi. The results
of the Cambridge exam came some months later. My mother was
particularly pleased that I had got a distinction in English.

⌒

For the five months after I arrived in Rangoon in December 1950
and while I was waiting to go to College in June 1951, I led
a life of leisure and laziness, and was thoroughly indulged by
my mother. How we enjoyed each other's company! We talked
endlessly about everything except my father. But Rangoon I
detested. Burma had been independent for three years, but there
were no signs of progress, or even of rebuilding the city. Rangoon
was not a safe city, and in the evenings and nights there was a
curfew in many areas.

On Christmas Eve, we attended a Carol Service in the cathedral
in the city. It was where Anne and I were baptised. We returned by
bus, and were walking from the bus stop to the school campus at
7.30 in the evening. Three men walking behind us said something
to my mother in Burmese. I turned around to look and saw one
of them holding a revolver to my mother's back. I gasped.

'Don't make a noise,' my mother said. 'Just give them your
watch and gold chain and keep walking.'

I did that, and she gave them her handbag, chain, bangle and earrings. They took her purse, opened it and took out the money and returned the purse and the handbag. They told us to keep walking, and just as suddenly as they appeared, they disappeared. We were very shaken, and told the guard at the school gate. He told us it was a frequent occurrence, and there was no point in reporting the incident to the police, as they were corrupt.

I did not want to stay on in Rangoon, but my mother felt obliged to stay till the end of the school year in May. I did, however, feel secure in the comfortable little bamboo and wood house on stilts, inside the school campus. The sound of the night watchmen moving around at night, with their sticks and lanterns, gave me a sense of security. Several of my mother's older pupils became my friends, including the serene and gentle San San Nu, daughter of the then Prime Minister U Nu, a fine man. They liked to practise their English on me. The highlight of the weekday for me was at noon, when about twenty food stalls would be set up by vendors under a huge canopy. Before staff and hordes of students were let loose to buy their lunch, I would go to inspect the stalls, and after much dawdling, choose lunch for my mother and myself. It must be due to the continuing isolation of Burma that its culinary delights have not been experienced outside the country in the same way as Indian, Chinese and Thai food. Burmese food is varied and exceptionally tasty. My mother would often ask a few of the poorer students to join us. As I lived with her, I was coming to realise what an extraordinarily generous person she was, sometimes foolishly so.

I learned there were to be two forthcoming athletics meetings in Rangoon, where one did not have to belong to a team and could enter as an independent. These were meetings of the Burma Athletic Association and the Burma Olympics. I entered for both the 100-metre and 200-metre sprints, coached by Alfred Uncle. Competing with Burmese and Chinese girls, I came first and second in the two events in both meetings.

Two years earlier a temporary rift had occurred between Alfred Uncle and my mother. He had married Sucie, my first cousin on my father's side. Her father was my father's older brother.

The marriage was arranged by my aunt Jessie. My mother was neither consulted nor informed of the impending alliance, and only heard about it when the engagement was announced. In my community, it is customary for the engagement to take place only after all wedding arrangements have been finalised. It is usually just a week before the wedding, and sometimes on the morning of the wedding. My mother was incandescent with rage, and left speechless when she received a telegram from Alfred: 'Engaged today to Sucie, Amrithraj's daughter. Marriage next week.' The telegram was sent from Madras while Alfred was on holiday there and staying in Annie Lodge. He was thirty-four and Sucie eighteen. They shared a birthday on 5 August. Amrithraj, according to my mother, was an unsavoury character. He had two daughters: Radha, the elder, a beautiful, intelligent and charming girl, who had died in childbirth, and her sister Sucie, who had picked all the short straws. Small and puny, unattractive, with a squint, she lacked charm. She was poor at her studies, and had left school early. Her marriage prospects were poor. She was only a few years older than me, and I remember playing hide and seek with her before my parents separated. All contacts with my father's relatives had stopped after my parents' separation six years earlier.

Amrithraj approached Jessie and proposed Sucie for Alfred. She was at first taken aback, but not only did Amrithraj extol Sucie's homemaking skills, he convinced Jessie, that such a marriage would bring the two sides of the estranged family together, and reconcile my mother and father. She put it to Thatha, who by now had tired of trying to find a bride for his youngest son, and asked Jessie to consult my mother and Alfred. If they had no objection, he would not have any. Jessie did not consult my mother, as she knew what my mother's response would be, and overruled Samson's objections. Jessie convinced Alfred that Sucie was a suitable girl. The marriage was arranged hurriedly.

After the wedding Alfred returned to Burma with his bride and brought her to visit my mother in Rangoon. My mother was polite but cool towards them. One day she asked Alfred what could have possibly made him marry Sucie, and he replied, 'So that Anne and Lindy could have a father again.' My mother said her marriage was dead, and could never be revived, and he had been foolish not to have consulted her before agreeing to marry Sucie, and that he had unnecessarily sacrificed his own happiness.

Sucie brought her firstborn to see us after we had returned to Madras. I felt sorry for her, as no one in the family seemed cordial towards her. I tried to be as nice to her as I could, and enjoyed playing with the baby, a very beautiful little girl. She came several times on her own, with the baby, to see us. She bore three more children, and they grew up without knowing us. Alfred continued to visit us on his own when he was in Madras, and never looked happy. It would be nearly half a century later, years after Alfred's death and my mother's death, that his son Appu would contact me, and that I would meet him for the first time, and I would see Sucie again, now grey and wizened. 'Do you know, Lindy,' she said, 'you were the only one in your family who was nice to me? Do you remember you always walked with me to the bus stop?' I didn't remember, but I was glad that I had done so.

It was from Appu that I learned so many things about my father, how he longed to contact me and Anne, but was afraid of my mother. And that he would weep when he talked about us. Appu had been very close to my father all the time he was growing up, and after my father had retired from government service in Orissa, he lived in Madras, in a flat above Appu and his family.

'Why, Appu?' I asked. 'Why did he not contact us when we had grown up and lived away from our mother?'

'Because he did not wish to offend your mother,' he replied.

⌣

In May 1951, much to my relief, my mother reluctantly left Burma for good. She had always said it felt more like her country than India did. Annie Lodge would be our home again, and my mother took charge of running it. Thatha was delighted at out return. Even Samson Uncle was pleased to see us back, though it meant he would have to curb some of his slack ways, so as not to incur my mother's wrath.

When Thatha, Jessie Aunty and other relatives were told I was going to Lucknow to study, they were horrified, especially as there were such excellent colleges nearby. They thought my mother had taken leave of her senses. This was utter madness. Thatha told Jessie that my mother had always had absurd notions and ideas. First, she had sent me to study for years with foreign white children, but that at least was only 200 miles away. This was 1,500 miles away, and two whole days by train. In fact, this was a foreign country with all those North Indians speaking strange languages. Why, if I were to get ill, I'd be dead before my mother reached me!

Our tailor, a Muslim called Abdul Wahib Sahib, aged about sixty, was duly summoned to sew some smart clothes for me. Patterns were from Western magazines and catalogues. He sewed for Europeans and Eurasians and was highly recommended by friends. At fifteen, I insisted that I would continue to wear Western-style clothes, unlike my cousins who had moved into half saris and saris, ensuring that their legs were covered down to the ankles. Modesty is very important in Indian culture. I had never worn Indian dress. My mother continued to encourage me to wear Western clothes, as I had done in Bishop Cottons. We were not allowed to wear Indian clothes there. My grandfather, relatives and neighbours strongly disapproved of my wearing Western clothes. They would say to my mother, 'Lindy would look so nice in a half sari or sari. Is it not time she started wearing these?' A withering look from my mother would shut them up.

Abdul Wahib Sahib would arrive every morning at seven in a coloured checked *lungi* and overhanging shirt, which was the usual dress of poor and uneducated Muslims. He worked in the upstairs verandah of Annie Lodge, on my mother's treadle machine. The handsewing he would do sitting cross-legged on the floor on a reed mat. We provided him with his meals. He was silent most of the time, and we could not get him to talk about anything which was not related to his work, at which he was meticulous, and required many fittings of me. At exactly 4 p.m., he would put away everything and leave to catch the bus to his home in Thousand Lights, a bustling Muslim neighbourhood off Mount Road, the long spine through Madras. When all the work was finished to his and our satisfaction, he would state his price, which my mother paid without bargaining, the latter being the norm. He worked for my mother on and off for a further five or six years and then disappeared, not responding to my mother's letters asking him to come and do more work. She thought he must have died. But he turned up some years later, bent and emaciated, and said he had tuberculosis, and was being treated at the Government Hospital. He was destitute. By then I was working abroad, and barely surviving on £25 a month. My mother asked me to support this poor man by sending him a few pounds every month. This I did until he died two years later, even though he had made a good recovery from the tuberculosis.

Chapter 9

ANOTHER COUNTRY

The journey from Madras to Lucknow would take forty-eight hours by train. We were to take the Grand Trunk Express from Madras to Jhansi, a journey of about forty hours, then take another train to Kanpur (spelt and pronounced 'Cawnpur' by the British) and change again there for Lucknow. The Grand Trunk Express was India's most famous and exciting train, going from south to north, from Madras to Delhi, a distance of over 2,000 kilometres with barely a dozen stops, over forty-eight hours. A steam train, it lost its appeal many years later after it was electrified and the number of stops increased to over thirty, but it still managed to cut its time to thirty-six hours.

At the end of June 1951, my mother and I arrived at Central Station in Madras to catch the Grand Trunk Express to Delhi. It left at nine every morning and would reach Delhi two days later. Comfortable second-class berths in a four-berth compartment had been pre-booked for my mother and me. My grey tin trunk, my mother's suitcase and two holdalls with our bedding had been sent ahead. Before we left, Thatha prayed as usual for a safe journey, and that I would return home safely five months later for Christmas. I was going too far away to return home for the Diwali holidays in October. At eighty-one, he was convinced he would not see me again.

Central Station was always an exciting, noisy place, crowded with people. In addition to the passengers, there would be numerous relatives to see them off, screaming babies, children playing hide and seek between people, porters with red turbans, important-looking railway staff in white cotton jackets and ties, hawkers selling their wares, and mountain-loads of luggage. But it was the steam engines which would make our pulses race. Our engine had not yet been connected to the carriages, which were already on the platform. It had gone to have a drink. We could see it beyond the platform. It was hissing and cursing and disgorging vast clouds of steam, and then it came backwards towards the carriages and with a great bump connected itself. In India, there were three widths of railway tracks which determined the width of the train. Important routes were broad gauge, as this one was. There were four classes of travel: first, second, Inter and third. The first two were comfortable and well upholstered. These compartments had four or six berths in two tiers and these had to be reserved in advance. First class also had coupes with two berths, much favoured by British couples. All classes had a Ladies Only compartment. It was usual practice for Indian men to dump their wives, luggage and children into these, while they travelled in the less crowded general compartments, taking their ease, talking, eating, sleeping, smoking and playing cards. This used to incense my mother. In Ladies Only third class, there would be severe overcrowding and chaos, with screaming nappy-less incontinent babies, puking infants, food splattered all over, vendors and sometimes beggars taking up residence. Invariably verbal fights would break out between the women. Once on a short trip, I was in a third-class Ladies Only carriage, when to my horror I discovered a man sleeping under a berth, with two round covered baskets. He was a ticketless snake charmer with live cobras in the baskets. He was ejected at the next station.

The berths were one above the other in second class. Our names were on a list pasted on the outside of the compartment, and a ticket collector ticked off our names on his list after checking our tickets. The upper berth was specially selected for me for security, in case we had to share the compartment with males. We need not have worried. We had the compartment to ourselves until the early hours of the following morning when at Kazipet, in the Deccan, a charming middle-aged Muslim man and his beautiful daughter got in. They were from Hyderabad, nearby, and like me she was going to Isabella Thoburn College for the first time.

I did not ever tire of this long journey. Punctually, the train set off, and very quickly gained speed. We left the green rice fields and coconut palms, so characteristic of the south of India. We crossed scrublands, and then the scenery became dramatic as we went through the dense jungle of central India, near the Seoni district, made famous by Kipling's *Jungle Books*. We passed tranquil fields with grazing livestock and crossed mighty rivers, the Godavari and the Krishna. We carried our own water and ate in the first-class dining car. We sometimes had to spend three or four hours there, as the train had no corridors, and we had to wait for a station stop before we could return to our carriage. The stations were like markets, with colourful food and fruit stalls, hawkers walking up and down the platform selling to passengers through the open windows, and then of course there were the beggars and lepers.

We arrived in Jhansi at midnight the following day, and even at that time the heat was searing. Madras was hot, but this was different. Unlike in Madras, there was no sea breeze to break the heat. Apart from being a busy railway junction, Jhansi was famous for its warrior queen, Lakshmi Bai, the Rani of Jhansi, who gallantly fought the British during the Indian Mutiny in 1857.

The coolies who carried our luggage were tall and sturdy, with luxuriant moustaches and magnificent turbans, unlike the short, puny Tamil coolies with skinny legs. And they spoke Hindi, not Tamil. My high-school Hindi was quite inadequate. We were all Indians, but it was becoming obvious that ethnically we were different, North Indians being of Aryan stock and we from the south, Dravidians. I was beginning to feel not quite at home. We took a train to Kanpur, and from there, another to Lucknow. On this last leg of the journey, we crossed the Ganges. I felt a strange feeling of exhilaration going over this great river, a feeling that was to be repeated every time I crossed it. There were no burial ghats or crowds at this part of the river, just a stretch of clear fast-flowing water.

We arrived in Lucknow, a city of historical interest made famous by the Indian Mutiny of 1857 against British Rule. British troops and their families retreated to the Residency and were holed up for eighty-seven days under increasingly appalling conditions until they were eventually relieved. Indians like to call this the First War of Indian Independence. We took a *tonga* to the YWCA Guest House, where my mother would stay for the next fortnight, to see me settled. The staff and other residents of the Guest House were all North Indians, spoke English and were friendly, but they wondered why I had come all the way from Madras, which was well known for the high quality of its education. But they all agreed that Isabella Thoburn was an outstanding College and the Principal, Sarah Chakko, away on sabbatical leave in Geneva, a uniquely inspiring woman.

Next morning, my mother and I, with my tin trunk and holdall, arrived at the impressive Parthenon-like portals of Isabella Thoburn College (IT). Each of the ten simple columns represented a virtue of Indian womanhood. We were welcomed by a few second-year students, who had given up a fortnight of their summer holidays to help us with our induction. They spoke fluent English and occasionally lapsed into Hindi, which I found difficult to understand. The senior staff were mainly American Methodist Missionaries, and the youngest was twenty-six. The younger staff were mainly Indian.

The difference from my experience at Bishop Cottons was startling, even allowing for the fact that I was older. There, I was made to feel different and always conscious of the Raj. I belonged to an inferior race which had been conquered and ruled. I never felt comfortable being an Indian in Bishop Cottons. Here, it ceased to be an issue. The Americans emphasised our Indianness. This was an enormous relief, but I was not completely at ease. Those girls who had been to vernacular schools spoke to each other in Hindi or Urdu. I felt left out. And then there was their strange food eaten at strange times.

I was shown to my hostel, to the first floor, where there was a large room, which I was required to share with five other girls. Each of us had a bed, table and chair, as well as a curtained-off cubicle which had a wardrobe and a dressing area. Rooms opened onto a verandah at the end of which were shared bathrooms. It was all very spartan. We were expected to do our studying mainly in the college's well-stocked and furnished library, a block away. The dining room was on the ground floor, L-shaped and large enough for all 220 boarders to eat at the same time.

The campus was on a 30-acre site with extensive playing fields, catering for hockey, soccer, basketball, volleyball, softball and tennis. Best of all, there was a swimming pool. But to my utter disappointment, there was no athletics at any time of the year. On Sports Day team games were played. Compared to Bishop

Cottons, it was a dull day. We did, however, have competitive swimming, which I threw myself into, and I soon became the college champion at breaststroke but never managed to master the crawl.

The classrooms and laboratories were in the administrative block, which led on from the entrance portals. Men, apart from male servants, of whom there were a few, were not allowed beyond this point. Any visitors, including male relatives, even fathers, had to wait in the visitors' room and the student concerned was summoned by the chaprassi. In the middle of the administrative block was a magnificent newly built auditorium with a stage, and on the rear of it was an outdoor stage. There were comfortable dressing rooms and bathrooms, all intended for the production of concerts and plays, for which this college was famous. The new plush velvet curtains alone were reported to have cost ten thousand rupees, a princely sum in those days.

ſ

Initially, I was carried away by a totally new environment with new experiences every day. There was also much kindness from everyone, but by the end of the first week I was beginning to feel very isolated. The language was increasingly becoming a barrier. Those girls who spoke English all the time already had friends from their previous schools. My clothes, the newly made dresses, skirts and blouses, felt out of place. Nearly all the other girls wore Indian dress, mainly a tunic and baggy trousers called *salwar-kameez* with a *dupatta*, a thin shawl across both breasts and over both shoulders for purposes of modesty. Some wore saris. I did not possess any of these garments. I became conscious of my legs. I felt unable to ask my mother for a new wardrobe. I could not get accustomed to the food. Because of the intense heat, the day started early, and breakfast was at 6.15 a.m. It consisted of two hard, round tasteless biscuits, which we referred to as dog biscuits, and a weak cup of sweet milky tea. I soon discovered that for an extra charge I could buy two slices of bread and a pat of butter. Classes started at 6.40 a.m. At 10.45 a.m., there was what was called a refreshment break for forty-five minutes. We were given two *chapattis*, two dollops of a watery vegetable called *loukie* and some potato. We then returned to class, and on the first day of term I asked when we would have lunch. I was told that we had already had lunch. Classes finished at 1.40 p.m., and we returned to our rooms for a long siesta. We needed it in that heat. Though Madras had a hot, humid climate, it was relieved in the late afternoon by a cool sea breeze. This heat was dry, but persisted day and night.

At 3.30 p.m. we had tea; again, the same dog biscuits, which could be supplemented with bread and butter. This was followed on Mondays to Thursdays by compulsory swimming in summer, and games in winter. Dinner was similar to lunch, but with a bit of meat, usually goat. Out of deference to Hindus and Muslims, beef and pork were never served. I soon discovered that for twenty-five rupees a month, we could have a really substantial European-style meal in the evening, and I signed up for it. In winter classes started and finished two hours later. There were only cold-water taps in the bathrooms, and cold baths were very welcome in the summer. We bathed several times a day.

Bathing was in the Indian style. A bucket was filled under the cold tap, and one sat on a nearby wooden stool. With a dipper, one poured water over oneself, soaped all over, and then rinsed off the soap with copious amounts of water. Once it got cold, we would go out on to the verandah and yell for the hot water man to bring a bucket full of hot water to the bathroom. As we took our baths in the evening after games, constant shouting would be heard for the *bhisthi*, a most willing and amiable man. He was wiry and middle aged, and could adeptly balance a bucket of very hot water at each end of a pole across his shoulders. Many of the girls lived on the first floor, and he could be seen swaying from side to side as he climbed the stairs, but never spilling even a drop of water.

At the beginning of my second week in IT, I started to feel miserable. I had made no friends to sit with at meals, or sit and chat with, or go for walks with on the campus. My mother came to visit me every evening and was aware of my unhappiness. I could not see how I would ever fit in and feel comfortable and happy in IT. But there was no turning back now. I could not let my mother down, even though I knew that if I had asked her to take me back to Madras she would have done so. I was also uncomfortable that I was a curiosity. The other girls wondered why had I come all this way to study. Why was my Hindi so abysmal? Did I speak Madrassi? They were ignorant about South India. There was no such thing as Madrassi. The language was called Tamil, and was one of the major Indian languages.

The staff continued to tell me how pleased they were to have a girl from Madras, especially the professor of Chemistry, a Dr Margaret X. Wallace, as she was always known. What the X stood for, we never did find out. A very large, jolly lady from Minnesota, she always had a smile on her face, and from time to time would unexpectedly burst into peals of laughter, for no obvious reason. She became my mentor. The two Physics teachers were as different as chalk and cheese. Manmohanath Zutshi was a small, stern Hindu bachelor in his fifties. 'You fool,' he would say if you blurted out a wrong answer. If you managed 90 per cent in a test he would give you a little smile. When I returned after one holiday from Bombay, with a very modern poodle haircut, he looked at me and said, 'You fool!' Eric Shipstone, on the other hand, was a local Christian (Indian Christians, particularly in North India often have European names). He was in his mid-twenties. A bit portly but handsome, with a luxuriant moustache, he had an eye for the pretty ones. Some six months later he made an offer of marriage to the parents of one of the second-year girls, whose aptitude for Physics was minimal. It was accepted, and she was happy to escape from college. My other subjects were Botany and Zoology. All these subjects were mandatory for entrance to medical college. IT was affiliated to Lucknow University, which had decreed that English and Hindi were compulsory for the Intermediate Science course, and examinations had to be passed in these subjects at the same time as the science subjects.

My English teacher, Fran Molesworth, was a bubbly blonde twenty-six-year-old American woman, sponsored by her Methodist Church in Maryland, USA, to work in India for three years. We students had learned our English under the Raj, and had endless arguments with her about spelling and pronunciation, and finally managed to convince her that it was her American English which was out of step in India. The college also required us to take a religious course, and I chose *Understanding Western Art through the Bible*, which Fran taught. I am forever grateful to her for opening up my knowledge of Western culture and my continuing enjoyment and interest in it.

Fran was also the sports mistress, and our paths crossed frequently. Towards the end of her three-year assignment in India, she met and fell in love with a Parsi man and they intended to marry, but she finally decided she could not marry someone who was not a Christian, and left India broken-hearted. Some years later she met and married a Methodist minister. Over the decades, we have remained good friends.

Isabella Thoburn College was founded by the American Methodist Church and heavily subsidised by them. Though the Christian religion was central to its ethos, it was never forced on anyone. The majority of students were Hindus, with a sizeable minority of Muslims. We came from all backgrounds and castes, from extremely wealthy to very poor, from Brahmins to untouchables, from very pale skinned to black. In the three years I was there, neither wealth nor caste nor creed nor colour was ever an issue, nor a barrier to friendships. But naturally girls tended to seek friends from similar backgrounds. One of the three hostels, Nishat Mahal, had only single and double rooms. An extra charge was made for accommodation. It was not available for first-year students who were randomly dispersed in the other two hostels. Most of the girls who lived in Nishat Mahal were wealthy Hindus who went to European-style schools, did the Cambridge Board examination, were sophisticated and spoke excellent English. They were well-groomed and wore stylish clothes. One of my room-mates in my first year was a Hindu girl from Calcutta, from a wealthy upper-class family. Her father had been knighted by the British. She found the spartan atmosphere of our room difficult, and on arrival gave herself airs and graces and expected some deference from the rest of us. But we soon sorted her out and she turned into a delightful girl.

At the end of the two-week orientation period, it was time for my mother to return to Madras. On the evening before her departure, we sat for the last time on the bench under the eucalyptus trees, near the swimming pool. I continued to feel lonely and isolated, though I was surrounded by other students. I had a lump in my throat and could barely speak to my mother. She understood what I felt, and spoke many wise words of comfort to me. She said she still felt this was the right place for me, and if I could survive Bishop Cottons, where I always felt an outsider, I would eventually feel I belonged here in IT, and that it was just a matter of time before I made some firm friends. She gave me a warm hug as we parted. No kiss. Once again, I realised how deep our feeling was for each other. It would be five months before we saw each other again. She wrote me long letters every week, in her beautiful hand. She had a wonderful way with words. And there would be many parcels too, food and books. Anne also wrote to me often, telling me how much she was enjoying nursing. Annie Lodge did not have a phone as Thatha thought this was an extravagance. Students at IT were not allowed to use the College phone, except in times of emergency.

Apart from Nita, the girl from Calcutta, there were two other, more senior girls in my dormitory, with whom I established a rapport. They were best friends, but noticed my loneliness and would occasionally take me to the cinema or a café with them. There was also a girl called Shubha in my class. From Bombay, she was brilliant and eccentric, with a flair for mathematics. We shared an interest in politics and would rush every week to the library to see who could get first to the new copy of *Time* magazine. There was a definite slant in the College towards things American, rather than English, which I had been used to and missed. Shubha and I spent a good deal of our time in the library and invariably ended up chatting and arguing, and on a few occasions we were thrown out by the intense, efficient, dark-haired, monkey-like American librarian, Miss Williams. It was only years later when I became more thoughtful, and perhaps more wise, that I realised how much I owed to her and all the other missionaries who had given up so much, to go to an alien land, strange as it was, so that we might have a good education.

During one of the sessions in orientation week, I sat next to a girl who turned and smiled at me. I was struck by her beauty. She was fair of complexion, and I was startled by her large blue eyes.

'Are you Indian?' I asked.

'Yes,' she replied. 'Why do you ask?' I pointed to her eyes. She wanted to know where I came from. She said in Northern India and particularly in Kashmir, blue eyes, though slightly unusual, were not uncommon. I thought of my Thatha's sister and her blue-green eyes, so rare in that part of the world that they tragically sealed her fate. Rahat, as the girl was called, was a day girl and lived in a palace in Lucknow. She was from a prominent Muslim family, and her grandfather was knighted by the British. Rahat, like Shubha, became a lifelong friend.

I had hoped to continue with piano lessons and approached the Head of Music, an Indian, a Mrs Jordan. A talented, sharp-tongued lady in her late forties, she was always on the lookout for girls for her two choirs. The all-girl choir was called the Concert Chorus and sang for College activities. The other was the mixed choir of the Lalbagh Methodist Church, our local English church. There was also a Methodist Hindustani church in the city. The males in the mixed choir were local Christians of all ages. Mrs Jordan did not seem particularly interested in my wanting to take piano lessons. 'Can you sing?' she demanded to know.

'Er, I can read music and hold a tune,' I replied, hesitantly. 'But I don't have a voice good enough to be in a choir.' She insisted I have a voice test, without asking whether I wanted to have one or not.

'Right,' she said. 'You are in both choirs. Church choir practice is in the College Chapel every Friday at 6.30 p.m. Don't be late.'

'But, Mrs Jordan...' I started to protest. 'No ifs or buts. Be sure you are there.'

I shall be eternally grateful to Mrs Jordan for forcing me into the choirs. Not only did I discover how much I enjoyed singing, but it opened up the world of Western choral music for me. Mona Singh, one of my room-mates who befriended me, was in both choirs. She had an exquisite, powerful voice and was a contralto, often called to give solos. I was a soprano. I said to Mona that I did not really feel I was good enough to be in the choir, and could not understand why Mrs Jordan had chosen me.

'Mrs Jordan decides whether the face fits, and if she likes the look of you, you are in, and it is amazing what she can do with your voice. I wouldn't worry.'

Mrs Jordan and her family and extended family had an exalted view of themselves, because her father, Jaswant Rao Chitambar, was the first Indian Methodist bishop. I was to discover that American Methodists were different from English Methodists, who did not have bishops. The first Indian Anglican bishop was Bishop Gurushantha, who confirmed me in 1948. The Anglican church in South India became absorbed into the Church of South India in 1948.

In IT our exposure to the opposite sex was minimal. We were not allowed to go out with boys unless they were close relatives or family friends, and even then written permission had to be given by parents. At home, the only males I knew were my first cousins. We were discouraged from talking to their friends. I found all this quite normal. The constant male-chasing by English and Anglo-Indian girls in Bishop Cottons I had found quite unpleasant.

The subjects I had to study for the Inter-Science exams were Physics, Chemistry, Botany and Zoology. These subjects were mandatory for entrance to medical school, as were English and a second language, in this case Hindi, which was the only language on offer. With the exception of Hindi, I had no problems with any of the subjects. But I found Inorganic Chemistry very boring, as boring as the lecturer who taught it. I cannot remember her name but we referred to her as *Suffose*, as she could not say 'Suppose' because her teeth were in the way. We were cruel. Botany could also be dull, but the practicals were fascinating, especially when we cut fine sections of plant cells, which we stained and viewed under the microscope. Hindi was another matter, quite impossible. Our teacher, a lazy woman, could not understand English, and I could not understand her Hindi.

Hindi is a phonetic language and I could read it fluently, but I could not understand much of what I read. I needed to have it explained both in English and in Hindi, but this was not forthcoming. I was the only one in my class in this predicament. My friends sitting on either side of me tried to be helpful. They told me not to worry as no one had ever failed Hindi, and all one had to do was get the minimum pass mark. I banked on that, rather unwisely. My essays used to be returned to me covered with red ink. My vocabulary was improving fast, but it was getting the gender correct that floored me.

Mrs Mohan, our teacher would not give me extra lessons. She merely laughed at me.

⌄

The oppressive heat of Lucknow lasted well into October, when we broke up for the Diwali holidays for ten days. I remained in College with a few other boarders, who like myself lived too far away to travel home, or were too poor to afford the rail or bus travel. We spent a good deal of our time during the holidays swimming, or taking part in other sporting activities. Still homesick, I was not convinced I had done the right thing coming to this college.

Having lived in Burma and South India up until now, I had not experienced cold weather, nor had I ever owned a jumper or a cardigan. I was warned that this part of India experienced extremes of temperature, but I was unprepared for the discomfort of cold. There was no frost or snow, but minimum temperatures in winter were down to 5°C. There was no hot water in the bathrooms, and our rooms were unheated. The gallant *bhisthi* was exhausted providing buckets of hot water for our baths and washing. I wished I was in the warmth of the South, where the weather would turn cool during the winter months, but where there was really no winter, only hot season and cool season, the latter lasting a bare three months.

My friends took me to Hazrat Gunj, the shopping precinct, to kit me out with woollen cardigans and a long pale grey coat. The Gunj was one of the few areas that was not out of bounds for us. We were allowed out only on Friday evenings and Saturdays, and had to sign a register before we left the campus, and we were not allowed to go out singly. Apart from the cold, the shorter days were something else I had to get used to, and this added to my general sense of unease. I had by now made several friends, but they were really more like acquaintances. There was no one I felt to be close enough to confide in.

My mother continued to write long, comforting letters. Thatha continued to mourn my long absence and would constantly ask my mother when I was coming home.

Mrs Jordan was getting the choir ready for the annual Christmas Cantata in the Methodist Church. The girls had to wear white saris, instead of the cassocks and surpluses we wore on Sundays. I did not own any saris and asked my mother to send me one. I received a parcel with a white blouse, sari and long skirt which had to be worn under the sari, which was of pure Mysore silk, with a two-inch gold border running its entire six-yard length. On closer inspection, the border was composed of a line of woven gold elephants. The sari was exquisite, and wrapped in white tissue on which my mother had written 'Elephant Walk'. We had together seen a film of that name earlier in the year, and had enjoyed it. It starred Elizabeth Taylor and Peter Finch and was set in Ceylon. My mother was good at turning up surprises. My friends showed me how to wear the sari. They draped it around me, making careful pleats before the last bit went around, across the chest, and over the left shoulder to hang down the back as far as the knees. Would I ever learn to do this myself, I wondered, and would it stay on? It did.

We also had to do a recording of Christmas music, carols and excerpts from Handel's *Messiah*, which were due to be broadcast by All India Radio on Christmas Eve. I was so thrilled to be part of this, and I was able to hear the recording with Thatha and my mother when I had returned to Annie Lodge for the Christmas holidays.

The return journey to Madras from Lucknow was memorable and enormous fun. We travelled to Jhansi, where we picked up the Grand Trunk Express to Madras. There were about half a dozen of us, all with third-class tickets. As students, despite our parents' protests, it was not the done thing to travel in a higher class. My mother was aghast at the thought of my travelling in such cramped conditions for two days. Seats and berths could not be reserved in third class, and it was a case of first come, first served. She was also worried about the leering, lecherous males, and wanted me to travel in the Ladies Only carriage. On Indian railways, nearly every train has a Ladies Only carriage, which is always the dirtiest, smelliest and most crowded carriage on the train. The older girls who were experienced travellers had urged me to write to my mother to stop worrying, and that all would be well.

The coolies had made bonfires on the uncovered ends of Jhansi station, and passengers huddled around them. It was bitterly cold. As the mighty Grand Trunk Express roared into the station, there was a mad scramble for seats. The coolies with our luggage, precariously balanced on their bright red turbans, ran ahead of us to get seats in the Ladies Only carriage.

'No, No,' the older girls screamed, chasing after them and directing them to a general carriage, which effectively meant a male carriage. Once in, we paid off the perplexed coolies, and started to rearrange our luggage and settle in. The males around us looked concerned.

'Excuse me,' one said in English. 'You will be more comfortable in the Ladies Carriage.'

We took no notice. Another hiding behind his newspaper muttered in disgust, 'This is what happens when you educate females.'

One of my friends disappeared into the bathroom at one end of the carriage, and reappeared in her pyjamas. One by one the males around us started to move with their luggage to another section of the carriage, and soon we were left with ample space to sit and sleep.

At long intervals, the train would stop for half an hour at a big station. We would get out to explore the stalls and vendors, especially those selling all kinds of exotic food, strictly prohibited by our parents, and grabbing the opportunity to eat it. We would put a palm out to the fortune tellers, and persuade a snake charmer to give a quick performance. Cobras terrified me, but I never failed to be fascinated by them. Then the train whistle would blow, and we would make a mad dash to our carriage, occasionally getting into the wrong one, which meant a wait till the next stop, as carriages were not interconnected. Sometimes we would get into the dining car attached to first class, and meant only for first-class passengers, but we were never challenged, possibly because we spoke English to the waiters, and many of us had short hair, usually a sign of education, wealth and modernity. They assumed we were travelling in one of the two upper classes and would happily serve us. The food was always Western, English, as they called it, a hangover from the Raj. The waiters wore white uniform: long trousers, tunics with coloured braided cummerbunds and white caps. Table cloths and napkins were white, and freshly starched. The chairs were upholstered, a relief from the slatted wooden seats we had just come from. Lunch and dinner consisted of three courses: a soup, a meat roast with potatoes and vegetables, and a pudding. We thought it was all quite delicious. It certainly made a hole in our wallets. As the stops were so far apart, we could sometimes sit for hours in the dining car. One girl would agree to be left behind to look after the luggage and our seats.

All kinds of activities would be going on among us when we returned to our third-class carriage: sleeping, reading, playing cards, showering, and washing underwear and holding it out of the windows with their horizontal bars, so it dried in minutes. But it was talking, laughing and arguing which gave us the most pleasure.

One by one the girls would get off, until I was the only one left at Kazipet, the junction for Hyderabad and Secunderabad, famous Muslim cities, to face another fourteen hours alone before we reached Madras. To escape the constant stares of men around me—and no one can stare like an Indian man—I would move to the Ladies Only carriage, to suffer the rest of the journey. And as we moved closer south, it would get warmer and warmer and coconut palms and green rice fields would appear. Eventually, the train would slither like a long snake into the chaos of Madras's Central Station. Steam travel is much glamorised, but I have wondered if those who have not experienced it, and hanker for the return of those days, realise just how dirty and unpleasant it can be. Seats, berths, luggage, food, faces, hair, all get covered with fine coal dust.

My mother would be on the platform, and seeing me in my blackened state would hesitantly give me her bear hug. A servant with her would give me a long, cold drink of water from a thermos flask. The gardener and the cart man would take away the heavy grey trunk. In no time we would be on the number 11 bus, then would walk from the bus stop to Annie Lodge. Thatha would have been standing between the pillars of the porch, in front of the house for at least the past hour, gazing at the gate.

After being away for five months, my homecoming was all

I imagined it would be. I could shed my warm layers and walk barefoot again. But the first thing I was required to do was to have a bath, sluicing myself with hot water from the polished brass urn, with a maid to help me wash my hair.

Aunts, uncles, cousins, and Anne descended on Annie Lodge when they heard I had returned.

'I don't know why your mother had to send you away to those distant lands,' said Jessie Aunty. 'What was wrong with our Women's Christian College? You could have gone on the bus every day.' She had arrived with a large pan of her famous curried prawns.

'And how were those North Indians? Did they treat you well?' asked Samson Uncle. There were so many questions to answer. But the important one was from my mother.

'Do you think it was the right thing for you to have gone to IT?' she asked nervously, in case I said no.

'I can't think there could be a better place,' I replied. 'I still don't have close friends, but it does not seem to matter so much now. I know how the system works. But my Hindi is still very bad, and this worries me. I haven't picked up much, because my friends and I speak to each other in English; and the girls who speak to each other in Hindi, I have little in common with, so I am hardly ever with them. My Hindi teacher shows little interest in me. And I didn't imagine it would be so cold.'

Anne and I spent long hours exchanging our stories. She seemed very happy in her work, enjoyed the hostel life and had many friends. 'Everyone has missed you dreadfully. It has been so long, and Thatha is still furious with Mummy for sending you to Lucknow. They have had many arguments. You had better convince him that you are happy and she was right.'

On Christmas Eve, we made and put up streamers of coloured crêpe paper. A casuarina tree, the closest to a pine, was installed in the sitting room and decorated. On Christmas morning we went to the Anglican Cathedral, Thatha, my cousins, Anne and myself. Samson Uncle went to his Catholic church. My mother usually made some excuse and did not attend church. When we returned, there was the usual line of beggars of every description, squatting along the length of the street, waiting for their yearly offering. We were the only Christians in the area, and how they knew this was a mystery, but beggars have their own network. Our servants had made up food and clothes parcels for them. A few neighbours, all Brahmins, came to wish us a happy Christmas. If they brought us a gift, it was a bunch of bananas. Our presents to each other were minimal, usually a book. Lunch was always chicken biriyani and aubergine curry. The next day, the decorations and tree would be taken down. Christmas is a brief affair in India.

I returned to Lucknow early in the new year, and as a concession to my mother's concerns went second class as far as Kazipet, where I was joined by friends. As we crossed the Ganges, that holiest of holy rivers, we felt a great surge of excitement and patriotism. We threw open the carriage door, sat on the steps of the fast-moving train, looked far down at the pebbles though the transparent water, and shouted to each other, over the roar of the train, how proud we were to be Indian. What our parents would have said about this reckless behaviour, we did not dare contemplate. On one of our other trips, we got into conversation with the train driver, a burly white Anglo-Indian. He invited three of us to ride in the engine with him, until the next stop. We agreed. The heat and the excitement were overwhelming. Clearly against the rules, we came to hear later, that he was suspended for three months. One of his subordinates had reported him.

The new term saw an influx into my year of a new type of girl I had not hitherto encountered. They were from the American school called Woodstock in Mussoorie, a beautiful and popular hill station in North India. A Christian, international school, it served expatriates from India and South Asia, and offered various school qualifications recognised for entry by universities in India, America and Britain. A minority of the students were wealthy Indians. Girls who had taken the Senior Cambridge examination were allowed entry into IT in January, for Arts subjects only, as it was thought they had the ability to catch up with those who had started the academic year in the previous summer. Among them was a tall, white, slim, attractive girl I took to be American. She looked American, spoke American, dressed American and had an American name: Charlene. I soon discovered her surname was Chitambar and she was part of Mrs Jordan's family. Mrs Jordan was Charlene's paternal aunt, whom she referred to as 'my ant'. Charlene's grandfather was the first Indian Methodist bishop and much was made of this. Charlene's father was Indian and her mother a blue-eyed raven-haired, Irish American beauty. They had met and married while at university in America. Charlene was musically gifted, played the piano to concert standard, and had an exquisite soprano voice, with which she could convey a wide range of emotions. She and I were like chalk and cheese, and our paths rarely crossed, except for at choir practice. But we found it easy to talk to each other, and soon struck up a friendship and started to confide in each other. She was the first person I told about my parent's separation and the shame I felt. Charlene was the friend I had lacked all these months. I began to feel so much happier. She stayed that first year in an adjacent hostel, a few yards from mine, and was also assigned to a room with unfamiliar girls. She and I often swam together, and at weekends went to the cinema and occasionally enjoyed the rather expensive chicken mayonnaise we had discovered at a nearby restaurant. Our backgrounds were very different. Her schooling had been American and mine English, and we would argue endlessly on the merits and demerits of each system. She had a strong Indian identity from her father, spoke fluent Hindi and was at ease in a sari.

Charlene's father was an administrator in a coal mining company in Bihar. He, his wife and young son paid several visits to Lucknow and I was always included in their outings. My friendship with Charlene deepened and endured, and though inevitably we eventually went our separate ways, we kept in touch over the years, sharing each others joys and sorrows. And even as I write this more than half a century later, I am about to travel some thousands of miles to be with her for Thanksgiving in Maryland.

Charlene's close friend in Woodstock was a girl called Mary Chacko, who had joined IT with Charlene. Also of mixed race, an American mother and South Indian father, she took me on one short vacation to visit and stay in Mussoorie with some friends of her parents, an Austrian family. The family seemed plunged in some kind of gloom, and it transpired that their thirteen-year-old son had been dumped by his girlfriend, and he was inconsolable. Both were pupils at Woodstock. I was surprised that his parents had been so accepting of his having a girlfriend at this early age. I had a lot to learn about the differences in our cultures, even though my eyes had been opened at Bishop Cottons. In my Indian culture, except for in family units, adolescent boys and girls, and men and women, lived very separate lives from each other.

Isabella Thoburn College instilled strong Christian values into its students, regardless of their faith. We were constantly made aware of our responsibilities to the wider community, which was almost exclusively non-Christian. One such activity involved literacy classes for the illiterate poor and underprivileged. The list of students who volunteered for this was always oversubscribed. Twice a week, for half an hour in the evening, the gates would be open to all: rickshaw-wallahs, beggars, waifs, old men, anyone who wanted to read and write. Their enthusiasm and cheerfulness was inspiring, and for many of them who persisted, their lives were transformed. Unfortunately, I was excluded from being a volunteer because my Hindi was not fluent.

IT's attitude to servants was quite different from that in Bishop Cottons. In the latter we were not allowed to talk to any servant, unless it was an ayah. In IT we treated them as equals, and were reminded to be polite to them at all times, and to show our appreciation of their care for us.

Towards the end of the first year I experienced the fierce heat of northern India, with temperatures in excess of 40°C. Doors and windows would be flung open at dusk and at night we would drag our beds on to open verandahs, leading out from the dormitories. I would sprinkle my bed with water and lie on it. It was the only way to fall asleep. Sometimes a hot wind called the loo, from the desert, would be blowing, making sleep impossible. There was no air conditioning and table fans were not allowed in the dormitories. I used to sometimes visit the homes of day girls, and was interested in their way of cooling their houses. Doors and windows were tightly shut at dawn, and over them and the walls were hung fragrant mats called *khus khus tutties*, made from the roots of a grass called *vetiver*. All day, the gardener would be walking round and round the house spraying them with water, cooling the house through evaporation. It was very effective. At dusk, the doors and windows would be opened and stay open till dawn.

In May it was time for the long journey, in unbearable heat, back to Madras, for the two-month summer vacation. The trains had fans, but all they did was to circulate the hot air. Stripped down to what was decent, we would have several cold showers in the bathroom, and water ourselves in the carriage to the amusement of the other passengers. At every stop, we would rush out for iced drinks and watermelon—this, in spite of the fact we knew that ice was unsafe, because we could never be sure the water had been adequately boiled. We could have caught typhoid or cholera. Madras was another furnace, especially for ten days, called *kathri*, in May, linked to the new moon. We would all sleep under the sky on the terraces of Annie Lodge, on cool woven mats on the floor: men, women, boys, girls and whoever was visiting. The air would be so still, not a leaf would stir. There would always be a conversation in progress among ourselves, and then one by one we would fall asleep. In the morning we would be drenched with dew, and make our way, with our pillows, to our beds, but the great common enemy, the big yellow sun, would be rising. How we hated the sun. This would go on day after day with no respite. The late afternoon cool sea breeze would disappear long before dusk. And with the very high humidity, summers were unremitting torture. There was never a cloud to be seen, and I loathed the uninterrupted blue sky. I vowed that one day I would go and live somewhere where the sun rarely shone, but was there such a place on earth? Until I was eighteen, we had no fans as my puritanical grandfather considered them a luxury, and a *meerr* waste of money.

Chapter 10

THE FAVOURITE TEACHER

That summer, to our surprise, my mother announced that she had decided to teach again, and had accepted a resident post at a Christian school in Panchgani, a small hill station near Poona. The school year was to start the following January. No one had heard of Panchgani, and Thatha was not pleased. He had got used to her running Annie Lodge smoothly, providing his favourite food on time, especially caramel custard every night, and controlling Samson Uncle and the servants. Her elder brother Eddie's older sons, Edwin and Tom, had been living in Annie Lodge and were proving to be difficult. Eddie and his wife Violet had gone back some years ago to live in Burma, where he was a successful doctor. My mother had advised them that the two boys needed to have a parent around, so Violet had decided to come to live in Annie Lodge.

In my second year at Isabella Thoburn College, Charlene and I shared a room in the third hostel, Nishat Mahal, which had only single and double rooms. These were considerably more expensive than the six-bedded dormitories we had to live in as first years. Our room was adequately furnished but rather spartan, and Charlene used her homemaking skills to make it attractive and comfortable. And we bought a table fan. The only problem was that the communal bathrooms were regularly visited at night by a family of *bijous*, with long bushy tails the like of which I had never encountered. They were apparently civet cats. Often greeted with screams by the students, they were harmless.

Charlene was a dreamer and there was a general aura of absent-mindedness about her. But beneath it was a fine intellect and curiosity, and much warmth. She was often late for classes and appointments, and I was expected to get her to choir practice and church on time. She and Mona Singh, with whom I roomed in the first year, were our two main woman soloists.

These rooms were largely occupied by wealthy Hindu students, who had had a Western-style education like myself and Charlene. I could not help but notice how well dressed and beautifully groomed they were. Rich and sophisticated, they added another dimension to IT. Some of them had parents and grandparents who had been involved in the struggle for India's independence, and from the remarks they made, were clearly anti-English and anti-Christian. Though I had suffered considerable racism in Cottons and had been delighted to see the end of the Raj, I was an Anglophile and would rebut some of these remarks. I had always hoped that I would visit Britain one day. There were also anti-American undercurrents, and one hostile Indian newspaper headline, 'Chester Bowles out-bowled,' produced a certain amount of glee. Chester Bowles was the then American Ambassador to India.

IT was heavily subsidised by Methodists in America, yet we never gave any thought to this; nor did the missionaries ever seek appreciation or gratitude. We just exploited all the opportunities, advantages and privileges this institution gave us. It was only later, when we were adults, that we realised how fortunate we had been.

Sarah Chakko, the Principal, had returned from a year's sabbatical leave in Geneva. We were greatly looking forward to meeting this person about whom we had heard so much. A large dark and gracious woman in her mid-forties, she had enormous presence, and was from the southern state of Kerala. She was gentle, softly spoken and wise, and we quickly warmed to her; we were astonished that before long she knew the names of all the two hundred boarders.

'I am so glad you came to us instead of going to college in Madras,' she said to me, with a twinkle in her eye.

This second year, I so enjoyed being in IT, with so many friends, a best friend, several extracurricular activities: drama, choir, games, and swimming. I was doing well in my science subjects, though I was still finding Botany and Inorganic Chemistry a bore. But always, the cloud of Hindi was hanging over me. The Hindi teacher said I was improving, and no one ever failed to get at least 35 per cent, which was the minimum pass mark. Charlene and the other Woodstock girls were also struggling, but as they were Arts students, they had another teacher, a Mrs Singh, who seemed to take her subject very seriously, and gave them several essays a week. They could also speak Hindi.

During the Christmas holidays Anne and I helped my mother to get ready for her move to Kimmins School in Panchgani, a hill station nestled between five hills, and discovered by an Englishman, John Chesson, as a resort for the British during the summer months. With some difficulty we convinced my mother that it would be cold in January, and that she had to take warm clothes. She was to be provided with accommodation in the school grounds. She went to Poona by train, and then took a three-hour bus journey up several hairpin bends to Panchgani, which was accessible only by road. I looked forward to spending my summer holidays in this hill station.

I returned to Lucknow for my final term, during which I applied for admission to the Christian Medical College (CMC) in Vellore, a small town eighty miles from Madras, accessible by road and four miles from the railway junction at Katpadi, which served trains from Madras, Bangalore and other major South Indian cities. This residential, coeducational College, a private one, and affiliated to Madras University, was considered the finest in Asia and drew applicants not only from the subcontinent but from other Asian countries as well. Founded by Dr Ida Scudder, an American missionary, it gave preference to sponsored Christian students, who would after qualification go back to their communities and serve in Christian Mission hospitals. There were sixty seats to be contested, of which over 90 per cent were reserved for mission candidates. The rest were 'open' seats for anyone else of any race or religion. I applied as an open candidate. Unlike most Indian Christians, we had no affiliation to any local church or missionaries. My grandfather was a very independent man.

My mother and I assumed I would get into Vellore, and I did not apply to any of the other three medical colleges in Madras University, or outside Madras State. This was naïve of us, as competition for Vellore was fierce and fewer than 10 per cent of applicants would be successful.

The last term in IT was spent on revision. I could not be described as industrious or hardworking. I spent too much time on extracurricular activities and sitting, talking and arguing with my wide circle of friends. I was frequently pulled up by my teachers to work harder. I was blessed with an exceptionally good memory, and had the ability to stay up late at night and do intensive last-minute work. This always saw me through with good marks, but not my best.

The exams arrived, practicals first, in Physics, Chemistry, Botany and Zoology, followed a few weeks later by written papers in the same as well as in English, Hindi and General Knowledge, the last three being compulsory for all students in my year. In the Hindi papers, the instructions were in Hindi and not in English, as they were in previous years' papers. This threw me, and I ended up answering more questions than I should have. The topic for the long essay was 'Friendship'. Fortunately, I knew the Hindi word for it. I expected to scrape through the exam but knew it would bring down my overall average considerably giving me a second instead of a first class, which medical colleges in the country expected applicants to have. But Vellore had its own entry criteria, which was to prove my salvation. It would hold a competitive written exam for all applicants on 15 May in India's four main cities, following which one hundred students with the highest points would be called to a three-day interview, held in Vellore. As I expected to be in Panchgani at that time, I opted for Bombay, which was the nearest centre.

When it was time to leave Lucknow, I thanked all my teachers and promised to keep in touch with two of them. Sarah Chakko again said how pleased she was that I had come to Isabella Thoburn, and said she hoped I would become a doctor. Charlene and I wept copious tears at the station as we said our goodbyes, and vowed we would forever keep in touch. Our homes were over a thousand miles apart. I could not see our paths crossing again.

*

I took the Lucknow–Bombay Express for Poona, and got off at Kalyan station, a medium-sized railway junction, to connect to Poona. While I was sitting on my trunk, which was heavy with my textbooks, on the platform at Kalyan, a ticket inspector in a dishevelled white cotton coat came up to me and asked for my luggage receipt. I did not have one, not realising I had to. He asked my coolie to weigh the trunk. He said I should have had it weighed at Lucknow station, paid an excess fee, because it was overweight, and had it put in the brake van, not in my carriage. He demanded a fine, which was more than the money I had in my purse. He was clearly a bully and threatened to arrest me. He knew I was on my own and terrified. I showed him the contents of my purse, and pleaded with him to take whatever I had, except for eight rupees, which I needed to pay the coolies, and for my bus ticket from Poona to Panchgani. By now a small crowd, as is usual in India whenever there is some dispute going on, had gathered around us, listening to our conversation. The crowd was on the side of the underdog, me, and started to shout abuse at the ticket collector. He let me off. My mother had always encouraged me to be independent and fearless, and since I was eight, I had often travelled alone by bus and train on short journeys. She did not arrange to meet me at Poona, as I had hoped. I found the bus station; a coolie loaded my trunk on to the bus. I had a window seat where I could stick my head out if I felt travel sick. The drive up to 4,000 feet, when the flora changed to pines, was exhilarating, and even more so as we came round a hairpin bend, and the cool air blew against our faces. We had left the hot air of the plains below us.

My mother, in a pastel green sari, was at the bus stop to meet me, relieved I had not suffered any major mishap. She had written several letters to me about the school. A Church of England boarding school, Kimmins was founded in 1898 by one of its missionary agencies, and set up for European and Anglo-Indian children. The headmistress, Miss Yelland, was English and a graduate in her thirties, and had come from England a few years earlier. She was pleasant in appearance, friendly, intelligent and liberal in outlook, and my mother found her an amiable and cooperative colleague. She returned to England on furlough shortly after my mother arrived, and was replaced by the Deputy headmistress, a Miss Beavers, also an English missionary and who was everything Miss Yelland was not. A large, untidy woman in her fifties, she was primary-school trained and not a graduate. She was an evangelical Christian and could not accept that the

Raj had come to an end. She liked to emphasise the superiority of all things British. There were three young Indians on the staff. The rest were Eurasian, or English missionaries. My mother was the first Indian appointed to teach English in the senior school.

In Rangoon, my mother taught English as a second language. In Kimmins, she taught it as a first language. The pupils came mainly from the Bombay/Poona area, as well as from other parts of the country. Apart from a few Anglo-Indians and a couple of English girls, the rest were Indians, mainly Hindus and Parsis and from wealthy backgrounds. All were fluent in English, speaking it at home. This was not a selective school. The only criteria for admission for non-Christians were the ability to pay the fees and fluency in English. For my mother, it was sheer joy teaching English as a first language. She also taught Geography.

My mother's quarters were spartan but adequate, and she had advised the school in advance that her two daughters would be spending their vacation with her. She was given a small semi-detached bungalow with a wide, covered verandah, which did for a sitting/dining room. There was a large bedroom with three single beds, tables and wardrobes. There was also a bathroom. I wondered why her radio was on the far window sill overlooking the garden, instead of on her bedside table or in the verandah. The other semi was used by an Anglo-Indian widow, one of the matrons. All meals were brought from the school kitchen, and served by a bearer, provided by the school. His wife was our maid, and she often provided welcome additions to the meals.

My mother was an instant hit with her pupils, and was affectionately called 'Raju' instead of Mrs Rajan. An excellent, innovative teacher, she motivated them, including those who were lazy or not bright. She was also their mentor and friend. As strict as she was with Anne and me, she was liberal and lenient with them, a sort of Miss Jean Brodie. In their spare time, they would sit on the grass outside the far wall of her bedroom, and I soon realised why the radio had been placed where it was. She would switch on her radio to pop music. Anne and I were flabbergasted, as we had never been allowed to listen to this kind of music at home. The girls were always hungry, and she would go back and forth to the little local bazaar, and buy biscuits and fruit for them, even chicken *biriyani* on occasions, even though this was against school rules. No wonder they loved her. The wayward and disobedient ones were her favourites.

'You must never condemn them,' she would say. 'They need understanding. Do you remember, Lindy? You yourself were so often in trouble in Bishop Cottons, and you complained no one understood you, though what there was to understand, I never knew.'

But my naughtiness was minor compared to theirs. And I was never sullen and rude as they were. One such girl, Sheila Nanjappa, a Brahmin, became a firm favourite with my mother. Resentful, and often silent and disobedient, she was thirteen, slim and pretty with curly hair. Her father was a high-ranking official in the Indian Administrative Service. Her mother had married at seventeen and all four of their children had been sent away to boarding school when they were very young. Sheila was only seven when she came to Kimmins. She was often in trouble with Miss Beavers, the matron and other teachers, and my mother was the only one who could reach out to her.

⌣

The Vellore entrance exam was approaching and most of my time was spent revising for it, but my mother regularly dragged me away from my books to go for long walks with her, in the beautiful countryside, often onto Tableland, a plateau smothered with small white daisies. Out would come her Rolleicord camera and she would be clicking away. Anne had her short vacation at the same time, and joined us. We were so pleased to see Anne happy and growing in confidence. She was nearing the end of her four-year degree course in nursing.

I required somewhere to stay in Bombay, one of the centres for the Vellore exam, and was pleased when Shubha Divekar, the brilliant mathematician, my classmate in IT, asked me to come and stay for a few days with her and her family in their flat. I had never been to Bombay, and neither had I lived in a flat before, and it was an interesting experience. Perched on the fifth floor with a balcony, the comfortable flat was in Churchgate and above Bombellis, a well-known Italian restaurant, frequented by the rich and famous of all nationalities.

The exam for entrance to the Vellore medical college was held in one of the Bombay colleges, and consisted mainly of multiple-choice questions. This type of examination, an American invention, was unfamiliar to me, and to everyone else taking it. There were also psychometric tests, and a difficult English comprehension test, where we had to read a long article from a Physiology text book for medical students, and then answer questions, all in a very short time. The multiple choice covered the science subjects I had studied at IT, General Knowledge, and a bit of Scripture, but most of it consisted of intelligence tests involving convoluted mental gymnastics. I was completely exhausted at the end of it, but relieved that I finished all the papers, which I discovered later was unusual. It was impossible to know how satisfactorily I had done. My mother did not show any concern as to how I had performed.

Chapter 11

A QUEEN IS CROWNED

It was 2 June 1953, the day of the Queen of England's Coronation, and all of India was on holiday. Britain was riding high. The Australians were being slaughtered by the English in cricket, and word had arrived that morning via James Morris, a *Times* correspondent, that Everest had been conquered by the British expedition.

It transpired that the only radio in Kimmins High School was the one belonging to my mother. Miss Beavers had asked her if she and the other English missionaries could come to my mother's verandah and listen to the Coronation Service and BBC commentary. The radio was moved to the verandah and extra chairs were found, so that other senior staff could also join us. Any conversation during the service and commentary brought Miss Beavers's right forefinger to her closed lips, as she mumbled 'Hush'. Every time the British national anthem *God Save the Queen* was played, and this was happening frequently during the programme, Miss Beavers would stand bolt upright, and expected us to do the same. We would then sit down again. After this farce had been going on for about an hour, I got up and went into the bedroom, which was separated from the verandah by a single thin cotton curtain. I lay on my bed and started to read. Shortly thereafter, during yet another rendering of the national anthem, a gust of wind blew the curtain up, and Miss Beavers saw me. She was furious.

'What is Lindy doing, lying down during *God Save the Queen*?' she remonstrated. 'Tell her she must stand up.' My mother came into the bedroom to tell me what Miss Beavers had said, and asked me not to upset her any further. She asked me to come out, but I refused. My mother went back to the verandah. Again, *God Save the Queen* was played, and again Miss Beavers remonstrated with my mother, who left me alone. Miss Beavers gave up, but she and the rest continued to bob up and down like meerkats.

I had done satisfactorily in the medical entrance exam and

was asked to attend the three-day interview at Vellore, at the end of June. I had crossed the first hurdle. We started to make preparations for my departure.

And then the bombshell fell. I had failed Hindi. I had passed everything else with the required marks, but my marks in Hindi were so low that I was not even allowed a re-sit. My world collapsed. In the Indian system, failure in even one subject required all the other subjects to be retaken and that, too, only after one year, not any earlier. I just could not face it. The Principal, Sarah Chakko, wrote me a comforting letter urging me to return.

'At seventeen,' she wrote, 'a year seems an eternity, but I know how much you want to be a doctor, and the only way is to repeat the year, and we will do everything to ensure you pass the Hindi this time.' I was inconsolable. How did I know that I would ever pass the Hindi exam? The only consolation was that Charlene would still be there, as she was going on to do a BA in Lucknow. She had also failed Hindi, but was allowed an immediate re-sit, which she passed. My Muslim friend, Rahat with the blue eyes, was in the same boat as me, with equally abysmal marks, and had decided to return, as she too wanted to be a doctor.

My mother was sympathetic but did not fuss, and made me realise there was no other option but to return to IT. But first I wrote to the Principal at Vellore, to ask him to keep my place for interview the following year. He wrote back to say that as this was a competitive exam and interview, places could not be reserved, and he asked me to reapply the following year.

There were still a few more weeks to go before term started. One of my good friends from IT, Leela Singh, lived in Bombay and had come to Panchgani for a short holiday with her two older sisters, Sheila and Amrit, and a male friend, Zul. I told them about the Vellore interview and the Hindi debacle. They invited me to go back with them to Bombay for a couple of weeks. They seemed too modern for my mother, but Sheila Singh, a mature woman of twenty-five, was persuasive and assured my mother I would be well looked after and chaperoned. We drove off to Bombay on a beautiful sunny day, when the monsoon, in full force at that time, had decided to take a break. We drove across the western ghats, covered with dozens of tiny silver needle-like waterfalls glistening in the midday sun.

The Singhs, apart from their mother, a gentle Indian woman with simple tastes, were lapsed Sikhs from East Africa. Their father, an educated leader of his community, had run a very successful business in Africa, as many Indians did. He had died unexpectedly and the family relocated to Bombay. They lived in Malabar Hill, the most salubrious area in Bombay, with luxury flats and houses owned by wealthy Indians and Europeans. I was not used to this kind of lifestyle, but Mrs Singh made me very welcome and I spent a good deal of time chatting to her in the kitchen. She was plain and plump and wore shabby baggy trousers and a tunic. Her hair was pulled back from her face into a single short, weedy plait. She was nothing like her beautiful, sophisticated, Westernised daughters. Unlike her children's, her English was hesitant, but she made herself understood. She complained incessantly about her daughters. They were not domesticated. They were not interested in marriage. They smoked and were out late at night. They even wore shorts. Mrs Singh had received many offers of marriage for her daughters from wealthy families with suitable boys, but they showed no interest. Amrit was exquisitely beautiful. I could not stop gazing at her face. Zul, who had accompanied them to Panchgani, was interested in her, but she did not reciprocate his feelings. Both girls obviously wanted to choose their own mates, and had not as yet found suitable boys.

The Singhs' lifestyle was clearly different from mine. For a start, they wore slacks all day. I wore dresses or skirts and blouses. At night when they went partying, and this was nearly every other night, they wore silk saris and expensive jewellery. I wore no jewellery. I did not own any. I owned one sari, which was in Panchgani. They were keen to lend me their clothes, and took me to their wardrobes. My eyes nearly popped out. The wall-to-wall wardrobes, in their huge bedrooms, had hundreds of saris, of every hue and type, each on a hanger with a blouse to match. I was very slim, as were the two older sisters, so the cholis, the close-fitting blouses, were a perfect fit. Saris are five-metre-long sheets, and can be draped on anyone of any size. The first night, I wore a deep turquoise blue and gold sari, with a turquoise blouse. I did not normally wear makeup, but I was told it was mandatory, so I agreed to some lipstick. They wanted me to wear earrings but my ears were not pierced. They lent me their high-heeled slippers.

'You do look beautiful,' they said. 'Amazing what some nice clothes, and a bit of makeup can do,' they added. My mother would have had a fit.

And so, for my first party, we set off to the house of one of their longstanding friends. There were about a dozen people there, men and women in their twenties and early thirties, well groomed, well-spoken and well-behaved. The women wore saris; the men wore suits with ties. Soft drinks were in abundance. It was the time of prohibition, but the older ones drank whisky and brandy. The Singhs introduced me as 'Lindy from Madras' and Leela's college friend. They were all very friendly and a bit curious. I was not at ease. Zul kept an eye on me to make sure I was not feeling left out. I got talking to him. He was an Oxford dropout, having abandoned his studies after he got bit parts in films in England, and claimed to have acted in a few of them with Laurence Olivier, and other celebrities. When I told him about my ambition to be a doctor, he said, 'A woman like you was meant to be loved Lindy, not to have a career.'

'Can't I have both?' I asked. He smiled.

Many of the men were at Oxbridge. Their wealthy families could afford to send them abroad to study. I was impressed by their easygoing and confident manner. Their manners were impeccable. From their names, I gathered nearly all of them were Hindus; there was the odd Muslim. There was also one Christian man there, and he was married to a Hindu girl. Their parents must have given them a hard time. I drank Coca-Cola for the first time and did not like it. I had noticed crates of it in the Singh kitchen, and wondered what it was. At home we drank water, coconut or homemade lime juice.

At these parties there was a bit of ballroom dancing, a very un-Indian activity. The parties usually finished by midnight. Mrs Singh did not wait up for her daughters. And so the partying continued, and I grew to enjoy dressing up and meeting, very often, the same people. I found the men, in particular, interesting to talk to. I thought this was the kind of man I would like to marry one day. But he would have to be a Christian. Though not particularly religious, and with some shaky beliefs, Christianity underpinned the values of my family and myself.

The days in Bombay passed idly by, reading, listening to music, afternoon naps, chatting, going to the beach and eating delicious food prepared by Mrs Singh. I returned to Panchgani and in July to Lucknow. My mother and I would see each other again in Annie Lodge in December, five months later.

⌣

It was with some embarrassment that I returned to IT. People did not fail their exams. But I was welcomed with such warmth that any trepidation I had felt soon vanished. Charlene squealed with delight when she saw me, gave me a big hug and said she had managed to get our old room back.

Miss Chakko had ensured that my class had a different Hindi teacher, a Mrs Singh from the Arts side. A serious lady with round metal rimmed glasses, her English was poor, but she did try to do some of the teaching in English, and she and I managed to have a fair understanding of each other. She required three essays a week from me, and I did not mind that they were returned covered in red ink. She took time to explain my mistakes, and her criticisms were constructive.

The rest of the year quickly passed and I went to Madras to spend Christmas with the family. The excited anticipation of the long train journey had worn off. I was glad to get to the other end. Thatha had not seen me, nor my mother, for a year and longed for us to live closer to him. Violet Aunty had looked after him and Samson Uncle well, but Thatha and the servants said it was not the same as having my mother run Annie Lodge. In January, my mother and I went our separate ways, she to Panchgani, and I to Lucknow.

My mother was very keen to develop a really good library in Kimmins, and had been given a grant. To my horror, I discovered she had taken many of my childhood books, the *Brer Rabbit* and *Anne of Green Gables* ones, among several others, to add to what she had purchased.

'You are never going to read them again,' she said. I did not let her take *Tom Sawyer* and *Huckleberry Finn*. I was adamant I would read them again, one day.

I went back to IT knowing it would be my last term, pass or fail Hindi, but not knowing then that it would be the worst term I would experience there.

One evening after games we were going back to our rooms, to bathe before dinner, when we were urgently summoned to the College Chapel, a free-standing building of immense beauty, set alongside a eucalyptus path. We were perplexed as we went in. Miss Chakko came into the chapel, went up to the pulpit, faced us and announced quietly that one of the boarders, Shefali Biswas, whom we had known well, had died a few hours ago. There were gasps and sobs, and her close friends started to weep uncontrollably. I remembered speaking to her just a couple of days earlier. She was quiet, serene and beautiful, as she always was. She had developed a pimple near her nose, and had started to feel unwell, and had been admitted to the sick room. Her temperature had soared and she had become delirious. Transferred to the local hospital, she was diagnosed with fulminating septicaemia and was dead within a few hours. She was the only child of a widowed mother.

Miss Chakko spoke to us for nearly an hour, wiping away her own tears. She had a way with words and spoke of life and death, of God and the Resurrection, and of love and hope. We came away sorrowful, but comforted and uplifted. My love and admiration for Miss Chakko was boundless. We attended Shefali's funeral, which was delayed, because her mother had to come by train from Calcutta.

A month later, the college knockout basketball tournament was held. One evening, when the staff were playing against the first years, I was asked to referee the match. Whenever the staff played, there was always a big audience. Miss Chakko excelled in sports, and was always a key player in the staff basketball and tennis teams. She would not move very much, but was quick, and could shoot accurately from a distance. At half time, I blew the whistle for a short break. It was usual for the players to sit on the court for a ten-minute rest, and then start again. I saw Miss Chakko sit down, and then lie down full stretch. We were puzzled, as this seemed rather undignified and out of character. I walked towards her and saw her eyes were closed. She started to make some grunting noises. I shook her, and called out to her, but there was no response. Other staff members tried to get her to sit up, but she flopped. Male servants were hastily summoned to carry her to the sick room. The College doctor was urgently called. Word got around the three hostels that Miss Chakko had been taken ill. We did what we had done a month earlier, and drifted to the chapel and waited and prayed desperately. Half an hour later, the head student came in and walked to the front of the chapel and said quietly, 'Girls, Miss Chakko has passed away.' She was buried in Lucknow, in the same cemetery in which Isabella Thoburn was buried. Miss Chakko was forty-nine. Through Shefali's death, she had prepared us for her own.

I worked hard at Hindi, and Mrs Singh gave me a good deal of extra work. In the spring I broke my right index finger playing softball. It was splinted, and became very swollen and painful. I could not write with my right hand. Mrs Singh said I had to write an essay a day if I were to pass.

'Use your toes if necessary, but I must have an essay from you every day.' So I learned to write with my left hand. It was difficult enough learning to write English with the left hand, but writing in Hindi exercised my dexterity to the utmost.

In the midst of all this, Charlene had been ailing for some time with anaemia. Her parents took her home and she quickly recovered. I awaited her return, but she wrote to say she was not coming back. Instead, she was going to America to do a degree in Music at Oberlin University in Ohio. I was devastated.

The exams came around again. The Zoology practicals were tricky, as my fracture had not healed and my finger was still splinted. Exposing the venous system of the frog, and the salivary glands of the cockroach, were done with my right index finger up in the air. No help was given to me, nor any allowances made for my infirmity. The written papers posed no problems, and I understood the Hindi papers correctly this time, but still found them difficult. However, the gender of inanimate objects did not defeat me as before.

I wondered what I would do if I failed again. Without a university education, good career options for girls were very limited. Many of my friends were having marriages arranged for them, and seemed very happy. Some girls were already married. This most certainly was not an option for me, and the last thing my mother would have done was to arrange a marriage for Anne or me. She was deeply opposed to dowries, which were the norm in my community.

'Why should I bribe a man to marry my daughters?' she would say to my relatives. 'They are not blind, deaf, lame or dumb. They would be an asset to any man.'

Chapter 12

THE BEGINNING OF A LONG JOURNEY

I left IT for good in May 1954, and went to Panchgani for the summer holidays. I repeated the Vellore exam in Bombay, and was called to Vellore for the three-day interview once again. Word came from IT that I had passed all my exams creditably, especially Physics, and I had also scraped through Hindi. I was ecstatic. I spent the next fortnight partying with the Singhs in Bombay, and then got ready to go to Vellore. There was no certainty I would get in, in which case I would have to come back and apply to university somewhere else. I decided to take a suitcase to Vellore with enough clothes for the three days, and if I did get in, my mother would send my things in the grey trunk. But she would have none of this.

'Take all your things,' she said. 'I'm not sending anything later on. And while you are about it, make sure you take your tennis racket as well... and in its press.'

'But they will think I am overconfident, and that will go against me at interview,' I argued.

'If they don't take you, who else can they take?' she said unreasonably. She had obviously forgotten the Hindi saga.

My Muslim friend, Rahat Ahmad, also passed the Hindi, did the Vellore exam and was called to interview. I was so hoping we would spend the next five years together. But she failed to turn up. She got as far as Lucknow station with her train berth booked, but could not bear the thought of being parted from her large family. So she turned back. She went on to do a BA and became a business woman. She never married.

I arrived at Katpadi station to join several candidates waiting for buses to take us to the Medical College campus. We had to pass through the bazaar area of Vellore, colourful, bustling, noisy and congested.

The town was famous for its fort, which contained a magnificent Hindu temple. We then drove through a leafy residential area, and as the road took a bend a high security jail came into view. We were told it regularly had executions by hanging, and produced a reliable supply of unclaimed bodies for dissection in the Anatomy department.

The road leading to the beautiful College campus had little traffic and was surrounded by low green hills covered with rocks and bushes and a few trees. The hill across the road opposite the main college buildings was called College Hill, a favourite haunt for romancing medical students.

Our bus turned off the road into the campus drive, and came to a halt outside the main administrative block, an attractive stone building, surrounded by mature trees. A group of staff and students was there to greet us, as our luggage was unloaded. My embarrassment at having the largest trunk was compounded when a dignified elderly man, who I later discovered was the Principal, walked up to it and said gruffly: 'Whose is this?'

'Mine,' I said meekly, clutching my tennis racket.

'Some people are very confident of themselves,' he mocked, and added even more gruffly. 'And you have even brought your tennis racket.'

I felt dashed and humbled, and followed the porter carrying my trunk into the Women's Hostel, connected to the Administration Block by an open-roofed passage. I was shown my room, which I shared with three other girls. We were very nervous and barely spoke to each other.

The men were taken to the Men's Hostel, about 200 metres away on the opposite side of the road. The handsome newly built stone building was covered with colourful bougainvillea creepers and fronted by a circular lily pond. All the men had single rooms. There were large public rooms, and there were quarters for the warden and servants.

A couple of hours later, all one hundred candidates were summoned to the Assembly Hall, to be told how the three-day interview would be conducted. We would be subjected to various tests and activities, and at the end of three days we would be told whether we were successful or not, and if we were, we would be required to stay on, and not be allowed home until the end of the academic term. During the three-day interview, we would be known only by a number. We were to wear our numbered labels on our front and back at all times, except when we bathed or went to sleep at night. We were assigned to single-sex groups of about eight, with a Group Leader, who was a doctor, a staff member.

Dr Joy Paul, my Group Leader, a young pharmacologist, was cheerful and talkative, and quickly put us at our ease. Most of the candidates were mission sponsored, and were not required to get as high a grade as the minority of us, who were open candidates. The first night we had to attend a party in the Assembly Hall, so that we could be observed as to how we socialised. From the gallery above, some of the senior students were watching us. It was a spectator sport for them, as they joked and laughed at our expense. By our appearance and body language, they were laying bets among themselves as to who they thought would be selected, and who did not have a chance. In the previous year, there was a male candidate, a Parsi, who apparently walked around in a daze, with his mouth open. Bets were taken that in three days, he would be on the train on his way home. He did get in, and turned out to be the cleverest student the College had ever had, and went on to have a dazzling career and become a world-famous Professor of Gastroenterology. So much for first impressions.

The next morning after an early breakfast with the Group Leader, the real work started. Despite a few moments of extreme nervousness and desperation, I enjoyed all three days of the interview. The activities were interspersed with multiple-choice papers and psychometric tests. One of the tasks was to give a short talk without previous preparation on a topic, having been given a choice of two picked out of a hat. Mine were 'One Party Government' and 'The Four-Minute Mile.' I could have done either but chose the latter. Roger Bannister had been a medical student and I had an added interest in his achievements.

We were also required to work as a group. This was to observe our teamworking abilities and to weed out those with so-called group disruptive tendencies. Manual dexterity was tested by asking us to wrap awkward-shaped parcels in brown paper and tie them up with fine string.

There were also activities to test leadership qualities and organisational abilities. For one such, the group was given a huge piece of cardboard and told it was a sports field, and we were asked to organise a school Sports Day. With pins, sticks, stickers, paper, flags and Sellotape, we had to transform the cardboard. We thought we had done very well, but had marks deducted as we had forgotten to put in lavatories.

At the end of three days, we filed anxious and exhausted into the Assembly Hall to hear our fate. Only the successful candidates' numbers were read out. The suspense was unbearable. My number was called. I had to go to another room where the Principal was waiting to shake my hand, the same man who had made comments about my grey trunk.

'We expect great things of you,' he said. The Group Leaders stayed in the Assembly Hall to console and counsel those who had failed.

I sent my mother a telegram to tell her my good news, and she sent one to Thatha. I telephoned Anne in the School of Nursing, which was on the Hospital campus four miles away. I was so relieved for Thatha, my mother, Anne and Samson Uncle. They had invested so much hope in me.

This type of selection procedure that Vellore uses for aspiring doctors appears to be unique. Whether it succeeds in selecting the best kind of doctor is difficult to know. There is no doubt that Vellore has produced numerous outstanding doctors, practising in all corners of the world. They have received honours and accolades from all parts of the globe. Most were expected to work in Christian Mission hospitals throughout India, transforming medical care in rural areas and small towns. They are Vellore's true heroes. Without acclaim, and on poor salaries, they have devoted their entire careers, transforming the lives of poor people, not just by treating their diseases, but also by training health workers, setting up vaccination programmes, improving water supply and sanitation, and creating cooperatives and schools.

But what of the selection process itself? Which part or parts of it correlated with academic excellence at undergraduate or postgraduate level? Several years later, this was analysed and there was one area which consistently showed a positive correlation. This was the English comprehension test in the initial exam.

We returned to our allotted rooms, and during the evening of our selection we were summoned by the Women's Hostel Secretary to the Common Room, where senior girls had congregated. They told us this was Rag week, and ragging was about to start. We were to do whatever our seniors asked us to do. There was bullying of the worst sort, which turned out to be pernicious, barbaric and even at times malicious.

I failed to see any humour in it. Some of us who were labelled as 'Westernised' or 'forward' were given a harder time. An Anglo-Burmese girl, called Dawn Antram, from Rangoon, with whom I had already established a rapport, managed to escape after the first day, when she developed an ear infection with fever, after having been dunked in the lily pond. She was languishing in the sick room.

I could not help comparing this reception to the one I had had when I first went to IT. The week mercifully came to an end, and normal life started, but the ragging left a deep impression on me. I vowed I would get it stopped in future years, if I could. There were some girls I despised and could never relate to again. I was told I was picked on by some Tamil girls because they disapproved of me, a Tamil, wearing North Indian dress and having had a Western-style education. Unlike in IT, I could feel an undercurrent of prejudices. South Indians did not like North Indians, Tamils and Malayalees had a subtle deep seated hostility, Eurasians were too different from Indians, and so on and on it went. But we did learn to live amicably together in the Women's Hostel, and at no time did I feel that caste, state or religion was a major issue.

The second week our studies started in earnest. In the first eighteen months, we studied Anatomy, Physiology, Biochemistry and Statistics, after which we took university exams in Madras.

The Anatomy dissection hall was a very large open-plan room, entered from the Anatomy lecture room. The dissection hall was elevated and had no side walls. It was covered with an overhanging roof, supported by a few pillars, and was surrounded by a high-walled luxuriant garden with various tropical bushes, including oleander and perpetually flowering bougainvillea. So, as we dissected, we had views of the garden a few feet below, and we could take a walk in it whenever we required a much-needed respite. At the far end of the dissection room were formalin tanks, in which bodies and body parts were stored. Formalin not only preserved the tissues but hardened them, making them easier to dissect. Technicians in attendance would get the parts out for us, and lay them on concrete slabs for us to dissect. Each of us had a partner. Mine was Dawn and, unlike me, she was hardworking and diligent. We started with the upper limb, which would take over a month to dissect. I decided very soon that I did not like dissecting, so I let her do most of it while I read the procedure to her, from the manual by Cunningham, the Anatomy Bible. It described every detail of the part which we had to dissect, as well as exactly how to go about it. In another part of the room there were two small tables with scalpel (knife) sharpeners, and this provided another diversion. We chatted to fellow dissectors as we sharpened our scalpels. It was a good way of getting to know each other. I often volunteered to sharpen the scalpels of others, and when I returned to join Dawn she would have finished dissecting out an area, and would show me the structures she had carefully exposed. Many a romance started and blossomed during scalpel-sharpening.

The Professor of Anatomy was a missionary called Dorothea Graham, but she was referred to as DL. From a wealthy Northern Ireland family, she gave us an occasional lecture, but it was to the several demonstrators in attendance that we turned for help. They were young doctors, aspiring to be surgeons, getting a thorough grounding in anatomy as they taught and tested us. We would have frequent oral tests, and weekly marks out of ten would be entered on our individual cards. These would occasionally be scrutinised by the Professor and the Principal. After getting a string of one out of tens, I was summoned by the Principal.

'Just what do you think you are doing?' he asked in his usual gruff voice. 'We thought you would bring honour and glory to this institution. Instead you produce these disgraceful marks. You had better pull yourself together before the end-of-year exams.'

'Yes, Sir,' I said meekly, and walked away feeling rather ashamed. I decided to start doing some serious work, both in the dissection hall and in the evenings, instead of sitting in my room with my three room-mates and many others, talking and arguing.

There were four of us in Room No. 4, Saro, Amy, Lily, and myself, and we used to spend too much time reading both fiction and non-fiction books, mostly provided by my mother. She had given me a book, *The Healing Knife* by George Sava, also known as George Bankoff, a man of Russian origin whose parents had emigrated to Britain, where he had grown up and qualified as a surgeon. My room-mates also read the book, and we felt impressed and inspired. We decided to write to him to tell him how much we had enjoyed it. Back came a reply to say four more of his books were on their way to us. He had autographed them and written in them: 'With my best wishes to the potential doctors of Room Number Four.'

The end-of-term exams were held before we broke for Christmas, and the results came as a great shock to most of the students. Very few of the sixty passed, and I was one of them. But my dislike of Anatomy persisted.

Physiology was another matter. It was an exciting and living subject, but the two elderly professors, one Canadian and the other Indian were dull teachers. The demonstrator, Peter Zachariah, or Zach as he was affectionately known, a young Vellore graduate from the state of Kerala, was a brilliant teacher. I would always attend his inspiring tutorials, even when I was assigned to the American lecturer. Not surprisingly, he was made a professor at a young age, having got his doctorate from Oxford. The Indian professor insisted on segregation of the sexes at his lectures, girls on one side of the classroom and boys on the other. The only other person who insisted on segregation was the Tamil Pundit, an elderly orthodox, somewhat comical Hindu man. The boys would tease him by appearing late, and then sliding in to sit with the girls, near the door. The class would come to an abrupt halt, the Pundit gesticulating with his hands and ordering the offending boys to move to the male section. This class was compulsory for non-Tamils. I spoke Tamil fluently so naturally was exempted. It was essential that all students knew Tamil as most of the patients we would see in our clinical years would be Tamil.

Being compulsorily resident in our hostels, and as the Medical College was so isolated, we had to make our own social life.

For most of us it was the first time we were studying with the opposite sex, and that too in such close proximity. We took it in our stride and enjoyed it, but there were some shy girls and boys who hardly mixed. The sports field for football and hockey was on the Women's Hostel side of the road, as were the tennis, volleyball and netball courts. There was also much scope for walking, running and hill-climbing. It took twenty-five minutes to reach the summit of College Hill, from where there was a good view of the college campus nestled among trees. College Hill was a perfect place for courting couples, the large rocks affording privacy. A few couples paired in the first year and went on to marry after graduation, but most of us remained unattached.

The campus had several houses scattered about, all built of attractive stone, and those for the senior staff, including the missionaries, were substantial. Because of our isolation we lived as a close-knit community. Staff and students mingled freely. The staff were lucky in that they had an endless supply of free babysitters, us students. I was drawn to an Australian family when I joined the Student Christian Movement (SCM). The staff advisor was Dr Selwyn Baker, a very able gastroenterologist from Melbourne. In his early thirties, he belonged to the new generation of missionaries, to whom Indians could relate easily and comfortably. And for that, he was much admired and loved. His Christianity was of the more liberal variety and he encouraged us to think, to question, to argue and to disagree. His wife, Betty, was a physicist but there was no suitable employment for her, so she took to full-time domesticity, having two small children. The younger child was flaxen haired, so attracted a good deal of attention from local Vellore residents. The SCM was a very lively group, which was attractive to traditional and liberal thinking Christian students. A few of the more curious non-Christians attended some of the SCM functions. Older orthodox Christians did not quite approve of the free mixing of men and women at these events, and said SCM stood for the Society for Courtship and Marriage. I greatly enjoyed its activities: lectures, discussion groups, services, retreats, parties, workshops and group study. The other Christian group, the Evangelical Union (EU), was given a wide berth by me and my close friends. Its members were born-again Christians, fundamentalists, who were forever trying to 'save' us. They were encouraged by some young, aggressive Australian missionaries, and when we heard their conversion testimonies, describing the excesses of their past lives, it became obvious why they needed to be born again.

The Christian Medical College and Hospital in Vellore was a truly ecumenical institution, underpinned by about forty Christian denominations, some very different from others, and it was miraculous that they all managed to pull together in the same direction.

My friend and dissection partner Dawn was an excellent tennis player and would play mixed doubles, in her mid-thigh tennis skirt, nearly every evening. The tennis court was between the Anatomy hall and the Women's Hostel block, where single staff members, including Professor Dorothea Graham (DL), had their quarters. DL had to pass the tennis court on her way to her apartment. She would stop and glare at Dawn's skirt, and then walk on. She obviously disapproved of the length of Dawn's skirt. One day, she summoned Dawn, who was tall, slim and with a splendid pair of legs, and complained that her skirt was too short, and she was to take the hem down. We were indignant when we heard of this unnecessary interference, and told Dawn that under no circumstances was she to take any notice of DL. We were not having missionaries interfering with our private lives. The hem stayed up, and DL took to standing by the side of the court and shouting: 'Dawn, Dawn, put your hem down.' This sent Dawn's male partners into hysterics, and they would shout back: 'Hi, Dr Graham. Why don't you come and join us?' DL finally gave up. I mention this incident because there were older missionaries, particularly those from Britain, who felt it was their duty to treat us as children. Though the Raj had ended seven years earlier, the *Ma-Bap* attitude was difficult to shake off. DL was a person without guile, and from a wealthy aristocratic background. True to her Christian ideals, she had given up much to cross the seas to give of her services, so that Indian women could have a good medical education. We were not unaware of this, were grateful to them, and were prepared to make allowances for some of their unwelcome intrusion.

There was a small group of senior SCM students who went every Monday evening to a nearby village, to run a clinic for minor ailments. This group tried to get some of us first-year students interested in going with them. I had always been curious about villages, but had never had the opportunity to get to know any, and jumped at the idea of visiting one regularly, with about six other men and women. The village, Edayanjathur, was about two kilometres from the College, and to get to it we walked on a bund between emerald-green paddy fields, overlooked by coconut palms. The village consisted of neatly arranged huts on either side of dirt streets. There were also a few dwellings built of mud and brick with thatched roofs. The headman allowed us the use of a shed, where we kept patients' records, medicines, dressings and basic instruments such as scalpels and forceps. The building had a verandah, where we would see the villagers with their simple ailments and wounds. They were poor people who were mainly engaged in agricultural activities. There were a few lepers among them. We did not call them lepers, but leprosy patients. Some were badly deformed with missing digits or noses. They would appear after dusk. I started by being in charge of registering and record-keeping. Seniors did the clinical work. My work was not easy. Villagers would have one name only, and many were in common with each other. A woman would never give her husband's name. Not to utter your husband's name was considered a mark of respect. Streets had no name. Villagers did not know their house number, nor their age or date of birth. A conversation with a pregnant woman might go like this.

'How old are you?' Giggle. Giggle. 'Come on, you must have some idea.'

'Fifteen.'

'Don't be so silly. How can you be fifteen? You have already had five children.' More giggling.

'Oh, in that case, I must be seventy-five.' More giggles.

At this stage, exasperated, I would give up. Most of the women looked much older than their years.

These regular visits to the village were among the most rewarding things I did as a student, and I kept them up until my final year. This to me was a tangible expression of our Christian values. Not only did the village visits foster close friendships between ourselves, but they also gave us an insight into rural life, of which we were woefully ignorant. The vast majority of Indians live in villages, not in towns and cities. I had always lived in a city; my family was affluent; I was sent away to boarding school, and the only poor I knew were the servants. But we knew little of their families, who lived in villages, often at a distance. Most of the servants in Annie Lodge came from my grandfather's village near Tuticorin. We lacked sufficient curiosity to get more information about their early years and village life.

What I knew was from my mother, her siblings and, years later, from distant relatives. One thing that my grandfather did tell me was that most of the women in his village had long stretched earlobes, with huge holes through which were hung massive ornaments. Some of the earlobes would split or rest on the shoulder. This was very uncomfortable, but regarded as a sign of beauty. He considered this barbaric, and after retirement he had visited his village several times to repair these ears. He told me that after I qualified as a doctor, he expected me to go to his village and do plastic surgery on the ears, as he had.

⸎

Undergraduate life in Vellore was very pleasant and there was much socialising. A few students found their life partners in the first year, but whenever the religious, caste or language divide was crossed, there was considerable disapproval from parents. Some irate parents would come to Vellore to reprimand the Principal for allowing so much freedom. He would smile, shake his head and say it was not for him to interfere. He regarded the students as responsible adults. But he would speak to the couple concerned, and advise them gently that it was unwise to offend one's parents. Of the differences, it was the religious divide that caused the most distress. Christians were expected to marry Christians, Muslims Muslims and Hindus Hindus. And then there were Parsis and Eurasians to be considered as well.

The annual College Day was held a couple of months into the first term. It was a much anticipated event when the entire student body and staff came together. There was a tree-planting ceremony by the final-year students, men in white shirts and trousers and women in blue saris. In the afternoon, there would be a sumptuous tea in the luxuriant sunken garden around the lily pond, adjacent to the Women's Hostel. This would be followed by three hours of entertainment in the Assembly Hall. It would start with music and Indian dance, performed by some very talented students, which was followed by a full-length play. In my first year the Entertainment Secretary had chosen Oscar Wilde's *An Ideal Husband* and asked me to take the lead female role of Mrs Chiltern. It had been performed in IT when I was there, with girls taking the men's parts as well. I did not take part then, but had sat through many of the rehearsals as I was one of the prompters. I knew most of the lines. The part of Lord Chiltern was taken by a twenty-two-year-old final-year student, Rabindranath Azariah, a tall, dark, articulate, charismatic man. I knew him well as he was one of the leaders of our village team, an active SCM member. We would sometimes recite our lines to each other, as we walked on the bund to the village.

There was what was called a strict 'no touch' technique on stage. This meant there was no holding of hands, hugging, caressing or kissing between the sexes. In India it is not the norm for adults of the opposite sex to touch each other in public, or in the company of others, whether married or single, on the stage or even when saying goodbye. At the very end of the play, to my great astonishment, Rabin put his arms around me and gave me a great hug. The applause from the audience was thunderous. We expected a reprimand from the Principal, but none came.

Later that year the SCM organised a concert to raise money and we did a play from *A Man Born to be King*, a play cycle originally for radio by Dorothy L. Sayers. Rabin and I were again asked to do the lead parts.

My mother returned to her school in Panchgani in January 1954 with many ideas and plans for the English Department, not least the setting up of a well-stocked library. When I spent the summer holidays with her, she seemed pleased with the way her plans were working out, especially the first lot of students she had prepared for the Cambridge exams, who had excelled in English. The school had never had such good results in English and Geography. But I could sense she was becoming more and more irritated with Miss Beavers's meddlesome ways. With donations from some of the wealthy parents, my mother installed a set of *The Encyclopaedia Britannica* and encouraged her students, who were avid readers, to refer to it frequently. A few weeks later my mother was summoned to Miss Beavers's office. She was not even asked to sit down.

'I did not know you were a Communist,' Miss Beavers said angrily. 'What? Er...' said my mother, who was quite taken aback. She was interested in politics but had no political affiliations.

'Why did you not tell me you are a Communist,' continued, Miss Beavers.

'I am not a Communist,' my mother said. 'What is this all about?' 'Why have you installed the *Encyclopaedia Britannica* in our library?

It has Darwin's views on evolution, which Communists believe. They are quite contrary to Christian views. I strongly disapprove of them. I am writing to my mission head office in London to ask them how you should be dealt with, and I will let you know what they have to say. In the meantime, take away those dreadful books.'

Miss Beavers cut short my mother's reply, and would not listen to any explanation or reason. My mother wrote a letter to Miss Beavers, explaining why it was important for the school to have an up-to-date library. She added that she saw no conflict between Christianity and Darwin's theory of evolution. Back came a fierce reply from Miss Beavers, accusing my mother of deliberately using difficult words, which she had found difficult to understand. My mother showed me this letter. I could only assume that Miss Beavers had had a limited education in England.

The other two English missionary members of staff, who had always been very friendly and cordial towards my mother, and had complimented her on raising the standard of English in the school, became distant and cool towards her. The other staff were very supportive of her, but would not speak out.

At the end of the school year, my mother decided, after consulting me and Anne, to resign from Kimmins, rather than put up with the rantings of Miss Beavers. What my mother did not know then was that following Miss Beavers's complaint about her to the Mission Board in England, they had decided to recall Miss Beavers to London and offer her early retirement. They had arranged for Miss Yelland, her young predecessor, who was in post when my mother joined Kimmins, to return as headmistress. Anne and I were adamant that my mother should not reconsider her decision. We wanted her to return to Annie Lodge. Violet Aunty had once again returned to Burma to be with her husband Eddie. The unreliable Samson Uncle was running Annie Lodge with the cook and gardener, and neglecting everything and everyone including Thatha, who was now eighty-four.

My mother's pupils and many of the staff were distraught at her leaving, especially her naughty girls, and in particular Sheila Nanjappa, mentioned earlier. Sheila had taken to spelling her name 'Shelagh', probably after some heroine in a novel she had read, until her young, glamorous mother reprimanded the school for allowing this and demanded that the name revert to the original spelling. Sheila never let go of my mother, and became her third daughter.

Thatha was overjoyed at my mother's return. The house was shabby and the garden neglected. At last, she and I would live within a few hours of each other, and I would be able to spend an occasional weekend with her. Vellore was eighty miles from Madras. After morning classes on a Saturday, I would take the noon train to Madras, get a taxi and be home by mid-afternoon. My mother would be standing on the upstairs front balcony, with her arms on the railings, her chin on her hands, looking out for me to arrive. After dinner with Thatha, my mother and I would go into the city and to a 9 p.m. cinema show, much to his disapproval, as he considered it inappropriate for women to be out at that hour. We would return safely by taxi. The following evening, I would return to Vellore, getting the last bus from Katpadi station, and be in my hostel by 10 p.m. In all, a very satisfactory arrangement.

We had our Sports Day for both men and women in February, when it was still relatively cool and, unlike in Isabella Thoburn College, Sports Day meant athletics. A few weeks earlier, when I came in a pair of shorts on to the track to practise, there were gasps from some of the women students. No female student had ever been seen in a pair of shorts in the college, and there was strong disapproval from all quarters. The Principal saw me and merely grunted and smiled. Girls wore trousers and tunics. Some even ran in saris, and very fast too. News quickly got to my sister at the School of Nursing on the hospital campus that her sister was running around in a pair of shorts and shocking everyone. Anne too had worn shorts in Bishop Cottons. She merely laughed, but said to me, 'Make sure you win. The disapproval and giggles will then stop.' I won the 100 metres and 200 metres and came second in the high jump, but failed to win the championship by a point. I had taken the advice of two male classmates and scratched from the 50 metres, as they said I was a slow starter and told me to do the obstacle race instead, a silly non-athletic event, where I came to a complete stop. Halfway through the race, I was required to drink a bottle of fizzy pop. The girl who won the high jump picked up courage, and also wore a pair of shorts, but got into trouble with her fellow evangelicals, as they did not think God would approve.

Easter morning was memorable in Vellore. It was very hot by then. We would climb College Hill before first light and find a cool spot. During the Easter Service the sun would rise through the spectacular crimson sky. The previous Friday, I would have attended the three-hour service, my favourite, and never failed to remember the horror of that Good Friday in Mandalay in 1942.

By the end of April, other than my class, there were very few students left in the College, most of them having gone to Madras to do exams, or home for a brief vacation, or on resident hospital postings. The important end-of-first-year exams were looming, and we found it very difficult to study in the heat. Every window and door in the hostel was open in the evenings, but it was as hot outside as it was inside. The large rocks in the proximity of our hostel reflected the unremitting heat of the day. Hoping for an occasional breeze, I took to studying outside the common room, under powerful outdoor lights, until one night I saw two huge black scorpions doing a mating dance on a rock a couple of feet from me. I made a hasty retreat and studied indoors after that. I had not worked consistently during the year, forever procrastinating.

I had to do a considerable amount of last-minute cramming, but blessed with a retentive memory, I comfortably passed all the exams. Again the failure rate was high, but this did not stop anyone from moving on to the second year.

I decided that though I had passed my college first-year exams, my knowledge of Osteology (the study of bones) left much to be desired. I needed to improve on it, as I would be examined in it during the university exams in Madras later in the year. So when I took my grey trunk home for the summer holidays, it contained a half skeleton, including the skull, together with my copy of *Gray's Anatomy* which had a comprehensive section on Osteology. I intended to do some serious study during the holidays. My mother was amused, and doubted if I would look at even a single bone. I also felt compelled to learn to play the second movement of Beethoven's Piano Sonata No. 8, Op. 13 in C Minor (*Pathétique*), something I had wanted to do for years. It was my favourite piece of music, described as the greatest piece of musical consolation ever written. For this, a piano had to be hired for the six weeks, from Museé Musical, the only Western classical music shop in Madras.

'Why can't you learn it on the organ we have at home?' asked Thatha, who thought it extravagant to hire a piano.

'It can't be played on the organ, and any way our organ has only five octaves,' I said.

My mother agreed, and the handcart driver was summoned, and he and a servant were sent to collect the piano. The organ was banished temporarily from the sitting room. Amid much commotion and instructions from everyone, including Samson Uncle, the piano was carefully carried into its place.

The summer heat in Madras was overpowering, with the temperature rising to 42°C day after day. My friend Dawn came to spend a week with us. One afternoon, when my mother was out, the maid came upstairs to say that two young men had come to visit us. She had shown them into the sitting room. They were standing at the doorway when we came downstairs. They were our Vellore classmates. I was annoyed they had arrived without warning, and worried that Thatha would disapprove of us being visited by male friends, and would ask them to leave. I warned them, and hoped I could get rid of them before he appeared. He spent most of his time in his room, but had the habit of coming into the sitting room to read the time on the large Thomas Seth clock. He suddenly appeared. I explained to him that they were our classmates, had found themselves in the neighbourhood, and had decided to call. He looked them up and down, and asked them their names and where they were from. He then proceeded to quiz them on Osteology. They were taken aback, but were bright boys and answered all his questions. He was impressed and asked them to sit down, and offered them coffee, but they declined and politely left. I was relieved. My mother laughed when we told her about this visit. Thatha did not like me studying in a co-educational institution, but because Vellore had such a good reputation, he did not protest. I had to remind myself of my family's orthodox views, and that it was important that I try to avoid hurting their feelings when I possibly could.

The summer holiday came to an end. These were the longest holidays we would ever have. My mother was right. The bones never did come out of the grey trunk except when she wanted to take some photographs. But I did learn how to play the second movement of the *Pathétique*.

We had five months before our first university exams, the pre-clinical finals in Anatomy, Physiology, Biochemistry and Statistics. Our demonstrators, tutors, lecturers and professors tried to impress on us that we needed to work very much harder than we had done the previous year. I was full of good intentions, but threw myself even more vigorously into extracurricular activities and onto the stage again, and once more had the lead female part, this time in a George Bernard Shaw play. I missed not having Rabin to play opposite me, but he had now qualified as a doctor and was thinking about getting married to the girl he had been engaged to for seven years. But he never did marry her.

I had been going to the village clinics for a year and was beginning to do minor procedures, such as dressing wounds and lancing abscesses, and besides, as a regular attender, the village team depended on me, and I felt, even with the university exams looming, I should carry on going to the village. And then there were the social activities of the SCM. We had some inspiring guest leaders, such as Harry Morton, an English Methodist, and Geoffrey Paul, a missionary priest in Tamilnadu and Kerala, whose son-in-law, Rowan Williams, would one day be Archbishop of Canterbury. Paul Devanandan, an Indian intellectual, also led some worthwhile retreats. He edited the journal *Religion and Society*, which was one of the pioneers of Hindu–Christian dialogue. They were riveting speakers, and SCM discussion groups allowed for argument, doubt and uncertainty, something that the Evangelical Union abhorred.

For several months now, most of the students spent nearly all their waking hours studying and disapproved of the small minority of us who did not diligently apply ourselves to our studies. But four weeks before the exams, I gave up all extracurricular activities and used every moment I had to study, staying up till two and three in the morning, often only needing four hours of sleep at night. It was Anatomy that I struggled with, trying to remember the boring details. But under pressure, I could read very fast and retain what I had read after just one reading. Most of my classmates were revising for the fifth and sixth time. The knowledge that was required of us was frighteningly vast, and there was little doubt that luck would also play a part in how we performed, as it was not possible to know everything.

These were known as the 1st MBBS (Bachelor of Medicine and Surgery) exams. We sat the written papers in Vellore, and had to go to Madras Medical College (MMC), one of three medical colleges in Madras, for the practical and oral components. The examiners were senior staff from these colleges, as well as from my college, but there was no guarantee that we would be examined by someone from our own college. In our written papers all questions would be compulsory. There would be no choice.

The day for the written papers arrived. We were all speechless with nervousness. I had not managed to cover the whole syllabus, and hoped I would be lucky with the questions, which were all of the essay type. Multiple choice had not been introduced in these exams. I thought I had done well enough in the written papers to pass, though I was a bit vague on one or two sections of a six-part question. We were given our dates for the practicals and viva and I was fortunate that mine were not in the first week. This gave me a bit more time to cram, especially Osteology.

We took the train to Madras. Two large rooms were made available for Vellore women students in the Women's Hostel of MMC. The furniture for our belongings was sparse, and we were required to sleep on the floor. I could have stayed at home in Annie Lodge, four miles away, but it was useful to be with other students, as we were learning all the time from each other. We would return from our practicals and viva and tell each other what questions were asked. As the subjects were so vast, there did not appear to be any repetition of questions, but we had some idea of the trend of thought of the examiners, and their attitude towards us, which was not always polite.

The rooms resembled the platforms of Madras Central Railway Station. We rolled out our bedding on the floor. Sleep for us was almost impossible. The lights in the rooms would be on all night, students having different times of waking and sleeping and studying. It was all truly dreadful. Tempers were frayed, and we were stressed out of our wits, though the word 'stress' had not entered our vocabulary. My mother came to visit me and was so horrified at our living conditions; she begged me to come home. She saw a moving long black line on one of the walls, and on closer inspection found they were bed bugs. She went and bought some DDT and sprayed them.

My first exam was a viva in Physiology. The short hair I had when I started as a first-year in Vellore had been allowed to grow, and I now had two plaits. I looked absurdly young. Two male MMC students, also waiting for their viva, were sitting on a bench next to me outside the examiners' office. They looked at me, and then at each other, and one said to the other mockingly, 'Looks as though we have a prodigy in our midst,' and they started to laugh.

I was livid. Just then, I was called in. My heart was pounding. There were three middle-aged male examiners, all rotund and in different stages of baldness. All were immaculately dressed in suit and tie.

One smiled at me and said, 'You look very young. How old are you?'

'Twenty,' I said.

And then, after a pause, he continued, 'Can you tell us the physiological changes taking place in a student facing a viva examination?'

I was taken aback, but after a moment or two, I composed my thoughts and started to answer quickly and fluently.

'Very good,' he said.

He proceeded to ask me some standard questions, all of which I answered easily. He smiled again and said I could go. That was one hurdle I knew I had cleared.

And then there were the dreaded practical exams. In Physiology, among other things, I was required to demonstrate the role of calcium on the heart muscle of the frog. There were about ten of us in a queue, each to receive a beating heart, as a technician removed it from a frog. Each of us had already assembled a rotating drum, covered with graph paper, attached to an ink pointer. The heart would be connected to the apparatus. As I carefully took the heart to the drum, I tripped and dropped the heart. I froze. The examiners, who were hovering around, looked at me in disgust. Horrified, I thought I was doomed; the heart would be irreparably damaged, and I would not be allowed another one. I stared at it on the stone floor. It was still beating. I carefully lifted it, attached it, and perfused it with the appropriate solutions, and it continued to beat away merrily, until it stopped in a contracted state, after I had run calcium through it. I had a perfect graph. I then had to do some experiments in Biochemistry which went off satisfactorily.

I had a day at home in Annie Lodge, before I returned for the Anatomy practicals. In the unfamiliar surroundings of the Anatomy hall, corpses in various stages of dissection were laid out on numbered concrete slabs. On a piece of paper, which we randomly picked from a box, was the slab number and the dissection required. There were four of us around each corpse. I had to demonstrate the insertion of a muscle. I was hoping for a limb amputation, as these were the easiest to do, the technician doing the sawing of the bone for women students. I found the muscle all right and traced it, and found its insertion. The examiner, a very glamorous lady professor in a flashy sari, quite unsuitable for a dissection hall, came around and asked me several questions which I was able to answer. So far so good, I thought. One more to go, and that was the Anatomy viva, which included the dreaded Osteology. The first part of the viva was again in the dissection hall. Two examiners took me to a partly dissected body and asked me to identify various structures, which they pulled up with forceps: nerves, arteries, veins, muscles, organs. I then had to go to the next room for Osteology. Girls who had already been examined told us there were boxes of bones along the corridor, each box containing bones of the same kind. The night before I had decided to study three bones thoroughly, one of them being the femur, the thigh bone, and chance it as far as the rest were concerned. As I walked along the corridor, one of the examiners shouted out to me, 'Pick up a bone, any bone, and bring it along.' I had my wits about me, and grabbed a femur. I was saved. Bones are more complicated structures than they appear to be, with grooves, articulations and attachments.

The relief at the end of the exams was indescribable, but having had to take many more exams, one thing I have learned. The relief when an exam is over is never as great as the apprehension, anxiety and anguish before it. Each time, I wondered why I ever decided to study medicine.

I packed my bags and went to Annie Lodge, and when I said to my mother that the exams were enough to give anyone a nervous breakdown, she replied mildly, 'I don't know why you bothered about them so much.' She assumed I would pass. One could never be sure. It was usual for a third of the Vellore candidates to fail, and we usually had the best results of all the colleges. The results would be announced in January, before I returned to Vellore after the Christmas holidays.

It was mid-December now, and I would return to Vellore in January. But I had a few days only before I was to embark on an exciting adventure, which I had known about for the last three months, but to which I could not give my mind because of the forthcoming examinations.

Thatha, Paati, and family, 1917

Alice Wason and Daniel Rajan, 1928

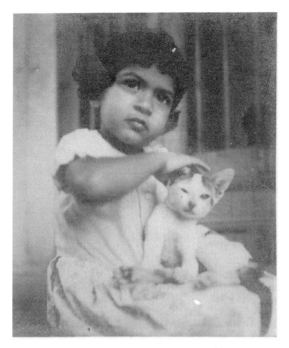

Lindy, three and a half years old

Biggy, Alfred, Alice, 1940

Lindy with Mother on the ship to Mandalay, 1942

Lindy, Bishop Cotton Girls' School,
Bangalore

Alice Rajan, 1950

Lindy, Burma Olympics, 1951

Anne and Lindy, 1953

IT College, Lucknow, 1953
(Lindy and Charlene, second and third from right)

Christian Medical College, Vellore

Room no. 4, first year medical students, Saro, Lindy, Amy, Lily

Lindy, 1956

Thatha, aged eighty-five

Lindy, 1958

Michael, 1958

Lindy and Michael's wedding, 1960

Lindy and Kiran, 1962

Kiran, 1968

Alpha

Lindy, Anne, and families, January 1972

Lindy and Alan's wedding, 1989

Kiran and Richard's triplets, Durham, aged seven

Alan

Chapter 13

HUNTING TIGERS

Rahat Ahmad, my Muslim friend from IT, who had also struggled to pass Hindi and had failed to attend the interview for admission to Vellore, had written to ask whether I would like to join her and her family on a tiger shoot in the Himalayan foothills over Christmas. She had invited two other classmates from IT: Shubha, with whom I had stayed in Bombay the first time I did the Vellore entrance exam, and Sheila Soota, a friend from IT and now a student at Lady Hardinge Medical College in Delhi. Many Indian parents would not have allowed their daughters such licence, but perhaps ours knew there would be a row if they did not, and they acquiesced. Thatha, of course, raised objections. Samson Uncle thought it highly dangerous. My mother said I was an adult and sensible. Shubha, Sheila and I decided to meet in Lucknow, visit IT and friends briefly, and then take the train, via Bareilly, to Kichha, a small village in the Himalayan foothills, where the Ahmads would have already set up camp.

Once again my mother was at Central Station, waving me goodbye on the Grand Trunk Express, but this time I was not alone. There were about eight of us from Vellore, all travelling third class, the others, going home for the Christmas vacation, getting off at various stops on the way to Delhi. That evening we reached Bezwada, a junction where the train stopped for nearly an hour. One of our party going to Delhi was met by her brother, who took her home for a shower and returned her in time, before the train set off again, The vegetarian café in Bezwada was famous for its food, and some of us decided to give it a try. We had to sit on very low wooden stools. A banana leaf was slapped down in front of us on the floor. A relay of men with buckets of varying size plonked rice, curry, vegetables, poppadoms and pickles on to the banana leaves. We had to eat with our fingers. The food was amazingly delicious, but it was so hot it blew our heads off. Andhra is famous for its pickles and we knew why. We forgot about the time. The train was about to start. The first whistle blew. We left the food and ran to wash our hands, and then on to the platform, but the second whistle had already been blown, and the train had started to move, rapidly picking up speed.

'Get on anywhere,' one of the boys shouted. I jumped on to the nearest carriage step, only to discover it was a first-class carriage. I begged the occupants to let me in, but they shook their heads, thinking I was a ticketless traveller. For the next two hours, I hung on, terrified, until the next station when we were all reunited in our carriage.

We approached Nagpur the next morning. One of our party, a tall, attractive, lively, Muslim girl, with straight glossy black hair down to her knees, was planning to get off in a few minutes. She disappeared towards the bathroom, and reappeared in a full black burkha with slits for the eyes.

'What's wrong with you?' we asked, amazed and amused.

'My brothers are meeting me, and they expect me to be fully covered,' she answered. 'My mother and sisters also wear the burkha.'

We had a happy visit at IT, meeting friends and staff. I missed Charlene. We took the overnight train to Bareilly, and changed for Kichha, a village with a small primitive station. Rahat warned us that the train would stop for only a minute, and to be ready to throw out our luggage to her servants, who would be on the dirt platform, and to jump out quickly. Indian trains don't wait for anyone. It was bitterly cold. The air was clear and the sky a vivid blue and cloudless. A jeep was waiting for us and we drove through fields of bright yellow flowers. In the distance were snow-capped mountains, the Himalayas.

We arrived at the campsite, a large clearing with several tents. Rahat and her family had arrived a few days earlier with a retinue of servants. We were taken to the women's tent, smaller than the rest. Rahat, her mother and father, her brothers and sisters, all younger than her, were in one large tent. Her older sister had recently eloped with a Hindu, and was not mentioned. Her grandfather, Sir Iqbal Ahmad, a genial man, and other male relatives were in another tent. There was a large communal tent with a roaring fire where we would eat our meals, freshly cooked. Lastly, a little distance away, was the servants' tent. All the servants were male: cooks, bearers, sweepers, watchmen and *mahouts*. And then there was something that made my insides churn with delight: four large elephants, tethered nearby, under a tarpaulin. What magnificent and mysterious creatures these are. The Indian elephant is more handsome than the African one. Its ears are smaller and its spine does not dip in the middle. I vowed I would own one, one day.

Our tent had three *charpoys* with mattresses, pillows, sheets and numerous blankets. The floor was covered with straw, which was also heaped up under the *charpoys* for warmth. A small bathroom, with primitive facilities, was attached to the tent. In the morning, a servant would bring hot water in buckets, which we had to use quickly for washing, before the water became cold. Bathing was not a priority. After a substantial breakfast, we would set off on the elephants, clambering up on to them, via their tail, which was held across by one of the men, and on to wooden seats. The men who were the serious hunters led the way with their rifles, and had the most experienced mahout. I was on an elephant with my tent mates, Rahat and her sisters. We were there for the ride. We chatted away, until we were asked by the men ahead to keep quiet, as we were frightening away the birds and animals. We went through fields, and then dense forest with streams and ravines. We mainly saw deer and birds. Now and again there was an opening, and the majestic, snow-capped mountains would appear.

No tiger was spotted that day, or the next, and the novelty of riding on an elephant wore off. Worse still, the side-to-side motion of the seats on the elephant made me queasy, until finally I vomited onto the elephant's back. This infuriated Shubha, an obsessive animal lover, and she reprimanded me for being so inconsiderate. I did not get sympathy from anyone. She also disapproved of killing tigers, as I think most of us did, so there was silent delight that none had been spotted. The next day, it was decided that we should go out at night as well. A young goat had been tethered to a tree in the jungle to attract the tigers. As we approached it, we could hear it bleating, and Shubha said in a very loud voice: 'Oh, the poor little thing.' The men were furious, as that would have chased any tigers away. We returned at midnight, empty handed. That night it was colder than ever. I had so many layers of clothing on, I could not bend; nor could we get much sleep.

At dawn the following morning, while we were still in bed, we heard Rahat's father, just inside our tent, shouting frantically: 'Girls! Don't ask questions. Just rush out of your tent. Quickly.' We leapt out of our beds and ran out, and he and two other men with rifles ran in.

After a few moments, we heard several rifle shots and then silence. We thought it must be a tiger. They came out pulling an enormous black hamadryad, a king cobra with part of its head shot off. One of the servants had seen the end of its tail disappearing into our tent, and had raised the alarm. These snakes can sometimes grow to eighteen feet. That night none of us slept, and were relieved we were leaving the next day. We were grateful to the Ahmads for giving us this experience and their limitless hospitality.

We got to Delhi, and Shubha and I stayed with friends of her father, bankers like him. They had been invited to a banquet for Madame Soong Ching-ling, Vice Chairman of the Peoples' Republic of China and widow of Sun Yat Sen. India and China had not fallen out with each other at that time. Our hosts said we could go with them as their guests. Shubha and I did not have suitable clothes for the occasion, nor did we have the money to buy any. Later we regretted the missed opportunity.

A telegram from my mother was waiting to say I had passed my exams. I took Shubha and Sheila to lunch at Gaylords, a popular restaurant in Delhi. But I could taste nothing, as I had developed a severe cough and cold the day we left Kichha. Shubha was having some sort of crisis. Having got a good degree in Physics and maths, we expected her to go on to a Doctorate in Physics, but she felt the urge to help mankind in a personal sense, and said she was going to become a nurse. Her parents were totally opposed to this. We told her she needed something more intellectual, to go back to Bombay and get the necessary Biology I.Sc. and apply to one of the Bombay Medical Schools. She was an eccentric, unorthodox person, and eventually qualified as a doctor. Her parents then set about finding suitable boys for her and her younger sister Alka, an organic chemist. Both girls resisted this, by being thoroughly objectionable when taken to tea at the homes of prospective grooms. They could not abide the thought of an arranged marriage. Their parents were distraught, but eventually left them alone. I did not expect Shubha to marry, but a few years later she wrote to me.

'Can you believe that there is actually a man who wants to marry me, and I want to marry him?'

The man in question, Sunil, was a splendid, erudite person who became a well-known neurosurgeon in Bombay, and delighted in his wife's eccentricities. Shubha's father refused to attend her wedding, because Sunil was neither rich enough nor did he belong to their caste. But it was not long before there was a reconciliation. This is not uncommon in Indian families when children marry against their parents' wishes. Alka too found herself an exceptional man, a scientist.

I spent a few more days in Delhi staying with Sheila in Lady Hardinge Medical College, before joining the Vellore group at Delhi Railway Station. Indira, the girl who jumped off the train at Bezwada to have a shower in her brother's house, was being seen off by her German mother and sister, the latter, a fine-featured beauty who would later find fame as Anita Desai, the novelist.

By the time we reached Madras, I felt very ill and feverish. Every breath produced a sharp pain in my chest. The rest of the group continued to Vellore for the new term, but my mother, who had come to spend a few minutes with me at the station, refused to let me join them, and took me home. The Brahmin doctor at the end of the street was summoned. With a stethoscope, he listened to my chest through my clothes, for purposes of modesty. He diagnosed pneumonia and pleurisy, gave me penicillin injections twice a day for a few days, refused to charge us, and put me right. I was back at Vellore within the week.

~

It was January 1956, and we were about to take the great leap forward. From now on, we would have to go every day to the Christian Medical College Hospital, four miles away, to study and train, but more importantly, we would be confronted with live patients. Our clinical years had started. But for a third of my class this was not to be, as they had failed either Anatomy or Physiology or both, and this included all my three room-mates. This meant retakes in the summer, and they would always be six months behind me. It was not a happy thought for them, or for me.

Before we were let loose on patients, we had to be primed on certain matters, such as how to approach them. We had to learn history-taking; this meant we had to find out the patients' complaints, symptoms and everything about these, such as the duration, severity, regularity, and so on. We had to know all their past complaints, treatment, operations, medication, family history and social history. All this had to be recorded under headings, in a legible, systematic way. We then had to learn how to examine a patient, system by system, in an organised way and record our findings. These fundamentals were essential in our training.

There was a language problem which had to be addressed. Vellore attracted patients from all over India, a country with numerous languages. Most of the patients were local and Tamil-speaking, but there was a significant minority speaking Malayalam, Telegu and Kannada, the South Indian languages, and Hindi, Bengali and Gujarati, the North Indian languages. Students would interpret for each other, as would relatives of patients. Everything was eventually translated into English. My Tamil was fluent and I could get by in Hindi. Many of the students had a flair for languages and were multilingual.

The day started after breakfast, with the first lecture of the day at College at 7 a.m. We were then taken by buses to the hospital where we remained until we were transported back, reaching College at 5 p.m. It was a long day. I would usually collapse onto the large square *charpoy* my room-mates and I had had installed in our room. Soon there would be half a dozen of us sprawled on it with our endless chatter. Every Monday evening I would drag myself to the village clinic, getting a second life, as we walked along the emerald-green rice fields. Other evenings, when I felt a bit energetic, I would go for walks with friends or climb College Hill. We were often joined by our male classmates. Nearly all of us were from single-sex schools, but despite this we found it easy to enter into comfortable platonic relationships. Our backgrounds could be very diverse, from the lowest to the highest caste, rich and poor, Westernised or vernacular, perfect English to adequate English. And we were Christians, Hindus, Muslims, Sikhs, Parsis and Jews. Most of the time we did not know who was what, and it did not matter.

The staff were equally diverse. Most were Indian, and the rest were from the United States of America and the white Commonwealth countries: Britain, Canada, Australia and New Zealand. The Americans were noticeably the most affluent. Nearly all were missionaries. Many had given up lucrative practices in their own countries. A few were paternalistic and controlling, but most were good, honourable and humble individuals, people of integrity, representing the best of humanity. They seemed to produce a lot of children, who were sent off to boarding school in the hill stations, where the curriculum was such that they could return to their respective countries for further schooling before they went to university.

Our first exposure to surgery was a series of lectures given by Hugh Somervell, professor of Surgery. Nearing retirement after many years as a missionary in South India, he had been in the 1924 Everest expedition which cost the lives of Mallory and Irvine. The other surgeon was Paul Brand, a most charismatic Englishman, who found world-wide fame in pioneering reconstructive hand surgery. Another missionary, John Webb, the Professor of Paediatrics, also gave up a lucrative career in England. A Balliol man, he was a dashing cricketer and sportsman, and very popular with students. My sister Anne eventually became his ward sister. The wives of many of these doctors were themselves doctors, but unlike Indian women doctors did little medical work while their children were young, despite having servants.

The pattern of our medical education was based on the British system, and though there was little difference in the way the British and American doctors practised, or taught us, for those of us whose thoughts were prematurely going in the direction of postgraduate education, it was Britain that occupied our thoughts. North America, Australia and New Zealand seemed very far away.

In our first year of clinical medicine we were called third years. We were assigned to what were called Firms, in Medicine and

Surgery. Each Firm was headed by a professor, and had doctors of all grades of seniority. There was a well-defined hierarchical order.

Each student would be assigned patients on the ward, which had about thirty patients, nearly all of whom would be lying on their beds. Some would have relatives sitting beside them or feeding them. We would have to take histories, examine them, look at the results of their investigations and present them to the Firm during ward rounds, when doctors, medical students and senior nurses went from bed to bed looking at and discussing patients. This was at first daunting, but we had to get used to it. Sometimes, only the middle-grade doctors were present, and they could be rude or sarcastic when questioning us, occasionally reducing a woman student to tears. We were also required to attend outpatient clinics of our Firms once or twice a week. These started at 7.30 a.m. and could last six hours, as the number of patients was huge. There was very little primary care, and few general practitioners. There was no referral system to specialists, as in Britain's National Health Service. These were essentially walk-in clinics, the clerks at registration deciding which clinic patients should attend. Their diseases varied, and were in all stages of progression. The experience we gained in a short time was immense. But what struck me most of all was the wretchedness of the human condition. Lectures were also held in the afternoons, and the quality varied, from the inspirational to the mundane. It was not uncommon for us to miss the odd one, bunking, as it was called. I would sometimes go and spend this time with Anne in the nurses' quarters, if she was having an afternoon off.

✓

In September 1956, just before my twenty-first birthday, I decided to spend a long weekend in Bangalore, where I had been at boarding school for six years, and had not visited since I had left in 1950. I visited my old school friend, Betty Josephs, and her parents, Anglo-Indians, who had been very kind and hospitable to me when I was a boarder. Betty and I had both decided to become doctors, but she had not been correctly advised when she chose her pre-medical subjects, and was therefore not eligible to apply for Medicine. She decided to do a BA in English instead.

Since she was a schoolgirl, she had been wooed by Ian Maiden, a maths master at Bishop Cotton Boys' School. She spurned him for years, but eventually, at twenty-one, married him. My trip was particularly memorable as Roma, the classmate I went with, and I spent most of our time with her brother, S, and his friend. They were young officers who had just completed their training at the Air Force Technical College. S was already a graduate engineer, and a few years later would qualify also as a pilot. I had not met him before. Dark, handsome, attentive and charming, I became aware that he was attracted to me. I was not surprised when he asked me, when we parted, if he could write to me. I readily agreed. He also asked me if I would attend his passing-out parade, at which his widowed mother and sister would be present. I declined as I did not think this appropriate. Letters from him came frequently, sometimes twice a week, and I would reply. He was a Christian, and we had much in common, but after nearly a year I felt the friendship was not going anywhere. He was warm, affectionate and complimented me often, but that was all, and he never mentioned the future, and there was never a hint of romance. But I had felt all the time that there was a future for us together.

A few months after I met S, I was at Annie Lodge, for the Christmas holidays. One day, when my mother was out, the maid came upstairs to tell me two men were downstairs, and wanted to know if anyone was at home. Apart from Thatha, I was the only one at home. I thought they must be students of Samson Uncle's. The latter had now gained respectability, since becoming a part-time lecturer at the Engineering College in Guindy, a Madras suburb. I went downstairs and was horrified to find it was S and his friend. Thatha could emerge from his room at any time, and he would definitely disapprove of my being visited by men, especially if he knew they were from the Forces. Prejudices ran deep in my family. Acceptable men were doctors, engineers or lawyers. If they were not considered bright enough, they became teachers or priests. Careers in the Forces were frowned upon. I said to my two visitors that if my grandfather appeared, as he well might, I would introduce them as medical student classmates from Vellore. They were indignant.

'What's wrong with the Air Force?' they asked. 'We are officers.'
I explained that Thatha would strongly disapprove of my meeting young men outside of my College environment. They were not pleased, but agreed, and sure enough, Thatha appeared just then. As planned, I told him they were my classmates. I was terrified he would start asking them medical questions, as he did when two of my male classmates had visited two years earlier. My current visitors were distinctly uncomfortable, and to my great relief left almost immediately. I had told my mother and Anne about S, and that I had met him again when he paid a flying visit to Vellore. They seemed to like what I had told them about him, and they would always refer to him as 'Your Airman'.

∿

Anne's career in nursing continued to progress very satisfactorily, and her services were much in demand, both in the wards she had worked in, and by the physicians and surgeons she had worked with. She had particularly enjoyed Paediatric and Cardiothoracic nursing. She was a good communicator, and lectured frequently in the School of Nursing to undergraduates and postgraduates.

Anne decided that Paediatrics was the field she wanted to specialise in, and in 1956 she applied for and won a Rockefeller scholarship to do a Master's degree in Paediatric Nursing at Boston University in America. As the scholarship came through the School of Nursing, she was asked to agree to work in Vellore for five years after her return. My mother felt this was too long a period to be tied down, and asked her not to commit herself, unless she was very sure. Anne was adamant that Vellore was the only place she wanted to spend her working life, as no other hospital in India could meet its high standards and give her the same fulfilment. She was twenty-four and had no attachments. She was still a serious person, but had more vitality and more of a sense of fun than she had in her morose teenage years. She had also developed a dry sense of humour.

As expected, Thatha, Jessie Aunty, Samson Uncle and other close relatives disapproved of Anne's plans. They could not understand, why, yet again, my mother was sending off one of her daughters to far off places. It was time a suitable boy was found for Anne to marry. Going away to America would lessen her chances of a good match; the younger the bride, the wider the field of suitable boys. My mother, in her usual way, soon saw them off. Jessie Aunty said rather sadly to me that she hoped Anne and I would find good husbands one day, because it was quite clear that my mother was not going to find them for us.

We got ready for Anne's great adventure and made several additions to her wardrobe, including some colourful South Indian silk saris. I was very sorry to see her go, but so happy that she looked forward to it with such confidence. It was her first trip to the West.

Anne travelled to New York with a friend, Violet, a contemporary at Vellore, who also had a Rockefeller scholarship to study for a Master's in Nursing Administration. In New York they were invited, with other foreign students, to have breakfast at the Waldorf Astoria with the Mayor. She then flew on to Boston, where she shared an apartment with students from Asia and Europe.

Anne excelled at Boston University, getting straight A's, as they say in America, in all her subjects. We had long, detailed letters from her, telling us how good life was. She made several lasting friendships and found the Americans to be generous and warm-hearted. There was one family, in particular, who invited her several times to Kennebunk in Maine. They taught her to eat lobsters and to drink Martini and Drambuie, all of which were new experiences.

Anne fell in love with a young Indian engineer, studying for a Doctorate in Engineering in Boston. He too was Tamil, but a Catholic and from Madras. It was a serious relationship, and they would have married but for the fact that Anne was not prepared to renege on her bond to work in Vellore for five years. He was not prepared to live in Vellore, and his parents were unhappy that she was not from a Catholic family. My mother had no time for them.

'I shall never marry,' declared Anne.

In the summer of 1957, we were to take our next lot of university exams, the second MBBS in pharmacology (the study of drugs), Pathology (the study of disease processes) and Medical Jurisprudence and Toxicology (Legal Medicine and Poisons). Patient contact was not a part of these subjects. Pharmacology was exceptionally dull, and no amount of inspired lecturing could make it otherwise. The Professor of Pharmacology was the Principal of our College: Dr David, the gruff man who greeted me when I arrived for interview for admission to Vellore in 1954. He was fond of me and often singled me out. We did not dare bunk off his lectures. He summoned me one day and, with a twinkle in his eye, said that the mother of S, my Air Force friend, had been visiting the College, and had come to see him, to enquire what sort of person I was. She clearly saw me as a possible prospective daughter-in-law.

The Professor of Medical Jurisprudence and Toxicology, Dr Asirvatham, a highly charismatic man and a fast talker, made his subject come alive, even though Toxicology could be boring. So fascinating were his lectures that there was hardly a vacant seat in the lecture theatre. He never requested us to sign the attendance register, 'because I know all of you are here today'. His lectures would be interspersed with all sorts of personal anecdotes. The one I liked best was about his sabbatical at a famous university in Carolina. He was a very dark-skinned Tamil, with straight black glossy hair and sharp features. His story was that on his first day at the university he saw two water fountains, one of which was labelled COLORED. Perplexed by this, he asked one of the students passing by what was special about it. Was it orange juice, or some other juice.

The student replied, 'Don't you know? It is for people like yourself who are coloured. You have black skin. You are not to drink from the other fountain.'

Seething with rage, Dr Asirvatham went to see the head of his department, who was very apologetic, and said that the notice was meant for negroes, and not Indians, and suggested that he wore a turban so that people knew he was Indian. White people would then not mind his using their fountain. He refused to wear a turban and drank from both fountains. No one objected.

Pathology consisted of various components, and was my favourite subject. But the Microbiology (the study of bacteria and viruses) part of it did not fill me with enthusiasm. The latter was taught by the professor herself, a lame, morose, middle-aged American missionary, who rarely smiled. She had a soporific, monotonous, deadpan voice, and was very strict with the attendance register, so it was unwise to miss her classes. Parasitology, a much smaller subject, was much more interesting, and the antics of some of these worms, wending their way around the body, was remarkable. And some of them had amazing names, such as *Dracunculus medinensis* and *Diphyllobothrium latum* which, with a bit of practice, we could roll off our tongues. Nearly everyone in India seemed to be infested with some worm or the other. Within Pathology, I found Histopathology (the study of abnormal or diseased tissue) the most fascinating. Despite many resolutions, I was still spending too much time on extracurricular activities, and not enough time studying, but Pathology I did study very hard, not just restricting myself to the standard text books, but frequently reading around the subject. I was in the running for the class prize. The Head of Department, Dr Small, was an American, a Seventh Day Adventist, from California. We had about a dozen staff and students who belonged to this sect, and they strictly observed the Sabbath, to the extent that on the rare occasion that a university exam was held on a Saturday, they would refuse to sit it, even if it meant they had to wait for the next exam, six months later. They were highly principled, disciplined, gentle people, who did not try to inflict their religion on others. We used to say they were the only Christians who practised what they preached, except for one lively doctor who found it difficult to live up to his sect's standards. We called him a seventy-seventh day Adventist. Dr Small had a flair for teaching, and years later, as a postgraduate, I found him inspirational. The other professor, Dr Job, an Indian and a Vellore graduate, equally able, had a special interest in research into leprosy. He gave the impression of being perpetually amused by women students. After a class exam he had set, I thought I had written the perfect answer paper. I was furious to get a mark of only 70 per cent.

I marched up to him, paper in hand, and said 'What have I left out that you have given me only 70 per cent?' He was taken aback.

'I never give any paper more than 60 per cent. You are lucky.' This seemed to be usual among Indian teachers generally: mean with their marks, unlike the American ones, who were far more generous, often giving 100 per cent.

The university exams arrived, and after the written papers we once again made our way to Madras for the practical exams and viva, for yet another week of excruciating anguish. All the examiners who tested me were external, and I did not know any of them. I had not encountered any problems, and thought I had done very well, particularly in the Pathology viva, which lasted twenty minutes, twice as long as usual. Long vivas were for candidates who were deemed to be a borderline pass, or for those who were eligible for a distinction, depending on how they had performed in their written papers. My viva covered various topics, the last of which was Hepatitis A, and the last question was whether I knew anything about recent epidemics. As luck would have it, I had been in Delhi, following the unsuccessful tiger shoot eighteen months earlier, and had stayed with my friend Sheila Soota, a medical student. Delhi then was in the midst of a big Hepatitis A epidemic, caused by a contaminated water supply, which was widely reported in the national press. I had gone to the wards with Sheila, and seen some of these patients. I was able to wax eloquent about the epidemic at the viva, and as I was about to leave one of the examiners said:

'We are delighted that your general knowledge is as good as your knowledge of Pathology. Good luck for the future.'

The others nodded. I was certain the class prize was mine. I went home and told my mother how well I had done.

'It's about time you shone in something' she said.

But it was not to be. I failed Pathology. The Principal was as shocked as I was, and went to see the Chief Examiner to check the records. The Chief Examiner told him that I had got a mark of five out of fifty in the viva, and had barely opened my mouth. To this day I believe it was a clerical error on the part of the examiners, and I was given someone else's marks. Nearly two thirds of my class failed that year, including some outstanding students, and we never knew why. I passed the other two subjects with a second rank in Medical Jurisprudence. Fortunately, failing these exams did not hold us up. I re-sat Pathology six months later and passed.

Chapter 14

THE ANGLO-INDIAN DOCTOR

'Do you know,' said Doris Nathaniel, one of the Anatomy lecturers, 'there is a young doctor in my department who is very interested in you. He is a demonstrator, and shortly to go to England, to train to be a surgeon.'

I had heard something along similar lines before about other students and doctors, and I had not been interested, but sometimes curious.

'Who?' I asked.

'Michael Cartner,' she replied.

'I thought he had a crush on my friend, Dawn, a couple of years ago,' I said.

'That was then,' she said. 'He asked me if I thought he had a chance with you. He seems smitten.'

'No,' I said.

Michael Cartner was Anglo-Indian and had qualified as a doctor even before I had joined medical school. Quiet and unassuming, he was known for his sense of humour and was very popular with students. He was Warden of the Men's Hostel during the two years he was an Anatomy Demonstrator. Two years earlier, he had invited Dawn to dinner. We teased her about him, but she was not interested. At five feet six and a half inches, he was half an inch shorter than her. Short and stocky, he had been a boxer in his student days.

'No,' I repeated to Doris. 'I am definitely not interested.' 'A pity,' she said. 'You will not find a finer man.'

Some weeks later, I spent a weekend at Annie Lodge, as I was now in the habit of doing once a month. This suited me very well, and made my mother and Thatha very happy, though he continued to disapprove of our late-night cinema trips. I returned on the Sunday afternoon to Vellore, as I usually did, and as I got off the train, I saw Mike Cartner standing on the platform.

'Hello,' I said. 'Have you come to meet someone?'

'Yes,' he said. 'You.'

I was taken aback.

'How did you know I would be on this train?' I asked.

'I heard you had gone to Madras and I assumed you would return this afternoon, and I've been hanging about for the past few hours. Please let me come back with you to the college,' he said sheepishly.

Annoyed, I walked on towards the bus stop, but he hailed a taxi and asked me to get in. I thought this rather extravagant, but so as not to make a scene I meekly got in with him. I thanked him when we arrived at the college, and kept walking towards my hostel.

'Can I see you tomorrow evening?' he said. I felt very uncomfortable. He sensed this.

'Please. At six o'clock. We can go for a walk. I'll come to your hostel,' he said.

'Oh, all right,' I reluctantly agreed.

Michael Cartner lived in the Men's Hostel across the road from the Women's Hostel, and as Warden was given a free flat. He was twenty-seven, and had qualified from Vellore some years earlier. After house jobs, he had gone to work in an American Methodist Mission hospital in Kolar, a town forty miles from Bangalore, where his retired parents lived. Called the Ellen Thoburn Cowen Memorial Hospital, its Director was a pleasant, soft-spoken American missionary called Esther Shoemaker. So impressed was she by Michael that she asked him if he would train to be a surgeon in America, then return, and develop the hospital, and take over as Director when she retired. She had been at the hospital for over thirty years. He opted to go for his training to Britain rather than America, as his younger brother and sister had emigrated to England, and it was possible that his parents too would do so. To prepare for the Primary examination of the Royal College of Surgeons, he had decided to spend a couple of years as a Demonstrator in Anatomy in Vellore. The first part of the exam required a thorough knowledge of Anatomy.

Mike's students never missed his lectures, and enjoyed his simple, clear, anatomy demonstrations, often interspersed with humour. In one embryology class, he was drawing on the blackboard as he was teaching the development of the male and female reproductive systems, superimposing a diagram of one on the other, to show the similarities and differences. At the end of the lecture, he leapt onto the table at the front of the class, and yelled, 'Vive la difference,' much to the delight of the hand-clapping male students.

Our first walk was rather short and we were both ill at ease. The college campus was extensive, and apart from the main road in front, there were no boundaries. Beyond the college buildings, at the rear, there was endless scrubland with a few trees, and large flat, grey rocks with smooth surfaces. We sat on one and talked. Mike said he noticed me three years earlier, when he was working in the paediatric department in the hospital, and I was a first-year student. He had come to college functions, but thought I was too young to approach. When we got up to leave, I told him very politely that I saw no future for us together. He said nothing and we parted.

S, the Airman, continued to write to me, and I wrote back. And Mike continued to arrive at the Women's Hostel every evening, and ask the porter to take a note to my room, asking me to go for a walk. I would send back a note politely declining, and he would go away. After a couple of weeks, I became irritated and decided to go and meet him, and tell him to stop this. But he was so pleasant, so kind and gentle, and so funny, that I felt unable to hurt his feelings, and agreed to go for an occasional walk. The walks became more frequent, and slowly, I came to enjoy them and to like him, and then to love him. We had much in common. He was good company, well-informed and erudite, and we laughed together a lot.

My three room-mates were always excited when I returned from my walks, and asked me endless questions about him. They got to know him and liked him a lot.

'If you won't have him, we will,' they would say.

If anything makes you keen on a man, it is knowing that someone else wants him.

Mike did not ever propose formally. He would talk endlessly about how he saw his life unfolding, his hopes and ambitions, and how these could be fulfilled if I was with him. He promised me a fulfilled life as well. I told him about my parents, something I had felt too ashamed to tell anyone else. To my relief, he brushed it aside, except to say he was sorry. His parents had had a very happy marriage. Indian families take a dim view of divorce and separation, and do not like their children to marry into such families.

Mike asked if he could meet my mother. He said he knew that Indians disapproved of Anglo-Indians, and expected my family to feel the same, and more so when it involved marriage. I assured him that my mother was an unusual Indian and did not have these prejudices, though she did have others. She did not think much of marriage as an institution, and thought it was unfair to women, but she realised it was necessary for most women, and for the raising of children. She generally disliked men, and it was not just because of my father. She and I would argue about marriage. She insisted that all women should have careers and be financially independent of men. I would say that for a woman it was possible to have a satisfactory marriage and a worthwhile career. She said that was true in theory, but it did not work out that way, because men were so selfish. I was to remember this in later years.

I knew it was time to tell my mother about Mike. I wrote to her about him; I found this easier than speaking to her. I wondered what her reaction would be, but I need not have worried. She wrote back to say that anyone I wanted to marry must be very special indeed, and would be acceptable to her. And she ended her letter, 'But what about your Airman? I think you are more emotionally involved with him than you realise.'

Yes, but what about the Airman? But after much thought and sadness I had already resolved this in my mind. Yes, I was very fond of him, but by now he should have made his intentions, if any, plain. I also felt that a life in the Forces was not for me. And furthermore, his sister, my classmate, had become distinctly cool towards me. And I knew they were a close family. I wrote to S and told him that I was intending to marry Mike. He was completely shattered. He had assumed our friendship was progressing, and that we would eventually marry. He had not stated his intentions towards me as yet, because as a newly qualified engineer he said he had little to offer me, but saw our future together. He wrote me a sad but polite letter, and wished me happiness. Eighteen months later, when he knew I had married, he asked his mother to find him a suitable bride, and made a satisfactory marriage. His career was exceptionally successful.

The year was also memorable because, much to Thatha's distress, my mother decided to move from Annie Lodge. Her brother Eddie's wife, Violet, had moved back to Annie Lodge to be with her sons, two of whom were going through a troubled late adolescence.

The previous year Thatha had given my mother two acres of undeveloped farm land in Tambaram, about twelve miles from Annie Lodge. It was a lonely spot, but on the main road used by buses to go into Madras city. The only neighbours for miles were a couple on the opposite side of the road; she had been in College with my mother in Rangoon. Their daughter was Anne's classmate at Bishop Cottons, but had now become a nun, to the distress of her parents. Lakshmi and Deb Prasad were a strange, eccentric, quarrelling couple. Though Hindus, we would hear them singing Christian hymns, sitting on a bench outside their house. I wondered how my mother, with a low tolerance threshold, would cope with them. They had built a house and adjacent flat some years ago. They lived in the latter, and my mother rented their house while she was in the process of building a small house for us, which she called Alpha. Tambaram town itself was a small bustling place, on two sides of the railway line used by trains to the tip of Southern India. Tambaram was famous for a large Air Force Station, and the finest men's college in Southern India, if not in India itself: Madras Christian College (MCC). Part of Madras University, it was founded by Scottish missionaries in 1837, and occupied a 365-acre site three kilometres from Alpha.

The building of Alpha posed many challenges for my mother. Relatives thought she was yet again up to one of her crazy ideas. Why did she want to live in such a lonely area so far away from Thatha? She knew nothing about building a house, and would be cheated by the builders.

Before the construction of Alpha, the boundaries of the garden were established and a barbed wire fence erected all around. The municipal water supply did not come anywhere near Alpha, and the Prasads had to build a well in their garden, which supplied them through a water pump. Alpha, too, needed its own water supply, and a well had to be sunk. Samson Uncle, who had declared himself to be a water diviner, offered his services. My mother was very sceptical of his self-proclaimed gift, but he delivered. Water gushed from the site he had chosen, after only a few feet had been dug. There was a generous spring below, and even decades later, when other wells would run dry in the summer, ours served us and our neighbours abundantly.

My mother was an obsessive gardener and was excited that she had been presented with a blank canvas for a garden. She could not wait to try out her ideas. She was very keen on trees and shrubs, rather than flowering border and bedding plants. She planted, coconut and palmyra palms, mango, guava, pomegranate, sapota, limes, Japanese cherry, cassia, jacaranda and a variety of bamboos.

We were concerned that my mother lived alone in Alpha, and begged her to hire one of the servants to stay the nights with her, but she declined. She was fearless and insisted that the servants return home to their families every evening. One night while sitting and reading, she looked up and in the mirror on the opposite wall saw a semi-naked man directly behind her. She screamed loudly. There was no one to hear her. He snatched the gold chain from her neck and ran away. We were relieved he had not attacked her. This prompted her to build servants' quarters on the premises, a hut with thatched roof and an outside bathroom. A live-in gardener, Joseph, and his wife, Annamarie, were hired from a village to live in the newly built hut. Catholics, they arrived with one baby and after a few years, when baby number four arrived, my mother said unless they stopped at that they could no longer live on the premises. Joseph, though a Catholic, agreed to a vasectomy, which was carried out in a private birth-control clinic in Tambaram, all expenses paid by my mother. Six months later, Annamarie was pregnant once more. Furious, my mother marched off to the clinic, and threatened to sue the surgeon for incompetence and demanded her money back. A young, mild-mannered doctor, he said how sorry he was, but there was no absolute guarantee that a vasectomy would work and so far, he had not had any failures.

Shortly afterwards, the head gardener, and my mother's right-hand man, told her that during Joseph's periodic overnight visits to his village, Annamarie was entertaining male visitors in her quarters. She was summoned by my mother and asked if this was true. At first she denied it, but later admitted it and promised she would stop this. After the birth of this fifth child, there were no further pregnancies. Joseph and Annamarie worked for my mother for several years; all their children finished school, and with my mother's help and influence learned a trade and became independent.

ſ

The year 1957 was an exceptional one. Apart from studying for the three subjects already referred to, we were well into ward work and clinics and we were rapidly acquiring vast amounts of knowledge. It was all very enjoyable. Our teachers kept emphasising how important it was to get a thorough grounding of the basics. Paul Brand, the pioneering hand surgeon, took great pains to show us how to keep our gloves sterile as we put them on. Other doctors taught us the art of easy venepuncture, getting into a vein at the first attempt, and how to feel the edge of a liver or spleen. Discipline, accuracy and thoroughness were paramount. Slipshod ways were not acceptable.

The core clinical subjects were Medicine, Surgery, and Obstetrics and Gynaecology. Public Health Medicine was also considered important because of its relevance to social conditions in India. We would be tested in these four subjects in the final examinations before we qualified as doctors. But this was still some time away.

I continued to help at the village clinic every week. We were always on the lookout for new recruits, and usually managed to get students who were members of the Student Christian Movement, of which I was now President. I played tennis when I could. My interest in athletics had dwindled, mainly due to tiredness. But I did anchor the 4 × 100 metre relay both for my House on College

Sports Day, and for the College team when we competed in Madras against the other medical colleges. We never failed to win.

I always made time for Michael, going for evening walks two or three times a week. My friends and I felt safe when he came swimming with us to a huge well among rice fields. He came more as a chaperone, and would sit on one of the steps higher up, quietly smoking his pipe. He would bring little gifts for me, mainly Rolo chocolates, which, because they were imported, were extremely expensive. My friends said this was a sure sign that he loved me.

It was time to take Mike to meet my mother. I took him home to Tambaram one weekend. My mother and he took to each other instantly. She liked his gentleness and unassuming ways. Jessie Aunty and Samson Uncle thought he was a wonderful man, and found him easy to talk to. He never met my grandfather, who was still living in Annie Lodge. But I told him all about Michael, and took his photograph to show him. He looked at it long and hard and said:

'His physiognomy is not bad at all. I hope his nature is as good, and I hope he will earn enough to look after you properly.'

I missed not having Anne in Vellore to talk to about Mike. I wrote to her frequently and she said she remembered Mike very well, when he worked on the paediatric wards, and said what a splendid young doctor he was.

Mike wanted me to meet his parents, who had retired to Bangalore from North India several years earlier. Mike and two siblings had been to boarding school in Bangalore, to Baldwins School, a Methodist establishment, considered not to be in quite the same league as Bishop Cottons, but we did the same state exams. I was nervous about meeting Mike's parents, and told him they would disapprove of me because I was Indian. Anglo-Indians did not marry Indians, especially Anglo-Indian men.

'Nonsense,' he said. 'They know all about you and want to meet you. My mother is a wonderful person and will love you. I want you both to be good friends.'

After getting approval from my mother, I went with Mike to Bangalore. His father was a doctor, and had been a radiologist in the army, where he had spent his entire working life. He was pale skinned, but not as pale as his wife, ten years younger than him, a beautiful woman with a peaches and cream complexion and grey-blue eyes. Though fair skinned, Mike and his elder brother did not look Caucasian, as did their mother, sister and two brothers. Mike always maintained, much to his mother's annoyance, that there must surely be an Indian ancestor. Their ancestry was supposedly English, Irish, Scottish, Italian and German, but several decades later family studies showed that there was a Prussian ancestor on the Cartner side, a missionary in Kerala, who had married an Indian Muslim woman and converted her. This made Mike one-eighth Indian.

The Cartners lived in a modest flat, having lost most of their money in an ill-thought-out farming venture on the outskirts of Bangalore. They were welcoming, but reserved. Mike's sister, Delicia, was visiting them with her two small children. She had emigrated to England three years earlier, with her husband, Eldon Walker. She was exceptionally beautiful, slender, with deep blue eyes, chestnut-brown hair and her mother's complexion. I had seen Delicia at inter-school events; we had been contemporaries for a few years, but we had never met. She was a diving champion and known in Bangalore for her beauty.

Delicia was very friendly and admired my saris, which I wore all the time I was with her family. Mike's family did not say very much, and the weekend was uneventful. On the train back to Vellore, Mike assured me that his parents had fully accepted me. But this was not so, as I later discovered.

Delicia had come to Bangalore to try to persuade her parents to emigrate to Britain. Michael was in favour of this, especially, as his two younger brothers, Geoffrey and Owen, both bachelors, were already there. She had also come to leave her two children with her parents for a year, and go back to work full time, to enable her and her husband to buy a house in London. Michael's parents decided to move to England after a year, to stay with Delicia in Isleworth, in Middlesex, Greater London. Michael's elder brother, Desmond, a pilot working for Air India, the international airline, was to relocate from Bombay to London in a few years.

Michael repeatedly assured me that not having any family in India made no difference to his intention to live in India permanently, after he completed his postgraduate studies in Britain. I had made it plain to him that, were we to marry, I was not prepared to make my home anywhere other than in India, and that if he wanted to settle where his family was, that was quite understandable, and we should go our separate ways. Mike said that after going to university he felt more Indian than Anglo. He spoke Hindi, Tamil, and Kannada like a native, unlike the typical Anglo-Indian, who would not and could not speak any Indian language, either grammatically or with a correct accent.

I was into my final year in medicine in 1958. There was an exam in Ophthalmology (eyes) to take early in the year. A good deal of emphasis was put on this subject, as eye diseases are a major problem in India, especially among the very poor. The Professor of Ophthalmology was a tall, thin, hyperactive, middle-aged American called Victor Rambo. He had an obsession about exercise, and the body being the Temple of God. Lectures would start with him leaping about on the stage, waving his arms and legs, in front of the class, and exhorting us to do likewise. We would sit motionless and stare at him, much to his irritation. In addition to a considerable amount of practical work, we were required to study a textbook, which was usually read by postgraduate students. As it was a single subject, I prepared well, and passed.

The play to be performed for College Day that year was *The Barretts of Wimpole Street*, a play by Rudolf Besier written in 1930. It is about the real-life romance between the poets Elizabeth Barrett and Robert Browning. The Entertainment Secretary asked me to take the lead role of Elizabeth Barrett. Final-year students did not take part in extra-curricular activities, as they were expected to spend their time on the wards and studying. I had not been on the stage since my second year. This was my last opportunity and I agreed, encouraged by my mother. Michael strongly disapproved, as I would have to spend the evenings at rehearsal, instead of spending time with him. The college Principal also disapproved. However, I went ahead and started memorising my lines before rehearsals were due to start. A week later, I came down with a severe dose of influenza. Rehearsals were postponed. I recovered, but within a few days relapsed, and when I relapsed yet again, after a few weeks, I very reluctantly had to pull out of the play. I went home to Alpha to recuperate. The fever and intense malaise recurred for ten weeks, by which time I was convinced I had some serious underlying disease. Michael was distraught with worry, and came to see me whenever he could. He urged me to return to Vellore to be properly investigated. It finally came to light that I had had para-typhoid, and it had now burnt itself out without treatment. The Principal suggested, that because I had missed nearly a term, I postpone my final exams for six months.

'You have the minimal required attendance, and you are so bright, I am sure you can pull it off, but you have a lot to make up. I strongly urge you to postpone your final exams. However, I leave it to you.'

I thought long and hard, and in the end, decided to go ahead and do the finals as I had originally intended, in December. I could not face waiting another six months. Besides, all the plans Michael and I had made for the next two years would be disrupted. I did not think I would have difficulty passing three of the four subjects, barring some really bad luck. But it was Medicine which was my worry, a vast subject in which we had had some poor teaching. However, on to the scene just then burst two young enthusiastic physicians, recently appointed lecturers. Both were Parsis from Bombay and had just returned from England, having passed their membership exams from the Royal College of Medicine. They were not Vellore graduates, but had wanted to work in a centre of excellence on their return from England. They transformed the teaching of Medicine in Vellore. They also introduced us to a new textbook of Medicine by Davidson. It read like a story book, as far as I was concerned, and such a change from the voluminous, dreary books we were used to. These young lecturers gave us extra tutorials and night classes, and infected us with their enthusiasm.

In our final year, we had resident hospital postings in Medicine, Surgery and Gynaecology/Obstetrics. This meant we had to live in the Women Doctors' Quarters on the hospital campus, four miles from the College. Michael, who lived on the College campus, found this separation tiresome. He would cycle to visit me, but I was often called away for an emergency, as I was required to shadow a junior doctor on call. This sometimes meant I was up all night, and the next day I would have to be at lectures and clinics, as well as doing work on the wards. In the evening, when Mike came to visit me, I would be so tired, I would not be very good company. But having been through it himself, he understood.

Michael left for England a month after his parents, and a few weeks before my finals. I had hoped to go to England after I had passed my finals and graduated, and be married there. I would then do the two mandatory six-month house jobs in Medicine and Surgery, and get my United Kingdom registration.

The Madras Government and University had introduced a new rule, to the effect that after we passed our finals we would be awarded our degrees only after we did a year's unpaid internship. This was for two reasons: firstly, the hospitals where we did our training would get our services without having to pay for them; and secondly, it was made compulsory that we spend three months of that year in rural hospitals or clinics, thus ensuring that some of the villages nearby would get much-needed medical care. It had always been difficult to get young doctors, or any doctors, to work in villages. We grumbled, but there was nothing we could do about it. It meant Mike and I would have to wait an extra year before we married, and we would be separated for sixteen months. It was naïve of us to think we would be the same people after this time, especially as we would be exposed to very different situations. Our parting left a great void in my life; it was almost like a bereavement, but I was also relieved that I could single-mindedly devote myself to preparing for the forthcoming exams.

The nightmare of practical exams and vivas was upon me again. I had done more than satisfactorily in the written papers. In the former, I had to get past sixteen examiners, of whom only two were from Vellore, Tamil women professors nearing retirement age, and who were disapproving of me. They felt I was too modern, not a credit to the Tamils, because I wore North Indian dress, sometimes sleeveless, had a pony tail, ran in shorts, mingled freely with the boys and so on. However, I attended the practicals and viva suitably dressed by their standards, wearing a white cotton starched sari and sleeved blouse, modestly pinned in the appropriate places so as to cover my bare midriff. (Bare midriffs are considered quite normal in India, except for some in the older generation, who disapprove.) My hair was scraped back into a neat little bun. The idea was to be as little conspicuous as possible. Both the Vellore examiners recognised me and gave me a hard time in the vivas, but they were partnered by polite male examiners from Madras.

I came away from the last exam spent and exhausted, and swore I would never take another exam in my life. In fact, I decided if I failed and had to re-sit, I would abandon medicine, and do something else. I had done my best, and felt the results could go either way. They came out just before the new year, and I had passed all four subjects. As always, the relief was enormous, but never as great as the anguish that preceded the exams. The overall pass rate was exceptional, and much of the credit had to go to the two young Parsi physicians who tutored us, as Medicine usually had the highest failure rate of the four subjects.

I sent a telegram to Michael, and one to Anne. The Indian telephone service was abysmal. At Christmas, it had taken Michael four days to get a call to me from London. I went to tell Thatha the news and he was choked with pride. Samson Uncle gave a little laugh. My mother was restrained in her praise.

'Well, that's that,' she said, but I could tell how pleased she was.

Chapter 15

STARTING AT THE BOTTOM OF THE LADDER

After a brief respite at home, I went to College to see my room-mates who were at least six months behind me, and said goodbye. I moved my belongings to a single room in the Women Doctors' Hostel on the busy hospital campus. My mother always bemoaned the fact that my accommodation in Vellore was so spartan, but I was glad of it. It was all part of our rigorous training to accept hardships. We ate in the hostel canteen and the food was exceedingly good. Board and lodging were free.

I could describe my internship with just two words: work and exhaustion. The working day would start at 7 a.m., and about twelve hours later I would return to the hostel. At 10 p.m. I would be back on the wards for a final round before going to bed. But life was enjoyable as there was great camaraderie among the doctors.

Every three or four days, I would be on call, which meant I would be working on the wards all night as well, or assisting in the operating theatre or in the labour room, depending on my posting.

Vellore had a superb reputation, with up-to-date facilities and advanced technology. Patients came not only from nearby towns and villages, but from all parts of India, Asia and the Middle East. There were outpatient clinics in every specialty every day, run by various Firms. So great were the numbers that the clinics would sometimes last many hours, starting at 7 a.m. and running well into the afternoon.

My first posting was in Medicine and I was in a Firm headed by a young Australian missionary for whom I used to babysit when I was a student. Selwyn Baker, unlike the older missionaries, was very informal, and had an easy relationship with Indian colleagues. The coffee break of the Firm was usually taken in one of the scruffy cafés on the congested road opposite the hospital. He had no qualms about tucking into hot Indian food with his fingers.

Other missionaries did not quite approve of this. Brilliant, and exceptional in his research, especially on tropical sprue, Selwyn was granted large sums of money by the Wellcome Foundation.

If every opportunity is taken, the learning curve of a young, inexperienced doctor is almost vertical. Despite the final-year clinical postings, I started off unsure and frightened. I soon gained confidence in diagnosing and carrying out various procedures, such as pleural taps and lumbar punctures. As a final-year student, I had become adept at venepuncture and setting up intravenous drips.

After three months, I was moved on to Surgery and worked for a brilliant Indian surgeon, H. S. Bhat. I enjoyed the atmosphere of the operating theatre and assisting in operations, but found Surgery dull compared to Medicine. The sub-posting which I found memorable was the three weeks I spent in hand surgery. Unfortunately, the famous hand surgeon Paul Brand was on furlough in England. His very able assistant, Mary Verghese, worked from her wheelchair. As a final year student, she had been returning from a class picnic when the coach she was in was involved in an accident. Mary sustained injuries to her back and became paraplegic. Depressed and without hope, she was rehabilitated by Paul Brand and trained by him to become a very fine hand surgeon. Nearly all the patients I encountered were suffering from the ravages of leprosy, and many had their lives transformed by pioneering hand surgery.

Surgical outpatient clinics were particularly exhausting, but the wide range of conditions we saw in a morning could be phenomenal. Lumps and bumps of every description would turn up: large, small, smooth, knobbly, wrinkled, weeping, ulcerated and stinking, benign and malignant. And there would be huge hernias and elephantiasis, affecting not only the legs, but the scrotum as well. I remember seeing a man with a scrotum larger than a football. It was the wretched human condition again, from which a doctor can never escape. Most of the patients were very poor. Many were treated free, and others on a sliding scale. Some went home untreated because treatment could not be afforded, or their condition was hopeless.

There was a young Muslim mother called Assina. Madonna-like, she was breathtakingly beautiful. She had brought her six-

month-old baby girl, as bonny as herself, with the brightest of
black eyes. The baby was chubby and looked healthy, but had
developed a smooth, warm swelling on one shin. It turned out to
be a bone infection due to tuberculosis. Her lungs were clear of
the disease but her mother, though symptom free, had tuberculosis
in her lungs. Her husband, a rickshaw driver, and her four-year-
old son were clear of the disease. They were ready to go away,
as they had no money for treatment. I asked them to wait and
ran to the Social Work Department and managed to arrange free
treatment for them. I saw Assina and her baby a few more times,
before I left the Department of Surgery, and they were responding
very well to treatment. I often wondered about them. Five years
later, I returned to Vellore to visit Ann (who had discarded the 'e'
at the end of her name, on returning from America, much to the
annoyance of my mother). I hired a rickshaw to take me to the
market and back, and while I was paying the rickshaw man he
said: 'Amma, do you not remember me? I was Assina's husband.
You treated her and the baby. They had TB.'

'Yes, I do,' I said, remembering very well. 'How are they?' I
asked.

'They are both dead. They recovered well and we completed
the treatment. But the TB came back, but they would not give us
any more free treatment. We went to the Government Hospital,
but it was no good. They died quickly.'

He then went on to tell me that Assina was married at thirteen
to a sixty-five-year-old man and had a baby son. She was very
unhappy and ran away. He found her wandering with the baby.

'She was so beautiful. I wanted to marry her even though she
was a Muslim and I am a Hindu. We were very happy together,
and we had the baby girl. Now I am bringing up her son, though
he does not know I am not his father.'

After three months in Surgery, I moved on to Obstetrics and
Gynaecology, the posting I was not looking forward to and which
I least enjoyed. As far as I was concerned, every impending birth
was a potential crisis, which could turn into a catastrophe. I had
seen too many disasters when I had my final-year student posting.
We worked in pairs, men and women doctors. The reason was that
many patients, especially Muslims, refused to have a male doctor

attending them. We were required to be completely gowned up in the Delivery Room. Our hair and part of our faces were covered with caps. Men were not allowed beards, and masks covered their moustaches. They were not allowed to speak in case they gave away that they were male. We found all this very funny, but it was a serious matter and unethical; yet it was the only way men could gain essential experience. During one such charade, with the birth imminent, the patient gave out a bloodcurdling scream. She seemed to be in excruciating pain, and we expected the head to pop out. But instead, the patient leapt from the couch and ran into the next room. Apparently, my partner's mask had slipped, exposing a luxuriant moustache. Both mother and baby survived this ordeal.

As always, the clinics were huge. They were mostly free, so as to encourage women to come to antenatal clinics, and we were constantly faced with their ignorance of their ages and dates. Most were very poor and malnourished, and worn out by repeated pregnancies and lactation. We tried to persuade them to be sterilised, especially if they had a male child, but we were seldom successful.

The Gynaecology Clinic produced its own horrors, women having neglected themselves, and seeking medical help only when they were desperate. Often, the diseases would be so advanced that they would be beyond help.

And so, I arrived at the last stage of my pre-registration internship. This was in Public Health. I had to move to the Rural Hospital, which was not far from the College campus, and nearly five miles from the hospital I had been working in. The purpose of this hospital was to expose us to working in a village situation with very limited facilities. We were expected to use our wits and to innovate, where necessary. We carried out minor surgery using old-fashioned anaesthetics, such as ether and chloroform. A tea strainer covered with gauze would be placed over the patient's nose, and the ether dripped over it. It worked.

Much time was spent visiting the surrounding villages, researching into the villagers' health and the factors adversely affecting it. Again, we did this as partners, male and female, as this made us more acceptable to the villagers. My partner and

I studied the incidence of vitamin A and D deficiency in school children, as well as the post-natal nutrition of mothers. We were also allotted families where there was someone with a chronic illness such as tuberculosis, or there was a pregnant woman. We were required to follow them up for three months.

In one such family there was a girl called Kanti, aged sixteen, well advanced into her first pregnancy. She and her farm-hand husband lived in the same village as her parents, but she had come to live in their house for the birth, as is the usual custom in India. Adjacent to their hut were two enclosures for pigs. Kanti was a cheerful, buxom girl, and her pregnancy was supervised by the village midwife, a middle-aged woman with no formal qualifications, but highly experienced and regarded. She had agreed to be supervised by a nurse midwife, part of our team from the Rural Hospital.

When we visited Kanti one day, she was standing, smiling, at the entrance to her hut. Her bump had disappeared.

'What was it?' we asked excitedly. 'A boy,' she said, proudly.

When we asked her if we could see him, she pointed in the direction of the pigs.

'What!' we exclaimed.

There he was, rolled up in a bundle of rags in one of the enclosures, squirming and making baby noises. The pigs were in the adjacent enclosure.

'What madness! Why?' we asked.

'So that the Gods will not be envious and cause him harm,' said Kanti's mother.

We asked about Kanti's diet and were told she was being given rice and stick curry, as recommended by her grandmother. We asked to see this curry. An earthenware pot was produced. It contained a watery brown liquid with short, thin sticks. Its nutrition value must have been zero. As it was only for the first seven days after birth, the nurse midwife suggested we refrain from any adverse comments. Both mother and baby flourished.

'Roadside' was one of the great innovations of Ida Scudder, Aunt Ida, as she was affectionately called. She was the American founder of the main hospital and medical college. Twice a week, a very large van equipped with drugs, dressings, surgical instruments, ground sheets and anything necessary for a small mobile hospital would go deep into rural areas, often with no road, just a dirt track. Another van would follow, with an experienced public health doctor, an intern, a couple of nurses and clerks, a pharmacist and a porter. As this was a regular feature, the villagers would be expecting us, and crowds would be waiting. We would work under the shade of a large tree, often a banyan. Shrubs would provide privacy, if needed. Seriously ill patients would be taken back to the main hospital.

The first patient I was confronted with had severe toothache. It was obvious that the decayed molar had to come out. I summoned Dr Benjamin, the senior doctor.

'Take it out,' he said.

'But I don't know how to,' I replied.

'Oh yes you do. Didn't you have a short dental posting in your fourth year? Try to remember, and put it into practice.' And he walked away.

With the help of one of the nurses, I injected a local anaesthetic, waited, and then extracted the tooth, roots and all, without much difficulty, the nurse giving me the correct pliers. The grateful patient went on his way.

But there were the usual horror stories too. A young man was brought in, paraplegic and depressed. Some months ago, he had fallen off a coconut tree and had obviously broken his spine. He had lain in his hut until his relatives had heard about Roadside. He was riddled with bed sores, and his testicles were exposed through his ulcerated scrotum, covered with maggots. I had to walk away. He was taken to the main hospital for rehabilitation and plastic surgery.

A pregnant fourteen-year-old arrived in a bullock cart, in a moribund state. She had been in labour for three days. The dead baby's arms, torso, and legs were protruding from her, but the head was stuck inside. It was too large to come through her small pelvis. The exhausted uterus had stopped contracting. She was in shock with a low blood pressure and was rushed to hospital, but died on the way.

After the long day when the last patient had been seen, we would pack up and return in the dark. There would be silence in the van. It was not just because we were exhausted, but also because of a sadness that overwhelmed us. I wondered if, even in a hundred years, anything would really improve. Nevertheless, it was worthwhile and, in a strange way, fulfilling.

During the three months of our rural posting, for a short time, we had to live in a village thirty miles from Vellore. Three of us interns shared a very basic house, more like a hut, with some nurses, who were already stationed there. We accompanied them on their house visits. Our living conditions were quite primitive. There was no electricity in the outdoor lavatory, which we tried not to use after dark. If we had to, we took an oil-filled lantern. We were horrified to find that we were sharing the lavatory with other creatures and, at times, the local cobra.

After arriving in this village, we were introduced to the local grandee, a formidable matriarch in her fifties and the wife of a wealthy landowner and agriculturist. Unusually, they were Christians. We were invited to their palatial home, where two adult sons were slouching around. Obese, with their shirts hanging out and cigarettes hanging from their mouths, they seemed to be useless young men. We were getting used to our simple vegetarian meals, when we started to be supplied with delicious dishes from the grandee's house. One of the nurses said we owed this to the lady of the house becoming interested in me for one of her sons. I quickly let it be known that I was to marry in a few months. The food offerings promptly stopped.

⁙

I was coming to the end of my internship and my thoughts were becoming focused on my forthcoming marriage. During the fourteen months we had been apart, Michael wrote to me three or four times a week, briefly, on airmail forms. I tried to reciprocate weekly. I was so touched by his devotion that it never occurred to me that the longer we were apart, the more his doubts were growing as to whether we were doing the right thing getting married. His parents and three of his four siblings had settled happily in England, and his older brother, Desmond, an Air India pilot, had moved his wife and three children to live permanently in England. Michael's horizons, experiences and ideas had all expanded widely during the short time he had been in England, and he was being relentlessly pursued by the nurses he worked with, even though they were aware he was engaged to be married.

I finished my internship and went home to Alpha to spend the next two months with my mother, 'doing nothing' as she put it. She, Ann and I were to leave for England four days before my wedding, fixed for 23 March 1960.

My mother was delighted to have me home; it was the first time in several years that we were to be together for such a length of time. We were both concerned that Thatha was being neglected again in Annie Lodge. We did not think he would agree to leave it to come to live at Alpha, but once we suggested it, he jumped at the idea. It was decided that he would move to Alpha on my mother's return from England.

The following month, my convocation was held at Madras University, together with the graduates from the other three medical colleges. We were all awarded a second class, there being two classes only, first and second. No one was deemed good enough to get a first. A girl from one of the other colleges got all the gold medals. Tall and attractive, her details, including the gold medals, were advertised in the matrimonial column in the broadsheet paper the following Sunday. Suitable grooms were invited to apply.

Always thin and now thinner, I needed, my mother decided, fattening up. We interns often skipped meals, as there was no time to eat. Fast foods were not available. I was a poor eater anyway. An unorthodox but excellent cook, my mother innovated tempting meals. Breakfast would sometimes be a big bowl of home-made ice cream. I would sit on a red stool in the kitchen, and we talked and talked while she cooked. In Annie Lodge, we always had at least one cook. In Alpha, my mother insisted on doing all the cooking, and she often cooked for the servants to make sure they were adequately nourished.

'How do you expect them to do a full day's work, if their bellies are not full?' she would say.

And she fed the workmen too. Samson Uncle and Jessie Aunty thought my mother was being taken for a ride. But she was a hard taskmaster and expected the servants to be as meticulous as she was. Trivial inadequacies would trigger off her rages. The maid was sacked because she did not make neat envelope corners while making the beds. Illiterate servants would be reprimanded for mispronouncing English words, for which there was no Tamil equivalent. One who consistently said 'bruce' for 'brush' was sent home for the day. 'Butter' would be called 'vutterr' and 'twenty', 'tontee'. Once we had grown up, Ann and I were no longer intimidated by these rages; they would send us into hysterics. Out of my mother's sight, we would roll about laughing, and the servants, seeing us, would smile, and perhaps not feel so battered.

Often servants were sacked on the spot. They would be reinstated after a few days. They kept coming back because they were paid generously, working conditions were pleasant, and they knew my mother cared deeply for them and their families.

⌢

'If I am getting married and going abroad, I had better learn how to cook,' I said one day, without any enthusiasm.

'Rubbish,' said my mother. 'If you don't want to cook, there's no need to learn. I don't know why women think they have to cook, if they don't want to. Besides, Michael says he eats in the doctors' mess. You can do the same.' So I went to England without knowing how to cook anything, except boil an egg.

During the two months with my mother, it was a great luxury having the time to read. The house was full of books. Every week, my mother would go to the British Council Library and to Higginbothams, a well-stocked bookshop on Mount Road in Madras and never did she come back empty handed.

In the evenings, when the heat had abated and the sea breeze had set in, we would walk in the garden inspecting the progress of various plants. We would sit out on the lawn and drink iced lemon juice, and neighbours would drop in for a chat. As dusk approached, large fruit bats would arrive, and there would be the wholesome smell of wood smoke from villagers cooking their evening meal. It would then be time to go in as mosquitoes would start to whine and bite. After dinner, we would go to the top terrace, which was too high for mosquitoes, and gaze at the starry sky. If we were lucky, we would see a few shooting stars. My mother was very good at recognising the constellations, a skill that always eluded me.

Decades later, she would still be up on the terrace at night, and when I would pay my annual visit to her, at about 10 p.m. on my last night, there would be a roar in the distance, and a few minutes later high in the sky there would be the twinkling lights of a Jumbo Jet making its way westwards. She would know I was in that aircraft, and wonder if she would see me again.

⌣

My trousseau had to be put together. I decided to abandon my *salwar-kameez*, the North Indian dress, and wear saris for work and trousers for leisure in England. It was not acceptable in Britain, at that time, for women doctors to wear trousers in hospital. Michael said resident doctors, as I would be, had their laundry done by the hospital, which meant my saris for work would have to be hardy and washable. I did not have many of them. Cotton saris are difficult to wash and iron, so I decided to take only silk ones. There are a variety of silks in India, from fine ones—Benares, Mysore and Kashmir—to heavy ones—Tussar and Kanjeevaram—the latter made and widely worn in South India.

A sari is a single piece of cloth five and a half metres long and 120 cm wide. It is worn with a blouse, or choli, with a bare midriff. One end is tucked into the tight waist of a long skirt, taken round the body, then pleated by hand, again tucked into the skirt and then wound round the body, across the breast, and over the left shoulder so the other end, or *munthani*, hangs loose. It takes thirty seconds to put on. It needs no pins.

Wedding saris can be very elaborate, with much gold. Hindus wear red. As a Christian, I would wear a white Benares sari with a narrow gold border along the length of it. The *munthani* was heavily patterned with gold. Small gold motifs were scattered throughout the sari. The choli material was similar to that of the sari. The shop owner, from whom I had already bought several saris, arranged for matching material for the choli to be specially woven for me in Benares, 1,500 miles away. My mother did not approve of midriffs, so I barely showed mine. As wedding saris go, mine was quite plain.

I went to the holy town of Kancheepuram to buy several heavy silks, which I intended to wear for work. Jessie Aunty lived there, where her husband was the headmaster of a large Christian boys' school. She knew some of the weavers and suggested that we ask them whether they would weave some saris of my own design and colour. They were hesitant at first, as the loom wove three at a time and they were not sure if the other two would sell. They decided to have a try with one, a deep magenta body with a contrasting black border and *munthani*. I was delighted with it, and the other two went to their showroom and sold within a week. The weavers were keen to try some more. I asked for a 'peacock' sari of blue-green shot silk, where the warp and weave were in the two different colours. There was no border on either side, so that it would make me look taller. The *munthani* was bright pink with gold polka dots, and the main part of the sari had bright pink polka dots. This too was an instant hit. But the best one was deep raspberry, with small gold dots. The border was the same raspberry but shot with gold, as was the *munthani*. It was exquisite. But it lay at the bottom of my sari box, unworn, for nearly thirty years, when it would be worn again for a very special occasion.

My request for simple gold earrings and two gold bangles was considered frivolous by my mother, but after Ann's intervention she took me to her mother's jewellers in Madras, and these were made to order in 22-carat gold.

Since coming to stay in Alpha, I had visited Thatha as often as possible. He had always made it plain that I was very special to him. Despite his increasing deafness—he was nearly ninety—we had some very good conversations. On the morning of 3 March, I made my usual one-hour trip by bus, from Alpha to Annie Lodge, to see him. I walked up Wason Street to the house. I opened the gate, and the gardener came running towards me, tears streaming down his face. I knew the worst had happened. Samson Uncle too came out, and said Thatha was found dead in his bed early that morning. Neither of our houses had a phone. Samson Uncle asked me to return to Alpha immediately, to tell my mother that he had made arrangements for the funeral to take place that same day at 4 p.m. It was usual practice for funerals to take place as soon as possible after death, because of the heat and the paucity of adequate mortuary facilities in local hospitals.

The bus on my return journey to Alpha stopped at a bus stop halfway, and was adjacent to another bus going in the opposite direction, which had also stopped. To my surprise, I spotted my mother in it. She had decided to make a trip into town. I leapt out and got into her bus, and gave her the news. She was quite unemotional.

'We will both go to Annie Lodge and see what is going on,' she said, obviously not quite trusting Samson to make proper arrangements. But he had, and had sent servants and messengers to relatives and friends to tell them about the funeral. A box-like black hearse turned up at the right time, and we drove the three miles to the Christian cemetery at Egmore. A grave had been dug next to my grandmother's grave, the plot having been bought for him twenty-two years earlier, when my grandmother had died.

Samson Uncle, much to my mother's fury, had informed my father, who had now retired to Madras, and his two brothers about the funeral. Wisely, my father decided not to attend, but his two brothers were there. The older one, an odious man, opened a bottle of eau de cologne, and was about to pour the contents over Thatha's face in the open coffin. My mother began to remonstrate. She detested perfume. I firmly held her and pulled her back.

'No, Mummy,' I said. 'Just let it be.' And a scene was avoided. She ranted and raved later at Samson.

'What if the old man had turned up?' she said. This is how she referred to my father. Samson Uncle just looked sheepish. Jessie Aunty told him later that he had been foolish.

I had a profound sense of loss at Thatha's passing, and also many regrets that I did not spend more time with him when I was growing up in Annie Lodge. He used to complain to my mother that I did not visit him in his room often enough. When I did, from the age of six, he would ask me to read to him from the heavy King James Bible. And in later years, we would discuss medicine. He would look at my text books and protest at their size, comparing them to his. He never could appreciate the continuing explosion of medical knowledge.

My mother was relieved that Thatha had died before we were

to go to England. His health had started to fail since his return, a month earlier, from a trip to his native village, Kanandivallai, near Tuticorin.

Against my mother's and Samson Uncle's advice, he made this arduous trip about once every five years. It was an overnight journey by train, and then by bus. He would insist on buying a third-class ticket, and sit on a hard seat all the way. He would return exhausted, with massively swollen legs. The last time he went, he took a servant with him. My mother had bought them second-class tickets so they had a berth each. She had asked the servant to buy similar tickets for the return trip, but Thatha, in his '*meerr waste*' frame of mind, had made the servant buy third-class tickets. Thatha had gone specifically to donate a bell to the village church, the same one he had attended with the pastor who befriended him as a boy of sixteen. While there, he had the urge to bathe in the brick-lined well he used as a boy. With the help of his servant, he went down the steps to the water, and then panicked. He was unable to ascend the steps. There was a great commotion and a crowd gathered. Some men went down and brought him up. I had wanted to accompany him on this trip. Thatha and my mother were quite enthusiastic, but this time she was overruled by Jessie Aunty and Samson Uncle. They said I would be kidnapped and married off.

Part III

England

Chapter 16

A BUNCH OF GOLDEN DAFFODILS

On a searingly hot day, in March, my mother, Ann and I left Madras for London, breaking journey for two days in Bombay, to stay with Michael's brother, Desmond, the Air India pilot, and his wife, Violet. She was a warm, friendly Anglo-Indian woman, some ten years older than me. She gave me to understand that Mike's mother was not happy about the forthcoming wedding because I was Indian. Violet was not trying to make mischief, but was just warning me, and for this I was grateful. I was not altogether surprised.

The Air India flight took twenty hours. There were four stops, but being drugged on Dramamine, to overcome my air sickness, I could not share my mother's enthusiasm for the many sights on the way. The Anglo-Indian air hostesses, in Western uniform, were rather aloof. It was the British Airline, BOAC, that was the first airline to recruit Indian girls and put them into saris. They were a great hit with passengers, Indian and foreign.

Three days before the wedding, we arrived mid-morning at Heathrow Airport in London, to a completely grey sky, from which the sun appeared to have been altogether obliterated. How delightful it was, not to have a blazing sun. In the Customs Hall, a member of the ground staff handed me a bunch of flowers.

'A man waiting to meet you asked me to give these to you.'

These were flowers I had never seen before, except in pictures. But I had recited poems about them. They were daffodils. They were, of course, from Michael. We collected our luggage, and Michael took us in his car to our small hotel, in Richmond, Surrey. The occupants of the hotel seemed to be elderly long-term residents, mainly women, and they were clearly intrigued by our arrival, three sari-clad women.

My mother broke the ice and spoke to a friendly Englishwoman. She was surprised we spoke fluent English. On hearing we were here for my wedding, she wanted to know when and where it was to be held.

Our room was spacious but cold. Using pennies, Michael showed us how to light the electric fire in the fireplace. We thought it a strange way to heat a room, and stranger still, there was no attached bathroom, as we were used to in Indian hotels. The bathroom was at the end of a cold corridor, and had to be shared with other residents. It was unheated. The bath did not show any sign of recent activity; there were a few old cobwebs here and there. The British did not do showers, and would not for some decades. They did not appear to do baths, either.

Ann and I became increasingly cold, and took to our beds and covered ourselves with some rough blankets. My mother looked at us disapprovingly, and said she was going out. She returned three hours later, and told us excitedly that she had been to Kew Gardens, and that it was everything and more than she had ever expected, even at this bleak time of year. We were not surprised, as all her adult life she had talked about Kew.

'I wonder if they would give me a job as a gardener there,' she would jokingly say. Her other great wish was to go to the Chelsea Flower Show, the world's most famous display of plants and small gardens. This she would realise, as she had arranged to stay in England for two months till the end of May. Ann was to return a week after the wedding.

That evening Michael took us to meet his family and have dinner at Delicia's house in Feltham, part of Greater London. Mike's mother, now widowed, lived with Delicia, as did Owen, the youngest brother. In addition to Delicia's two small daughters, Desmond's two girls, aged six and ten, also lived with them, having been enrolled in school in England. Delicia's husband was a small, silent man handing out the drinks. All were polite, but not particularly cordial. Delicia offered to take me shopping for warm clothes the next day. Mike and I went to the flower shop to order a simple bouquet of white arum lilies for me, and a bouquet of pink roses for Ann, to match her dusky pink and gold sari. She was to be the only bridesmaid. I also ordered a wreath of small white flowers, for my hair, hoping they would be similar to the jasmine flowers I would have worn, had I been in India. For my mother, there was a single yellow rose, to be worn in the brooch which kept her sari in place, at her left shoulder. She had agreed to wear a pale green silk sari with a thin gold border. This was a concession to Ann and me, as normally she would only wear cotton saris.

Delicia suggested we go to the hairdresser on the morning of the wedding. We were not used to this. Ann had short wavy hair which was trimmed by one of her nurse friends. I had not cut my hair since before going to medical school, and it was now long enough for me to sit on. Very thick, black and glossy, it was the envy of my friends. I usually wore it in plaits over my head, but for special occasions it was pulled back into a chignon. The hairdresser was so taken with my hair, she invited passers-by into her establishment to look at it. She asked me if I would sell it to her. Neither of us liked the way the hairdresser had done our hair, so on our return to the hotel, we combed it out and reverted to our usual styles. Ann looked lovely in her pink sari. She was slim and blessed with a good figure. I wore a white and gold Benares sari. I looked thin, as I always did. And in concentrating on not being late, I forgot to put any makeup on my face, not that I usually did that. The residents of the hotel had gathered in the foyer and clapped as we left. We got to the church on time.

About forty people had been invited to the wedding at St Stephen's Church in Twickenham. I was given away by Rabin, the student I used to act opposite in medical school, some six years ago. He had married a nurse, one of Ann's friends, and was training to be a neurosurgeon in Bristol. The wedding guests included Mike's family, friends from Vellore training in the UK, some of my mother's friends and staff from Mike's hospital. The vicar, a Reverend Felce, and his wife were young and friendly. We had visited them the previous evening. Mike had attended his church and met him a few times before the wedding. We wanted some hymns, and though it was a midweek wedding, an organist was found, but he played so loudly that the singing was completely drowned out.

The reception was held in Mathiaes, a small restaurant in Kew. After tea, there were short speeches by Rabin, Mike and Mike's brother Owen, who was best man. The occasion was over.

I changed into a mustard and gold sari. Our luggage was already in Mike's little second-hand Renault, and we set off, supposedly for the New Forest, where Mike had booked us into a hotel for a couple of days.

As we drove off, Mike said, 'Why don't we go to Delicia's and surprise them all, and have supper with them, and then leave?' We did that, and certainly surprised Delicia. After a meagre dinner of mince and dumplings, we set off, and arrived in driving rain at a musty hotel, which we discovered was again inhabited permanently by curious elderly ladies.

For the next ten days we drove around Devon and Cornwall, staying in small hotels. They were varied: one delightful one was perched on a cliff top; some smelt of boiled cabbage or bacon. People were curious, but friendly. The sun never shone. I did not mind this, but I did not like the cold.

We were to end our honeymoon on the Isles of Scilly, but I could not face another journey by air, no matter how short, so we gave our two tickets to Ann and my mother.

Having been totally apart for the past fifteen months, Mike and I were not at ease with each other at first. It was just as well we had these ten days to ourselves, but what struck me most was his great attachment to his family, particularly his mother. In their presence, he sparkled. With me he was quiet. I was perplexed. He told me several years later that he felt so distanced from me after our separation that he had grave doubts about our getting married. But we learned to adjust to each other, as Indians are meant to.

Chapter 17

A NOBLE INSTITUTION

Michael was a junior doctor in the Senior House Officer Grade in general surgery, in a small district general hospital in Minster, Isle of Sheppey, just off the Kent coast and joined to the mainland by a drawbridge. Before coming here, he had been in a much larger hospital in Kent, doing Orthopaedic Surgery. He wanted to move to general surgery, his primary interest, and decided Sheppey would be a quiet place to start married life. The hospital grounds were very pleasant. At the rear of the hospital was a large apple orchard and beyond that a pebbled beach and the sea.

Hospitals such as this rarely attracted British doctors. They kept themselves to large cities and teaching hospitals with medical students. Britain relied heavily on foreign doctors to fill junior hospital doctor posts. As a general rule, a British doctor was always regarded as superior to a foreign doctor, regardless of the calibre of either. There was also an unsaid pecking order for junior doctors in the National Health Service (NHS) which went thus: English, Scottish, Welsh, white South African, Australian, Canadian, Indian, Pakistani, African. Among the dark-skinned doctors, paler skins were preferred.

This hospital had the core specialities. There were only three junior doctors in all. Michael was the Senior Resident Officer and worked in the surgical department. The other two were House officers, one in General Medicine and Paediatrics, and the other in Obstetrics and Gynaecology. All provided cover for the Casualty department, but Mike had overall responsibility for emergencies. There were three full-time consultants, and about half a dozen visiting ones from various hospitals in Kent. It was obvious Mike was held in high regard. The two surgical consultants Mike worked for said he was the finest young doctor they had encountered. He had gained much experience working in India, and his present grade was well below his level of competence. This meant he rarely had to involve his bosses during the hours of on call. His amiable disposition, dry sense of humour and competence endeared him to everyone, especially the nurses. The other two junior doctors were also foreign. One was a Coptic Egyptian, Dr L: obese and uncouth, we tried to avoid sitting with him in the communal dining room. The other was a shy young Muslim woman, Dr A, from Hyderabad, equally uncouth but in a different way. I was beginning to understand why there was prejudice against foreign doctors.

The doctors' quarters, a two-storey block, were adjacent to the hospital. There was a sitting room downstairs with a black-and-white television set. There were three bedrooms upstairs, two single and one double. Twin beds had been put in for Michael and me. Heating was primitive but adequate. There were two gas burners side by side, each encased in a vertical metallic box, about four feet high. They acted as radiators. There was always a faint smell of gas. Michael, who had given up smoking when we were courting because someone had told him I had declared that I could never marry a smoker, had started to smoke cigarettes soon after we married. When I expressed surprise, he laughed and said: 'You don't run after a bus after you have caught it.' He also said: 'Men are interested in the happiness of pursuit, more than in the pursuit of happiness.' I pondered on what he had said.

Michael's smoking in the bedroom was a constant worry to me. The connection between heart disease and smoking was becoming increasingly apparent. Besides, both his parents had coronary artery disease, his father having died from it recently. But Mike, at thirty-one, had no fears whatever for his future.

The four of us shared a bathroom. There was only one bath tub. Dr L regularly left his curly pubic hairs behind in the tub, and this would reduce me to tears. Every night Michael would wash out the bath, before I took mine. There was no kitchen in our quarters, just a kettle for making tea and coffee.

We had all our meals in the common dining room for hospital staff. Consultants would sit at their table, and the four of us junior doctors at ours. We would try to get to our table and serve ourselves quickly, before Dr L arrived, as he was in the habit of emptying all the food on to his plate. Dr A was five months pregnant, and would sit at the table with her feet drawn up on to her chair, and pick at her food. A strict Muslim, there was not much she was permitted to eat. She would remain silent. Food, accommodation and laundry were free for resident doctors. I was charged a fee for services provided to me.

I spent the next two months either in the sitting room, or in our bedroom. I had many thank you letters to write after the wedding. Television was new to me, and I watched it in the evenings, waiting for Mike to return from the hospital. He was very thorough and conscientious and spent much time talking to nurses and patients. I saw little of him.

Dr A's six-month appointment was to end in two months and I hoped to get her post. Michael had spoken about me to her consultant, Mr Schmelz (Mr S). I was required to do two house jobs for registration with the General Medical Council. This was mandatory to practise in Britain.

Mr S asked to see me. He was surprised at my fluent, nearly accent-less English. A Czech, he was in his late fifties, a gentle, pleasant man with a strong European accent.

'We in this hospital are so impressed with your husband,' he said. 'We are so fortunate to have a man of his competence in this small hospital. If you are one half as good as he is, I will be delighted to give you the job. Are you?' he asked.

'I hope so,' I said.

'It is yours,' he said, smiling. 'We will not be advertising it.'

I was relieved. It is always difficult for foreign doctors to get their first job in Britain.

⌣

My mother, in the meantime, was thoroughly enjoying England. She had booked herself into a bed and breakfast in Gower Street in London, and had established a good rapport with the landlady. She visited us a couple of times in Sheppey. She kept telling us what a wonderful country this was. She made several coach trips to various parts of the country. On one guided trip to the Lake District, she was with a group of South Africans. It was at the height of apartheid. Not used to having an Indian sitting with them, some of them did try to be friendly.

'You speaky English?' one asked.

She laughed and spoke to them. They were astonished at her knowledge of English, History, and Literature. The guide finally threw up his hands in despair and said:

'This lady knows far more than I do. Address your questions to her.'

My mother spent two months in Britain. She was enthralled by the museums, art galleries, Oxford Street, Selfridges, the parks, Foyles book shop, the Royal Festival Hall, theatres, and of course Kew Gardens. And she managed to get to the Chelsea Flower Show. She then spent ten days seeing a few cities in Europe. She vowed to come back to Britain. Foreign exchange at that time was a problem. Indians were allowed to take out only £3 per person, an invitation for flouting the law. When she asked the Reserve Bank of India if she could take out more, because her daughter was getting married, she was told that Indians should marry in India. Luckily, she had an English friend in the Niligiris in India, who arranged for her to have pounds in London and took rupees in India at the exchange rate prevalent at the time. This was probably illegal.

∫

For the two weeks preceding the taking up of my appointment, I shadowed Dr A. This included night calls. One night, there was a frantic phone call from the labour room. We were summoned urgently. Fearing some impending obstetric disaster, we rushed. The midwife pushed us into an ante room. In a cot was a small baby boy, completely swaddled but for the face. She undid the clothes and we gasped with horror. I had never seen anything like this. There were no arms. Instead, at the shoulders, were flipper-like fingers, two on one side, and three on the other. There were no legs. The buttocks were smooth and rounded with an aperture in between. The head and torso were normal. His eyes were wide open. We stood there speechless.

The mother of the baby was a sensible woman. In her late thirties, with other children, she was told that her baby was very ill, and she could not see him for the time being. This was 1960, when patients showed deference and accepted authority. She did not question anything, and just before she was discharged a week later, the baby was brought to her and the full extent of his abnormalities revealed. She too was speechless. She was advised to leave him in hospital till he reached an acceptable weight, and then after some weeks at home, he would be transferred to a rehabilitation unit in Essex. We did not know it at the time, but he must have been one of the first 'thalidomide' babies in Britain. It was very likely that the mother's family doctor gave her some thalidomide samples when she complained of morning sickness. The drug, developed in Germany, was also a sedative.

I started my job in the spring and was nervous at first, but I soon discovered how much easier it was working in the National Health Service than anywhere in India. Michael had told me what a splendid and noble institution it was. One could practise the best possible medicine and, most importantly, it was free at the point of delivery. The standard of care was uniformly high throughout the country, and the sense of goodwill and compassion of the staff was always apparent. Despite the long, arduous hours and deplorable pay, I felt totally committed to my work. The fulfilment was enormous. In the Obstetric and Gynaecology Department, there were only two doctors, Mr S and myself. He lived on the island, and on the rare occasions when he was not available, he was covered by two consultants from the mainland. At first I felt intimidated by male British consultants. They reminded me of the Raj. Many were aloof, arrogant and overconfident. Nurses were frightened of them. But as I became confident myself, I learned to look them in the eye, not always agree with them, and argue my point. I found they were not unreasonable. The nursing staff were very helpful and were headed by the sister midwife in the maternity ward. Tall, elegant, single and middle-aged, she told me she lived for her work.

After a few months, our consultants realised we were not having time off, so one weekend every month, they covered for us. We made sure we left the island, so as not to be called by the hospital. We would go to London and stay in a cheap bed and breakfast and go to the theatre if we could. We enjoyed going to Speakers Corner in Hyde Park. Michael would insist that we pay a visit to his mother and Delicia, and I was happy to do so. Occasionally, if it was a sunny day, we would make a trip to a seaside town. One weekend, I was wearing a sari and we were sitting on the pier at Southend. A middle-aged woman approached us.

'Why have you come to my country?' she asked of me. 'Because you came to mine,' I said. She walked away.

The one aspect of my work which I disliked was working in the Casualty department. Not particularly busy, except in the summer, when jellyfish stings were a problem, it was run by a fierce and over excitable nurse, Sister H. A handsome unmarried woman, she ranted and raved all day, terrorising the junior nurses. Quite soon after I joined the hospital, she summoned me to see a fifteen-year-old girl with abdominal pain.

After taking a brief history and doing a general examination, I could find no abnormality and was about to discharge her with reassurance. Sister H glared at me and said:

'Well, aren't you going to examine her internally to see if she is pregnant?'

'She is not married,' I said. In India women are virgins until they marry.

'On which planet were you born? Go on, get on with it.' And with that she threw a pair of gloves at me.

I could not bring myself to do it. I asked the girl a few more questions and was convinced she was not pregnant. I rang Mr S and he came to see her. He too decided she was not pregnant, did not examine her and discharged her. I became less and less intimidated by Sister H. One day when she was arguing with me, I told her to shut up. She was taken aback for a moment, then laughed, and we developed a good relationship after that. She was never around after 5 p.m., and rumour had it that she was regularly inebriated after six and was known for her raucous behaviour in town every night.

There was only one moment of real crisis when I worked in Obstetrics. A young woman in her first pregnancy was admitted in labour. The experienced midwife telephoned to tell me she thought it was a breech presentation, and seemed concerned. I went to see the patient and confirmed the midwife's findings. The labour was progressing quite fast. I rang Mr S to find he had taken a night off, and the obstetrician from the mainland was covering. I rang him, giving details of the patient's progress, and told him I did not feel competent to deal with the situation if anything went wrong. He said he would come straight away. A few minutes later he rang to say the drawbridge to the island was up, and would be for a few hours, by which time the baby was likely to be born.

'Do your best,' he said. 'I am sure all will be well.' And he rang off.

I was terrified. But all did go off well.

I was surprised at the large number of unmarried mothers, nearly all of whom were having first babies. And nearly all of them gave them up for adoption, leaving the island sad and empty handed. It was usual practice at that time for patients to be in hospital for ten days after the birth. I noticed these women had few or no visitors. The maternity unit sister told me that because of the stigma of being an unmarried mother, these women chose to come to Sheppey to hide their pregnancy, and after giving birth, returned to their homes without their babies.

Michael and I did not want to stay longer than six months in Sheppey and started to look for jobs in larger hospitals on the mainland, but we could find nothing where we could be together. We had to have a roof over our heads. We did not have a home and money was short. We then applied to hospitals in the London area, and realised we would probably have to work in separate hospitals. I was shortlisted for a post in a hospital in Ealing, and when I arrived for the interview I found in the waiting room three other doctors, a Chinese, an Australian and a West Indian, all of us hoping to get the same job. A little later, a smartly dressed white doctor, with an umbrella, walked through the waiting room, opened the door into the interview room and went in. Three male consultants were sitting at a large table. We heard him say to them: 'When do I start?'

The door was shut, and a few minutes later he walked out and left. Each of the four of us had a short interview and were told we were unsuccessful and that Dr H had got the job. I felt it had all been a farce. This was confirmed when I unexpectedly bumped into one of my doctor friends from Vellore, a Senior House Officer in Casualty, at the same hospital. I told him the story, and he was perplexed and said, 'But we all knew that Dr H had already been given this job.'

Mike and I felt that preference should always be given to British graduates, whether they were better or not than foreign ones. This was after all Britain. And this is what usually happened. What we did not like was the pretence that the British doctor was appointed because he was the best, when, on occasions, he clearly was not. It would have been more honest to say the British doctor was appointed because he was British. No one would have argued with that.

Michael succeeded in getting a post in Surgery at Lewisham Hospital in south-east London and I got one in Medicine in Stoke Mandeville Hospital in Buckinghamshire, close to London. The latter was famous for its spinal rehabilitation centre, but it was also a fine district general hospital, with many specialities. The other doctors in my grade were all white, male, and from the London teaching hospitals. For me to have got this job, I assumed that one of the appointees must have dropped out at short notice. Our jobs were starting only in mid-January. We had to find somewhere to live until then. We decided we badly needed a holiday. We booked a cheap double room with breakfast, for two weeks, at the Methodist International House in Bayswater in London. It was a truly dreadful place, largely occupied by noisy unruly students from Africa. There was bedlam in the dining room at breakfast every day, with a lot of shouting across tables. We had our other meals in the surrounding cafés around us, and enjoyed, within our means, what London had to offer. Christmas was approaching and London became an even more magical city.

We said our goodbyes to the staff at Sheppey. I think our consultants were genuinely sad to see us go. They and their wives were very hospitable to us, often inviting us to their homes for meals. They had given us glowing references for our next jobs. Mr S and his wife made us promise we would come back and see them.

Before we left Sheppey, one of Michael's consultants, a Mr MacG, but always referred to as 'Wee Willie', asked him if he would do a locum for a few weeks at his other hospital in Maidstone.

Mr MacG was an Ear Nose and Throat (ENT) specialist. Mike found him a genial person to work with, but one of the other consultants had warned him to avoid calling Willie after 6 p.m., as he had an alcohol problem. On one occasion only, Michael felt compelled to call him at night. The patient had developed post-operative complications, and was leaking fluid from the brain through the nose. Willie turned up in his Daimler. There were no breathalysers in those days. He staggered into the hospital, and swaying, knelt by the patient's bedside.

'My boy,' he said with slurred speech, to Mike. 'This man has the DTs—delirium tremens. What he needs is a stiff tot of whisky. Give him some and he will be all right.'

With that, he left. Mike arranged for the immediate transfer of the patient to a neurosurgical unit on the mainland. Mike used to say that on many occasions he did not cover for consultants, but covered up for them.

Mike agreed to take up the three-week locum post in ENT in Maidstone, provided there was accommodation for me as well. This was arranged. We took our few belongings and settled into the doctors' quarters. No sooner had we arrived than Mr MacG told Mike that they were still short of junior staff, and would I also do a locum. Mike explained that my knowledge of ENT was minimal, having had only a three-week posting as a medical student in this speciality, and it was unlikely that I would agree. Mr MacG said that all they required was a junior doctor to do the clerking, take a history, do a physical examination, organise blood tests and make sure the patient was fit for surgery. I agreed to do the locum. I was also required to attend clinics with other consultants, and my knowledge of ENT grew rapidly. A few days later, Willie asked me if I would assist him in a fairly major ear operation. I was very reluctant as he had a reputation for behaving badly in the operating theatre.

'Mr MacG,' I said. 'I understand you swear at your assistants and the nurses, and throw instruments around. I don't think I could cope with that.'

He laughed. 'My dear,' he said, 'all you have to do is to hold the head absolutely steady with both your hands. If you can do that, I promise I will not shout at you.'

I agreed, and for nearly two hours I did just that. Willie, in the meantime, yelled and screamed at the nurse assisting him, and even called her a 'bloody woman'. And there were instruments flying everywhere. I was glad he did not ask me to assist him again, but he told me I had done a fine job. He later told me he had wrecked the ear.

ʃ

We took ourselves off to Delicia's for Christmas that year, adding to the crowding in her small house. It was my first experience of a traditional English lunch. Mike's mother was a superb cook. We had roast turkey with the traditional accompaniments. The latter were tastier than the turkey, a bland bird. The flaming Christmas pudding followed. The Brussels sprouts fascinated me; they were like miniature cabbages. It felt more civilised than the chicken biriyani and aubergine curry we had in India, year after year, though in the last few years my mother and I had started going to a luxury hotel for a Western-style lunch, usually for roast lamb or chicken. Thatha did not take to this kindly, and nor did Samson Uncle. They had their usual Christmas lunch in Annie Lodge.

During our short stay with Delicia, her silent husband kept plying me with all kinds of alcoholic drinks, with which I was unfamiliar. Michael, a teetotal Methodist, smiled politely and declined them all.

ʃ

Once again we had to find somewhere to have a roof over our heads before we started our jobs in mid-January. Mike found a locum post in Lewisham Hospital prior to starting his substantive post there, but could get accommodation only for himself. I applied for a locum post at St Mary's Hospital in Plaistow in the East End of London, and was appointed over the phone by the Hospital Secretary. I was instructed to arrive the night before, and report to the housekeeper, who would direct me to my room. Mike dropped me off. We were both feeling low. For at least another six months, we would have to live apart. To make things worse, I told him I was still feeling queasy after drinking so much alcohol. But being teetotal he was not sympathetic.

My room was very small and spartan, with a hard single bed. There were four such rooms on either side of a narrow corridor, at the end of which was a cold bathroom, to be shared. There was no sign of life, and I did not meet any doctors. I assumed they were on the wards, or in the doctors' sitting room. Next morning I awoke early, and on my way to the bathroom I bumped into a large, red-faced, middle-aged, fully dressed woman with a cigarette hanging from her mouth.

'Good morning,' I said brightly. Looking surprised, she glared at me and said nothing. Strange, these English doctors, I thought.

I presented myself to the Hospital Secretary before going on to the wards. I had given him a brief curriculum vitae and he seemed happy to give me the locum post over the phone. As it was a short, temporary post, it was not considered important enough for any of the consultants to interview me. The incumbent, an Irish doctor, was on leave. The Hospital Secretary looked at me and was clearly disappointed.

'Oh, I thought you were English,' he said. My name and speech had not sounded foreign to him.

'Well, you can see I am not,' I said unhappily. I always wore a sari for work. He told me which wards I would be working on, and asked me to present myself to one of the ward sisters. I was welcomed and told I would be working for five consultants.

'You won't see much of them,' she said. 'They do a lot of private practice, and also work in other hospitals. What is your spelling like?' she added.

'Pretty good,' I replied, wondering why that seemed a priority.

'Dr G won't mind if you don't know much medicine, but he is very particular about spelling.' She then proceeded to tell me the likes and dislikes of each of the consultants. There was a very competent lady registrar to supervise me. She was an Indian from East Africa and wore Western dress. She remained very aloof.

During the time I was there, I was on call for six of the nights and one weekend. I worked very hard, and even on nights I was not on call, I seldom left the ward before midnight. I struggled because my indigestion and queasiness were not improving. I vowed never to drink alcohol again.

I met the other junior doctors in the dining room and doctors' sitting room, and discovered to my annoyance that my room was part of the maids' quarters. That explained the woman I encountered there. The doctors' rooms were spacious and comfortable but there was not one available for me, as the doctor I was covering for had left her belongings in her room.

After a week, one of the consultants summoned me to his office. He said a vacancy for a six-month post would arise in a couple of months, and they wished to offer it to me without interview. I told them I was due to start at Stoke Mandeville shortly. He said there would be more posts coming up and asked me to apply. It was a dreary place, in a depressed area. I had no intention of returning.

Mike and I spoke to each other on the phone every day. I told him I was still feeling queasy and he told me what antacid I should take. The ward sister was sympathetic, and she gave me a supply from the ward. I wondered if I would be strong enough for the Stoke Mandeville job, but I had no alternative. We had no home and money was scarce, and I needed to be registered. I had to work.

Chapter 18

A HARD LIFE

Michael collected me and my belongings and we drove to Stoke Mandeville, near Aylesbury in Buckinghamshire. Stoke Mandeville Hospital had started life as an infectious diseases hospital, and as its purpose expanded, the building was extended. It was now also the National Spinal Injuries Centre. It was a single-storey building, and to walk from the doctors' quarters to the wards along the main corridor took some time. Michael was concerned that I had lost so much weight, and said if my indigestion continued, to go and see a physician. He had contentedly settled in Lewisham Hospital.

My room in the doctors' mess was simply furnished with a washbasin, and was quite comfortable. But the walls were thin, and not sound-proofed. There were the usual communal bathrooms, and unlike at Sheppey, there were about twenty resident junior doctors, nearly all of them white, polite but not friendly. They were mainly from the London teaching hospitals. I was to work with Alan Gibbs, the Senior House officer. I was a pre-registration House Officer, which was the lowest rung of the doctors' ladder. Alan was a slight, pleasant, unassuming man, about five years older than me, and had qualified in London. I could not have asked for a nicer colleague. We both worked for the consultant, Dr John Lloyd-Hart (L-H). Again, I could not have asked for a better boss. Alan immediately took me under his wing, and took me to our two wards, one male and one female, and introduced me to the two ward sisters who presided over them. I also worked in two outpatient clinics, alongside Dr L-H, as he questioned, taught, teased and joked with me. A tall, lean man in his fifties, he was shrewd but a joy to work with. I was determined to be a first-rate House Officer. After a few days, he said to me, 'You are so thin and look unwell. But I cannot fault your work. Is anything the matter?' I smiled and said nothing.

In my first week at Stoke Mandeville, I went to the dining

room for lunch one day. Not having had any breakfast, because the smell of bacon put me off, I was feeling empty, and thought I would try an early lunch. None of the other doctors had arrived. I sat at a table, waiting to be served. A maid came up to me and said I could not sit there, because it was Dr Guttman's table, and he liked only his staff to sit with him.

'Who is Dr Guttman?' I asked, in my ignorance.

'What!' she exclaimed. 'Don't you know who he is? He's a very famous man. Everyone knows who he is.'

With that she walked away, and I found myself another table. I also found out that he was indeed a famous man, and also somewhat pernickety. I did not ever come across another consultant who decided which junior doctors should sit at his table.

Ludwig Guttman was a Jew who had left his native Germany in 1939 for Britain. In 1943 he was asked by the Government to set up the National Spinal Injuries Centre at Stoke Mandeville Hospital. He transformed the lives of patients with spinal injuries with his methods of rehabilitation, and brought hope to thousands. He was later knighted. He could also be called the Father of the Paralympic Games.

~

It was Michael who suggested that I might be pregnant. The thought had not occurred to me. All I could think of was alcoholic gastritis, brought on by Christmas excesses. Alan Gibbs was worried that I was eating so little, and I confided my suspicions to him. He wrote out a pregnancy test request form with a fictitious name, and sent it with a specimen to the laboratory, and the result came back positive. I was shattered. It could not have been a worse time to have a baby. I think Mike was equally shattered, but he put on a brave face, so as not to compound my woes. He told me not to worry and that all would be well, especially if the baby was a girl.

I wondered how I could possibly carry on. I felt so tired and weak, and retched every morning and felt queasy all day. Night duty was a nightmare. When I was on call, I would be seeing emergency medical admissions throughout the night, clerking and examining them, taking and sending off blood samples, often doing

ECGs on them, and dashing to the lavatory in between leads to get sick. Alan and I worked alternate nights and weekends, and he urged me to let him do some of my nights and weekends. But I could not take advantage of his goodness. This was my problem. On nights when I was not on call, I would be so tired that I would find it difficult to drop off to sleep. I would usually do a final ward round with the night sister before I went to my room, just before midnight. I told her I could do with a sedative occasionally, and asked for the new drug, which was found to be so effective. It was called thalidomide. She suggested we stick to an old one that was tried and tested, and gave me Doriden instead. Her caution and wisdom probably prevented a catastrophe, as I was at the stage of pregnancy when thalidomide inflicted its horrific damage. In those days, there were no rules and regulations. Staff prescribed for each other, but very responsibly.

'Don't worry,' Alan Gibbs would say. 'It will last only a few more weeks.'

And he was right. I started to eat again and put on weight and look normal. There were times in moments of desperation when I thought of leaving my job and going back to my mother to have the baby, leave it with her, and return to Mike and England. My mother urged me to do this. But Mike would not hear of it, and I did not want to be parted from him. Despite all these problems, deep within me there was a growing happiness. I hoped it would be a girl. When my girth was beginning to expand, I thought it was time to tell Dr L-H; he was very excited and said, 'Is there anything we can do for you?' Of course there wasn't. I was just so relieved he did not look or say anything disapproving, because that is the way male or unmarried female consultants would react, on hearing such news from their junior doctors. It would be as if something indecent had happened.

I carried on doing my best and became more and more exhausted, but I was greatly encouraged by Dr L-H's appreciation of my work.

'Isn't Dr C wonderful?' he would write at the top of the page in the patient's case notes. This would be when I had made a tricky diagnosis, before he had. He would tell the ward sister that I was the brightest star in his firmament, and embarrass me further by calling me 'my precious' or 'my jewel' during ward rounds. Alan Gibbs would stand in the background with a smile on his face. Dr L-H frequently commented on my memory. As we went from bed to bed on ward rounds, I would reel off every detail about the patient, without reference to the case notes, and he would ask how could I remember so much, just as Mr S did in Sheppey. I had always had a very good memory, but it was also due to the training I had had in Vellore.

Dr L-H and his wife were very hospitable and generous to their junior medical staff, taking us to the theatre and picnic dinners.

They once took me to the Oxford Playhouse, where we saw a young Vanessa Redgrave.

My six-month post was coming to an end. When the time came, there was the usual leave-taking. I was showered with gifts for the baby. I said a special goodbye to Alan Gibbs, who had in the meanwhile got himself secretly married. Dr L-H made me promise I would keep in touch.

⌣

Mike tried to get a hospital flat at Lewisham. These were usually provided at a subsidised rent for junior doctors and their families. None was available. But there was a likelihood that there would be one in Hither Green Hospital, nearby. A large house in the grounds of this downgraded infectious disease hospital was being converted into three flats, one upstairs for the Group Catering Officer (GCO) and two unfurnished ones downstairs for junior doctors. We were allotted one of them, and allowed to choose the wallpaper and paint. We did not know how we were going to afford the furniture and furnishing. Mike's nurses, always a source of information, said we could buy them cheaply from shops dealing with liquidated stock.

Mike was a very creative and imaginative do-it-yourself person, and with the help of Fablon and accessories from Woolworths made a coffee table from a cupboard shelf and bedside tables from wooden tomato boxes. The one luxury which I had coveted, and Michael insisted I had, was a large floral carpet from Wolfe and Hollander on Tottenham Court Road. We sanded the floorboards and painted them black, and the carpet looked splendid.

Our flat had a very large bed-sitting room with huge windows overlooking a large overgrown garden, a dining/guest room, a tiny box room, a hall with huge fitted cupboards, a kitchen and a bathroom. The thought of actually having a place of our own made us delirious with happiness.

My cooking skills were non-existent, thanks to my mother, who maintained that if a woman did not have an inclination towards cooking, or any other type of housework, there was no necessity for her to do it; she should pay someone else to do it. With the help of a couple of basic cookery books and some innovation, Michael and I managed to eat. Our flat looked out onto a large, neglected lawn, reached by a few stone steps from a path opposite the front door. On either side of the steps were weed-filled flower beds, and a rockery. The hospital gardener said he did not have the staff to tend our part of the hospital garden, but if we could do it ourselves, he would lend us the necessary tools and a self-propelled petrol lawn mower. Neither Mike nor I knew much about gardening, apart from enjoying the fruits of our malis' labours in India, and we knew nothing about English gardening. But we were very excited about restoring this garden, large though it was. We acquired a couple of second-hand gardening books and set to work. In three months it was transformed. Michael used a scythe to cut the long grass. He then tied one end of a long rope to the handle of the lawn mower, and the other end to a strong wooden spike in the middle of the lawn. Once the mower was switched on, it would go round and round, while he worked nearby. I looked after the flower beds and rockeries, and once the weeds were cleared, found they were well stocked. We had been fascinated by early spring flowers, and planted bulbs of daffodils, tulips, hyacinth and lily of the valley. This for Mike and me was the beginning of a lifelong love of and interest in gardens and gardening. My mother, whose long letters to me often referred to her own garden, which now, after six years, had matured, often spoke of her own delight in it. She said strangers would come to the gate and ask the gardener if it was a park. But she envied the ease with which we maintained our lawn, because of the British climate.

My mother wrote to say that Alpha, her house, was being extended. Cheena, Biggy's neighbour in Rangoon, who was a timber passer and had moved to Borneo, had retired to Madras, where one of his brothers lived. Cheena was running a substantial bookshop for the Christian Literature Society in Madras. He had kept in touch with us over the years, and when I was in school and in Vellore he would write to Ann and me and send parcels of magazines and chocolates, Kit Kat and Mars bars, which were not available in India. Cheena wanted to pay for the extension of Alpha and come and live there. He had a car and could commute easily into the city to his office. Ann and I were a bit wary at first, knowing how fiercely independent my mother was, and what Cheena would make of my mother's rages. But we were also glad that she would have company and more security. She agreed to the arrangement, and while all was not harmony all the time, the arrangement worked out.

Chapter 19

A NEW SMALL PERSON

Would it be a boy or girl? That was what everyone was asking. Mike's two married siblings had five girls between them. There were no boys in this generation. Mike's mother kept saying that the Cartner name had to be kept going, as though they belonged to something important like the Ming dynasty. Mike was very strong in his preference, and said he definitely did not want a boy. There was no doubt what my mother wanted. I did not care what it was, as long as it was normal and healthy, but secretly I yearned for a girl.

And a girl it was. In the early hours of 24 August 1961, Mike took me to the Mayday Hospital in Croydon, and left me there under the care of the registrar, who had qualified in Vellore some years before me, and her consultant, whom she had strongly recommended. The last thing Mike said before he left for work was: 'Make sure it is a girl.'

He reappeared at 10 p.m. that night, ten hours after the baby's birth, and ecstatic. The baby was no great beauty, but exquisitely formed with a thatch of black hair. She was brown like me, but would grow up to look like her father and have his temperament. After much arguing, we decided on the Sanskrit name, Kiran, which means a ray of light, a very suitable name. We did not know then that there was an Irish name, Kieron, which sounded somewhat similar, so people in England thought it was an Irish name. My mother reprimanded us for not choosing an English name. And we did give her a second name after Mike's mother and my sister, Ann. I would have preferred an 'e' at the end but it was not to be.

The hospital food was dire, and it was no wonder that hardly anyone was breastfeeding. My Vellore friends brought in tidbits for me and even some main meals.

'It doesn't work,' the midwives and nurses said to me, referring to breastfeeding.

I was in a room to myself, and I would see trolleys with dozens of little feeding bottles with formula feeds, going past to the large main wards. Some of the mothers I got talking to said the same thing to me, when they knew I was attempting to breastfeed. But I knew they were all talking nonsense. Bottle-feeding happened to be in vogue at that time. Kiran did not have a bottle until she was five months old, and that too because we were going to a wedding and she was left with her aunt for a few hours.

Those were the days when we had to be incarcerated in hospital for ten days, even after a normal, uneventful birth, but after many protests from me I was allowed home a day earlier. It happened to be a Saturday, and Mike was able to take me home that afternoon, after his ward round. Bags of wet laundry were studded around the dining room. Not wanting me to face a basketful of unwashed clothes, he had gone to the launderette the previous night. We had neither a washing machine nor a refrigerator, which was another reason I felt I had to breastfeed. Disposable nappies had just been introduced, so that solved the other problem.

We had barely got home from the hospital when Mike got into his pyjamas, announced he was not feeling well and got into bed. I was taken aback. But I learned later that this is not an unusual male reaction. There was no food in the house. The new pram had not been assembled and was still in its packing case. We had no cot, the idea being to keep the baby in the pram for the first few months, and at night, next to our bed. I was terrified of cot deaths, which were much in the news. I asked Mike to assemble the pram, so I could put the baby in it, while I went out to get some food.

'Put her next to me,' he said 'We can assemble the pram later.'

'No,' I said 'You will squash her by the time I get back.' I had my way.

I took a couple of shopping bags and got to the butcher and greengrocer before early closing. As I passed the Porters' Lodge at the entrance of the hospital, my favourite porter shouted, 'What was it?' 'A girl,' I shouted back. I had got to know all the porters as our flat had only an internal phone line. The hospital refused to put in an external line, or allow us to put in one. This meant that every time we got an external call, it would come to the Porters' Lodge and they would ring us on the internal line, and we would have to go to the Porters' Lodge to take the call. If I wanted to call anyone, I would have to go to a public phone box down the road. It was all very unsatisfactory, but like everything else, we just accepted the situation. The morning after I came home, Mike bounced back and went off to work. That evening, we went to see Mike's family. His mother visited me once in hospital and said very little. I thought she might be disappointed it was another granddaughter or that the baby looked like me. We asked Delicia to be a godparent. The others were Ann, my sister, and Mike's elder brother, Desmond. Kiran was christened in the local Methodist church when she was ten weeks old.

My mother had wanted to come to England for Kiran's birth and give me a hand for a couple of months, but I put her off. Flights were prohibitively expensive, and Mike's family were close enough to give me support. Besides, the extension to Alpha was being built and she needed to be on site.

It was back to cooking, cleaning, ironing and gardening for me, but there was now also a little person to care for. How different it would have been in India. After coming home from hospital, I would have been endlessly pampered. My hair would have been washed by someone. My body would have been massaged. I would have been fed home-made chicken soup and, most important of all, there would have been an ayah to look after the baby, so I could have adequate sleep. My mother was deeply disappointed that I had no help from Mike's family.

Mike was sometimes on night duty for five consecutive nights, in which case I would not see him for six days in a row. The English couple, both young doctors, in the adjacent flat were exceptionally unfriendly, not even reciprocating a 'Hello'. But the Catering Manager's wife, a plump pleasant lady, showed an interest in the baby, and even volunteered to babysit. I had no friends nearby and could not drive. The only people I spoke to were the porters and shopkeepers. Being the only foreigner in the vicinity, I must have been a curiosity. As I pushed Kiran in her pram to the shops, children would run up to her and have a peep. Sometimes, I would hear a shout from one of them: 'The Chinese baby is coming.'

Kiran flourished. However, she drove me to utter despair in the first four weeks, wanting feeding constantly, sometimes twenty times a day. Michael solved the problem by providing her with a dummy, something I was determined to resist but failed. At six weeks, she recognised us and smiled. Her stick-like legs filled out; she started to make little noises, kick her legs vigorously, and acquire dimples in various places, just like millions of babies the world over. But every change and milestone filled me with wonder and delight. This was a child who was not expected, and came at an inopportune time, but I quickly came to realise, then and forever, that nothing better could ever happen to me.

⏜

The winter of 1961 was mild with a few snow flurries in late December, the first time I had experienced snow.

Mike had still not passed Part I of the FRCS, despite two attempts. It was depressing to hear that there were doctors on their sixth attempt. Some of our friends had given up and gone into general practice. Mike was spending too much time on hospital work and not enough time studying. I decided to take matters into my hands. The exam demanded a very high standard in its core subjects: Anatomy, Physiology and Pathology. He was failing in the last two, subjects that I had enjoyed as an undergraduate. I decided to study these subjects myself and teach him when he came home in the evenings. He was quite happy to be taught and quizzed over meals. I was certain that once Part I was out of the way, he would pass Part II quickly because of his experience and expertise in surgery. Then we could return to India. I was not happy living in England.

⏜

Our fortunes improved in the new year. Mike passed Part I of the FRCS, and we won the football pools. The latter was not exactly a windfall, as thousands of others had also got twelve draws, but £250 was a princely sum for us. We could now buy a refrigerator and take a short holiday. Life was beginning to look up a little.

We hired a boat for a week to take us leisurely up the Thames. Powered with an outboard motor, it was well provided with three berths, a cooker, sink, fridge and lavatory. Hot and cold water were available, but there was no shower. Washing at the sink, and using public baths when we tied up near small towns, was deemed acceptable. We would also be able to buy food and the all-important disposable nappies. We invited Mike's mother to join us and she readily agreed. At sixty, despite having had a heart attack two years earlier, she was still very active and adventurous. I had a good relationship with her, and my fears that that this would not be so had not materialised. As it turned out, it would have been very difficult to have managed without her. We had to negotiate several locks, and as Mike steered his way into them, I had to run along the boat, and then leap up onto the platform to tie the boat. Someone had to control the nine-month baby, which was constantly trying to crawl off the boat.

The first night we tied up near Windsor. It was bitterly cold, the blankets felt damp and Kiran, in her carrycot wedged between two berths, kept sitting up and crying most of the night. Early May was not the time to embark on such a trip. That morning, we were woken by a man who asked if we had heard anything untoward during the night. We had not. He said several boats, tied up near ours, had had their ropes cut and were drifting down stream. Fortunately they had no occupants, but this was enough to ruin my sleep for the rest of the trip.

The next morning we set off again, and near noon the engine suddenly cut out. To his horror, Mike found the outboard motor had snapped off, and was half-submerged in the water. He could lift it neither up nor out. The boat had started to drift with the current, and then began to circle round and round in the middle of the river. Several boats passed us by. We shouted out to them that we were in trouble, and asked for help. Some laughed at us, and one shouted 'God help you' and carried on. Mike quickly changed into a pair of swimming trunks, grabbed a rope, tied one end to the boat, jumped into the river and towed the boat till he could see a suitable tree. He clambered onto the bank, pulled the boat up and tethered it to a tree. He then went in search of a telephone box to ring the boat company. It being a Sunday, they agreed to replace the motor only the next day, and took details of where we were.

We were running out of nappies and rang Delicia to tell her of our plight. She and her husband found their way to us that evening with a supply, and she brought enough food for us to dine together on the boat that night. The motor was replaced the next morning, but my enthusiasm for the trip had disappeared, and I was pleased when the week was over and we were back home.

⁓

The Chelsea Flower Show was about to happen. My mother repeatedly reminded me not to miss it. I too was very keen to get to it, and found some information about it. The first day was for royalty, the next for Fellows of the Royal Horticultural Society, and the remaining three days for the public. Mike had an appointment at the Royal College of Surgeons (RCS) in London that week, and said he would drop me and Kiran at the Royal Chelsea grounds, where the flower show was being held, then go on to his appointment, and pick me up again later in the day.

I had seen pictures of elegant hatted and gloved ladies attending this show, and had chosen to wear a suitable sari. I had to find something equally suitable for Kiran, but she did not have a pretty dress and they were absurdly expensive. Delicia had shown me how to sew from paper patterns. I made a trip to Lewisham market, got some pink fabric and a white daisy trim for the yolk for a few shillings, and made the dress in a day. Mike's mother had shown me how to knit, and earlier I had made a pink cardigan. With white shoes and socks to match, I had no doubt that Kiran would upstage every flower in the show. But alas, when we got to the ticket office, with me wheeling Kiran in her bucket push chair, I was told firmly by the man there that children below the age of five were not allowed. I tried to argue and plead with the man, but he said he was sorry, rules were rules. There were two policemen hovering around and listening to this conversation. As I walked away, one of them came up to me and said that he and his mate would look after the baby for an hour, while I went to the show. I was deeply touched, but I could not entrust this

precious possession to strangers, even if they belonged to that most
trusted and admired group, the British Bobby. I tracked Mike at
the RCS. He said he was leaving shortly, and would meet me at
the entrance to the show, take Kiran home and come back for
me some hours later. The show was a feast for the eyes. It did
not disappoint me, and I did not disappoint my mother. When I
was walking out, I heard a voice behind me say: 'Why, if it isn't
Lindy Rajan!'

I turned around to see three beautifully groomed Indian women
in expensive silk saris. They were three wealthy girls I had known
at Isabella Thoburn College, nearly ten years ago.

'How you have changed and how tired you look! Did you
ever become a doctor?'

They had all married well-educated, successful businessmen,
and were ladies of leisure, spending a month in Europe every
summer while their children were looked after in India. Not for
them the hardship of being a junior doctor in England, married to
a junior doctor, coping with a baby, poor, and most importantly,
not having any servants.

Chapter 20

IT WAS NOT FOR ME

With only one salary coming in, our financial situation was dire. Our old Renault's days were coming to an end. I was prepared to take any job. But I was inexperienced, and at my level, hospital work meant a number of nights on call and weekend work. There was no flexibility in the system. I was surprised at the number of married British women doctors who had never worked after registration. They were unable to combine motherhood with a career. Salaries were very low, and those who could afford nannies had rich husbands or came from wealthy families.

One day, while reading the *British Medical Journal*, I saw an advertisement for a course in London, in family planning, run by the Family Planning Association (FPA). If I completed the course, I could work in evening clinics around London. I applied for the course, consisting of three evening sessions, and was accepted. Between Michael's evenings off duty and the Catering Manager's wife, Kiran was looked after.

The family planning sessions were personally run by Dr Helena Wright, who had been President of the International Planned Parenthood Federation. Past retirement now, she was charismatic, outspoken, entertaining and uninhibited. She did not mince her words or ideas.

'British men are the best lovers in the world,' she said, and when someone said that it was Italians who had that reputation, she quickly replied: 'Nonsense. Don't you believe it! It is a myth that they are good lovers. They may be passionate, but they suffer from premature ejaculation.'

Dr Wright was adamant that a woman should be in control of her own fertility, and that meant being in control of her body at all times. The pill had just come in, but was hardly prescribed, so we had to learn about the physical barriers: caps, coils and condoms. There were three or four generous public-spirited women who allowed us to practise on them. All the while, Dr Wright would be supervising us and quizzing us on the theory of these procedures, their consequences and complications. I had done my homework before the course and was well clued up.

At the end of the last session, Dr Wright asked me to stay behind. She was very complimentary, and said she hoped I would do sessions in London and then devote myself to family planning when I returned to India. She had always had an interest in India and Indian women, and had visited India a few times.

At the end of the course, we were each given an envelope. This contained an assessment/reference form from Dr Wright, to be sent with our application if we applied to work in clinics. Certificates of competence would be sent to us, in due course, from the FPA. Mike wondered what Dr Wright had written about me and wanted me to open the envelope and read the form. I was reluctant. He said it was good to know what people thought about you, good or bad. I gave him the envelope and he opened it and smiled, and held up the form for me to see. None of the columns was filled in. Instead right across the form was written in capital letters: BRILLIANT! I sent the form to the FPA and received from them a certificate to say I had completed the course. I then applied for evening sessions in the FPA clinics. I had a brief reply from the FPA to say I had been given a white certificate, which meant that I could do family planning in my own country, but I did not have the competence to work in Britain. For the latter, I needed a blue certificate. I was furious, and Mike even more so.

'Wasn't it a good thing that I made you open that envelope?' he said. 'If they don't want foreign doctors, why don't they say so?'

I wrote to the FPA to say I was taken aback by their letter, and that Dr Wright had led me to understand that I was exceptionally able. Would they please refer to her reference, and if they had lost it, would they please get in touch with her, as I was certain she would remember me. Back came an apology, with a blue certificate and an offer of work in their clinics in London. I was wary of working in any FPA clinic after this, but as I was considering it, another advertisement in the British Medical Journal caught my eye. This was for a trainee general practitioner (GP) in New Cross, London SE14, covering the Lewisham/New Cross/Catford area, which was near where I lived. The main attraction was that there was no night duty or weekends, apart from a few house calls after evening clinic, which would end by 7 p.m. and on Mondays by 9 p.m. It was for four days a week and some Saturday mornings. Ownership of a car and ability to drive were mandatory.

⁘

Two months earlier, I had reluctantly started driving lessons at Mike's insistence. I was not a natural driver. I liked to be driven. A colleague had recommended a seventy-three-year-old man called Percy Minn. He had enabled several doctors to pass their driving tests. But the main recommendation was that he was cheap and his hours were very flexible to suit junior doctors.

'But what about the baby?' I said.

'Bring her along,' said Percy. 'We will put her in the back seat.'

But I declined, as this was now a very active, noisy and robust ten-month-old. The Catering Manager's wife came to the rescue. What I was to discover about Percy was that he loved to talk, and he disliked West Indians intensely. There were many of them in south-east London.

'Look, look,' he would shout. 'We nearly ran over him, didn't we? He was so black, we nearly did not see him.'

But that was not true. He resented their presence in England, as did most of the population. When I explained to him why they were in this country, he would not listen. He said he would not have one of them in his car, as they chewed garlic all the time, which also was not true. We had many West Indian patients in the practice.

'What about me, Percy?' I would ask. 'I am brown, I am foreign and I am an Indian.'

'You are a princess,' came the reply.

Percy would make me drive into side streets and park, and then talk and talk, and put the world to rights. I would suggest that we did some more driving, and off we would go, only to stop again for him to talk some more.

⁘

I enquired about the GP job by telephone, and was put through to the principal partner, Bertie Pereira. I was surprised to find he was Anglo-Indian. He had grown up in Bangalore and qualified from Madras University. He was surprised that I was Indian. I was certain I would not get the job, he an Anglo-Indian and I an Indian, aware of how prejudiced they were against us. But I was wrong. He was extremely friendly and very interested in my past history. He had been a Lt. Colonel in the British Army in India, and knew of Mike's father, who had also been a doctor in the Army. Bertie had asked to be demobbed in Britain, set up a practice and had asked two Anglo-Indian doctors to join him. The senior practice nurse, Ida, was also the manager. Ida lived with Bertie and his two children in a flat above the surgery, a purpose-built building. Bertie was estranged from his wife, also a doctor, and with mental problems. They were Catholics and she would not give him a divorce. Their children were very devoted to Ida, and she to them. Some years later when the divorce laws were changed, Bertie divorced his wife and married Ida.

'Well,' said Bertie. 'The job is yours. Start in a month when you have passed your test. You must have a car and a licence. When did you lose your Indian accent?'

I failed the test. And that is the end of the job, I thought. I rang Bertie to tell him.

'That's the end of my job,' I said ruefully.

'Of course not. You can start straight away. We have so many house visits within walking distance of the surgery, you could do those. You are sure to pass the test the next time.'

But I was not so sure.

Percy said I would need a few more lessons. But Mike took the matter into his hands. A few months earlier the Renault had given up, and was sold to a garage for five pounds. We acquired a brand new minivan, and because there were no windows, there was no sales tax, and we could afford it, for just over £400. Mike said he would give me driving lessons. Unlike most husbands who yell at their wives under these circumstances, he was the epitome of patience and merely laughed when I did something silly. We drove hundreds of miles, with me at the wheel. I passed the test and Percy took the credit. Two weeks later he walked into the Casualty department at Lewisham Hospital, complaining of chest pain, and dropped dead.

I had to quickly find a childminder, and the CM's wife knew of a lady, Mrs Hammond, living in a council house across the road, two hundred yards away. Her husband was a retired manual worker. They seemed very decent people, had five children, the youngest being twelve, and were keen to help. They were obviously poor. The house was shabby, with worn carpets, but clean. The going rate was a pound for the five-day week, and I offered two pounds and ten shillings.

My mother used to say that servants all over the world were exploited and underpaid, and it was up to us, if we had the opportunity, to treat them fairly. I dropped Kiran off at nine in the morning, and picked her up after the evening surgery, usually at about seven. On the days Mike was not on call, he would pick her up. On Tuesdays, my day off, Kiran stayed with me. The Hammonds were kind people and Kiran appeared happy with them. I did not mind that she was picking up a cockney accent.

⌒

I sat in with Bertie Pereira for a few surgeries, which were what clinics were called, and went with him on house visits. Having only worked in hospitals, I was struck by the difference between the two. I found very little of real medical interest in general practice. After a couple of weeks, I said to Bertie that surely 70 per cent of the work could be done by a competent nurse.

'My dear,' he said, 'don't make such statements. Do you want us all to be out of a job?'

After the first week, I worked on my own. The practice was very well organised, with four consulting rooms. There was an efficient appointments system with a choice of doctor, rare in those days, but patients could also walk in and wait to be seen. Nearby, there was an excellent investigation centre, again a rarity, where we could send patients for blood tests and X-rays. This made a big difference to the ease and quality of our work. We referred our patients to the local hospitals, including teaching hospitals. Guy's Hospital was our nearest.

Ida was a great source of practical information, and ran the surgery very efficiently with two nurses. I did the house visits on foot initially, and then used my car. I did not like doing them. I could not examine patients adequately in their homes, and most house visits seemed unnecessary. Bertie would not reprimand patients for unreasonable requests, even the habitual abusers of this service.

One day in early December, I woke up and could see nothing out of the window. I had experienced fog in London, but this was different. The air was a sinister, sour, yellowy-green. Not since the Great Smog of 1952 had Londoners seen anything like this. Michael had been on call the past three nights, so he was safe in hospital. I decided I could not possibly drive to work. I rang Bertie. He said his partners had rung in to say they could not get to the surgery, and there were no buses running. There was a very ill patient he wanted me to see. I could walk to the main road and perhaps get a bus that went past his street. Bertie thought there were a few buses still running on this main road. With difficulty, Kiran and I walked to the Hammonds, and with greater difficulty, I found my way to the main road, and waited at the bus stop. After some time, a bus came crawling along. The driver realised my plight and tried to help. He knew the street I was trying to get to, and said he would drop me off near it. He told me to feel for the front garden walls of houses, as I walked along the main road. When I reached the third gap, that would be the turning into the street I needed. It worked. After going into a few wrong gardens, I found the right house and was escorted into an upstairs bedroom. On a double bed, propped up by pillows, was a large fat Cypriot man, being ministered to by three women. He was grinning and looked quite well.

'What's the matter?' I asked.

He said he had been to a party the previous night, had indulged excessively and had indigestion.

'Drink some milk,' I said, and left the house. Coughing and spluttering, I walked all the way home. I decided then that general practice was not for me.

A few weeks later, I was at home one afternoon. The doorbell rang; it was Bertie. He was in the vicinity doing house calls and, wondering where exactly I lived, had decided to drop in. I invited him in for a cup of tea. His eye fell on the pram.

'Whose pram is that?' he asked.

'My baby's,' I said.

'What!' he exclaimed. 'You didn't tell me you had a baby. Why did you not tell me?'

'You didn't ask,' I said. 'And besides, you would not have employed me.'

He paused a bit and said I was probably right. His partners would not have wanted a young mother as they would expect her to be taking time off.

'But all credit to you. You have not had any days off since you joined. Wait till I tell everyone in the Surgery.' I was glad the news was out.

⁀

The winter of 1962/63 started gently. We were driving back home from Delicia's, after dinner on Boxing Day. There were snow flurries, and then a little more snow, and then the windscreen wipers were having to work really hard. I was excited and hoped the snow would settle. We woke up the next morning to a white world. It was simply stubning. In the fresh snow, I drove Mike to work, where he would remain for a week, dropped Kiran off at the Hammonds and drove to work myself.

We were fortunate to be living in hospital premises. The porters ensured paths to the gate and main road were cleared of the heavy snow which was continuing to fall. As usual, the first day after the Bank Holiday the Surgery was full, and there were house visits to be made. I returned home routinely, and then had to return for the evening Surgery. I was nervous using the car. It was dark, and I had noticed earlier that cars were parked everywhere, and some had clearly been abandoned. I took a stiff drink of Stone's Ginger Wine, the only alcohol in this Methodist house. I felt a glow and set off. Breathalysers had not been invented. There was no knowing where the road ended, and the pavement began, but there was an advantage when doing house visits, because one just parked anywhere. That evening Bertie let me off house visits, but it was nearly nine before I collected Kiran. We were both so tired, and as we often did, dozed in the bath tub together. Was it all worthwhile, I wondered, enduring so many hardships, constantly being separated from Mike, struggling more or less alone with a small child, not seeing my family for years, and their having missed out on Kiran's early childhood. They hadn't even seen her.

The Big Freeze, as it was known, lasted until early March and was the coldest winter since 1740. Temperatures plummeted well below freezing. The sea froze off Bournemouth on the south coast, and people were walking across hedgerows and the Thames at Henley. In the midst of this, Mike's younger brother Geoffrey, an airline pilot, decided to get married. The bride, a delightful girl called Betty Duley, and he were married in a small inadequately heated church in Littlehampton on a cruelly cold day. The small wood stove placed in the middle of the church belched forth smoke during the entire service.

⁀

Encouraging letters came regularly from my mother, extolling the virtues of Britain and the British, and were expected to help sustain me. Living in Britain was a lifetime opportunity, and I was expected to exploit this experience. Then, out of the blue, came a letter from Ann to say she was about to become engaged to a Tamil cardiologist in Vellore. I wondered why she had not mentioned him before. Perhaps she thought I would disapprove. The young man in question and I had been contemporaries at Vellore. He was two years ahead of me. Brilliant, handsome, flamboyant and cocky, he graduated when he was only twenty-one. He had come to Britain for experience, and after only eighteen months, again at a very early age, had passed the exams to become a member of the Royal College of Physicians. He returned to work in Vellore. His name was Israel Purushotham Sukumar, and he was called Suku by everyone. He was a Christian. My mother, who had an aversion to Tamil men, disapproved of this relationship, as did his parents. Suku, on his return from England, was much in demand as a suitable bridegroom. His parents had intended an arranged marriage for him, with a bride from a wealthy, prominent Christian family who would pay a handsome dowry. My mother flatly refused to pay a dowry on principle. She said she was not going to bribe a man to marry her daughter. My mother hoped the wedding would be called off. I wrote to Ann to say that, if she wanted to marry Suku, I would fully support her, and that she must stand up to our mother, who could be very unreasonable. We did not phone each other because calls were so expensive. In the four years we lived in England, we did not make a single international call. Suku was adamant he would marry Ann, and to his credit said he did not want a dowry. Ann was three years older than Suku, and this was another excuse for his father, an odious fundamentalist, to advise against the marriage. His mother was a gentle, meek woman, who quietly agreed with her husband.

The wedding took place in St George's Cathedral, Madras, with six hundred guests. I could not attend it as the airfare to India was prohibitive. I was sure that if the respective in-laws did not interfere, the marriage would survive. It did.

∫

Michael passed his final exam at his first attempt in the summer, to become a Fellow of the Royal College of Surgeons. He wanted to move on from Lewisham Hospital and have a year with more responsibility at registrar level, and got a post at Newmarket General Hospital. The job was to start just as I was finishing my year's traineeship in general practice.

I did not learn much medicine during that one year, but I did learn a good deal about human behaviour and, once again, the wretchedness of the human condition. There were many West Indian patients in the areas I worked in, and I came to know many of them, their culture and their ways, some of which I found very strange. I also realised how acutely they suffered from racial prejudice.

Bertie urged us to settle in Britain, and offered me a partnership in his practice. I was sorry to leave him and the other staff but I was convinced general practice was not for me. Somehow I could not cerebrate.

Chapter 21

GOODBYE TO ENGLAND—FOREVER

In mid-October we were ready to move to Newmarket, a town near Cambridge, famous for its stables and horse-racing. Leaving behind our furniture, carpets and curtains, to the delight of the Hospital Secretary, we got all our belongings into our mini-van. Michael was not able to leave his hospital before nightfall, so it was midnight before we arrived in Newmarket to collect the keys for our three-bedroomed hospital flat. Situated across the main road from the hospital, it was newly built and fully furnished, but the heating was centrally controlled, which meant that it came on according to calendar dates, and not according to the prevalent temperature. This was decreed by the hospital treasurer, Mr M. We were often desperately cold. Rent for the flat, as well as for heating, was deducted from Mike's monthly salary.

There were three other flats in the block, all occupied by junior doctors and their young families. They were English or Scottish, and it was such a pleasant change to be among friendly people with a great sense of humour, a British characteristic nowhere better seen than in the satirical television comedy series *That was the Week that Was*. We tried never to miss it, and it had us and Britain rocking with laughter. Our flats were built around what was to be a grassed quadrangle, suitable for children to play on. Instead it was now piled high with builders' rubble, including metal and glass. The flats had been occupied for over a year, but no attempt had been made to clear this rubbish. Repeated requests to the Hospital Secretary, Mr H, to clear the area had met with the response that Mr M, the treasurer, would not release the necessary funds. We were surprised at this negative attitude, as we had found hospital administrative staff to be sympathetic and helpful towards junior doctors, appreciating the severe stress we worked under.

A few weeks after we arrived, Michael asked Mr H to have the rubble dump removed, it being a magnet and a hazard for the

children living in the flats. Again, there was no response. Michael
made a large poster which read: 'THIS AREA IS ADMINISTERED
BY NEWMARKET GENERAL HOSPITAL MANAGEMENT
COMMITTEE.' He hoisted it onto a pole and stuck it in the
middle of the unsightly dump. Soon, passers-by on the road stopped
to read it and started laughing. Mr M and Mr H heard about it
and came to inspect the site. They were enraged. They ordered
Mike to take the poster down immediately. He refused. They
reported him to his consultant, Mr Taggart, whose response was
that Mike was the best registrar he had ever had, and he fully
supported his efforts to clear the dump. A porter came and took
the pole away. The following week, workmen came and cleared
the rubble, and the area was levelled and grassed over.

The following month, I was in the kitchen one night, having
just made a pot of soup, when Mike walked in from work. He
announced that John F. Kennedy had been assassinated. It has
been said that everyone knows where they were on 22 November,
and what they were doing.

Nineteen sixty-three, Philip Larkin notwithstanding, had
been a memorable year. The snow had lain till March, Ann had
married, Michael had become a Fellow of the Royal College of
Surgeons and our finances had stabilised, thanks to my having
found reasonably remunerated work as a GP. On the political
front, the country was riveted by the scandal of the Profumo
affair and the Great Train Robbery, and to a lesser extent by
the more important matter of the country's marvellous railway
system being axed. For me, as the end of the year approached, it
meant we would be returning to India the following year. Mike
had been in touch with Dr Shoemaker, the American missionary
Director of the ETCM Hospital in Kolar, near Bangalore, where
we intended to spend the rest of our working lives. She and the
staff were very welcoming. She hoped I too would work, and
wanted Mike to take over from her as Director. He wrote back
that all he wanted to do was work as a surgeon.

I was keen to work again before we left England. The only post
which might be available in Newmarket was that of a Senior

House Officer in Obstetrics and Gynaecology (OG), a speciality I had had experience of in Vellore and Sheppey, and which I did not like. I regarded every birth as a crisis and used to worry endlessly, and unnecessarily.

The post was to be advertised in a few months. I was enjoying the time I was spending with Kiran, who was two and a great talker. I went to see the consultant, to tell him I would be applying. He had heard about Mike, and to my surprise said I could have the job without a formal interview and without it being advertised. As it entailed much on-call and weekend work, I asked my mother to come and stay with us for six months. We would all return to India together. She jumped at the idea. In the meantime, I spent a few hours a week in the Pathology department assisting with a research project for one of the consultants. I came to know most of the technical staff, the 'backroom boys' of medical care, without whom hospitals could not function.

⌒

My mother was delighted to be in England again and enjoyed her lively, talkative grandchild. Kiran's life became more interesting. They went on train and bus rides, to the seaside, to Cambridge, and visited gardens and bookshops. My mother had a knack of making friends easily and was invited to many homes in Newmarket. The Chelsea Flower Show in May gave her as much pleasure as it had done four years earlier.

I did not enjoy my work. My consultant was rather grim and serious, and had some strange views. He was forever encouraging women, in the early months of pregnancy, to have abortions. These were the days before the Abortion Act of 1967, which made abortions legal up to twenty-eight weeks and was later modified. He complained that these isles—that is, Britain—were over-populated, and that we did not want more undesirable people. He would find some medical reason to justify these abortions. I remember one perfectly healthy working-class woman in her thirties, twenty-four weeks pregnant with her fourth child. She had had high blood pressure in her first pregnancy but not in the two subsequent ones, nor in this one. My consultant tried to persuade her to have an abortion, in case her blood pressure went up again. She and her husband were reluctant, but they finally agreed. I was deeply unhappy about this. I was opposed to abortion on principle, but felt, like war, it was sometimes necessary, but certainly not on this occasion. I discussed the situation with the nurses and fellow junior doctors, and said I was about to tell my consultant that I felt unable to assist him with the termination. They said it was unwise to cross one's consultant, and that I would lose my job. I was prepared to take the risk. Mike fully supported me.

I told my consultant that I felt what he was doing was wrong, and I could not assist him.

He said, 'I respect your views. I will do the abortion at the end of the operating list, and you can leave the operating theatre after the previous operation.' The matter was never mentioned again. To make matters worse, the porter who disposed of the body of the aborted foetus said it was squirming all the way to the incinerator.

But it was not just foetuses of the lower classes that were seen off. Another woman had been admitted for termination of her third pregnancy. She had had postnatal depression after her first, but not her second. She was clearly very upset at the thought of an abortion. She wanted the child badly. I suggested she go home. She took my advice. I asked my consultant why he had advised a termination.

He said, 'I know her family doctor well. She is one of these middle-class liberals who let their children run wild, running around barefoot, and climbing trees and falling off them. They are always in the casualty department with broken bones and things. They are a nuisance.'

'I knew someone,' I said. 'He had six children, and between them they have had several broken bones. They ran wild, walked barefoot, climbed buildings and hung upside down from trees. They have grown up into splendid adults. He was at one time the Hunterian Professor of Surgery at the Royal College of Surgeons.' I was referring to a pioneering hand surgeon. My consultant laughed. He did not refer to the woman again, nor did he reprimand me for discharging her. A few years later, when East Pakistan ceded from West Pakistan to become Bangladesh, many pregnancies resulted from rapes during the war. He offered his services to abort these pregnancies.

The gravest situation I was faced with while working in Newmarket concerned a Jehovah's Witness, admitted one night while miscarrying an eight-week pregnancy. Bleeding heavily, with a haemoglobin of 7 gms (normal: 12–15 gms), she refused a blood transfusion and made me promise she would not have one if she had to have an anaesthetic. I gave her my word. I believe that if adults wish to die for their beliefs, they must be allowed to do so. I also discovered from her case notes that three years earlier twins were born to her with a severe rhesus blood problem, and it was known that immediately after birth they would need life-saving blood transfusions. She and her husband refused to have them transfused. At birth, the babies were removed from their parents, made wards of the Court and transfused, and then returned to their parents. They survived.

I put up an intravenous fluid drip and urgently rang for my consultant, only to be told by his wife that this was his usual night off and he could not be contacted. This was the first I had heard that he had nights off during the week. She suggested I ring his covering consultant in Cambridge. When I rang him, he said he had no knowledge he was covering anyone, and anyway he was not on call. He hung up. It was well known that there was a long-standing feud between the two of them. They had not spoken to each other for years. The Cambridge consultant was a colourful personality but I disliked him. He came one afternoon a week to Newmarket and I assisted him, and looked after his patients. He once summoned me to his changing room in the operating theatre, and while facing me and talking, dropped his trousers. I walked away. He used to tell me how popular he was. He boasted that he was the only man in Britain who could go to his birthday dinner party with his wife on one arm and his ex-wife on the other.

By now, I was frantic. I decided to ring the Medical Superintendent (a role in the NHS later abolished), a consultant anaesthetist. I thought he would advise me and asked the switchboard operator to get him.

She was amused and said, 'Have you not heard? He has made the headlines in one of the tabloids and is lying low. He is not available till further notice.' He was involved in some scandal, his wife having run away with a policeman, and the divorce had just come through.

'Get on with it,' said Mike. 'You had better get her to the operating theatre and do a D&C quickly before she bleeds to death. Ring the consultant anaesthetist on call. Tell him the problem, and he will have to make an exception, and anaesthetise the patient even though the haemoglobin is so low.'

The consultant anaesthetist, a Catholic, further added to the increasingly desperate situation. As I started to talk to him, he interrupted:

'I know the patient's husband. He is my milkman. Just when I am on the verge of converting my Anglican wife of twenty years to Catholicism, he is pestering her to become a Jehovah's Witness. The house is full of these silly pamphlets. I don't care that the patient has refused a blood transfusion. I insist she have one. Send her blood specimen to the lab for an urgent cross-match. You can get her to the operating theatre and we can start straightaway, and give her blood at the end of the procedure.'

There was no time to argue and I did as he said. But I also spoke to the lab technician, whom I knew well, and made him aware of the problem. I pleaded with him to refuse to issue the blood when requested, and to say there was a compatibility problem. He agreed.

Once the patient was under, I quickly curetted her uterus and the bleeding stopped immediately. But she was even paler. The anaesthetist sent a porter to the lab for some blood. He came back empty handed. 'Damn,' said the anaesthetist, and walked out of the operating theatre. The patient recovered, and went home two days later with a supply of iron tablets.

The next day, I told my consultant what had happened the previous night. The experience had completely wrung me out. He showed no sympathy or interest. He just shrugged his shoulders and said, 'It was my night off.'

I had never been happy working in OG and I did not feel any different after my experiences at Newmarket. I wondered where I would end up, as I was yet to find a branch of medicine that satisfied me.

We started to prepare for our return to India. Mike ordered surgical instruments he would need. He also collected obsolete instruments and out-of-date medicines, which though not acceptable in Britain, would be of great use in India. There were several household items I could buy in Britain but were unavailable in India, and this was my last opportunity to get them. This included a double-drainer stainless steel sink and a Dunlop tennis racket. Mike had told me there were two good tennis courts in Kolar. I looked forward to playing tennis again after several years. My mother and I paid a visit to Oxford Street in London, where I bought her several robia voile saris from Selfridges. They stocked them for their Indian customers, for whom they were a great luxury.

Mike's brother Desmond, a pilot with Air India, made all the arrangements with their cargo section to fly our numerous pieces of luggage to Madras. The mini-van now had windows cut into its sides, and felt more like a car and was easier to drive. Mike delivered it to the docks for export to India.

We said our goodbyes once again. Robin Tagart, Mike's boss, said there was always a job for him, if he wished to return, and that there was a future for him in England as a consultant. My consultant said I was his most successful junior doctor, whatever that meant. He asked me to send him a pair of leather Kabuli sandals, the sort he had worn when he was in India during the war.

Packed and ready, we rang from the flat for a taxi to take us to Cambridge railway station, and as we drove out of the premises, there was Mr M, the treasurer, standing on the pavement, grinning, his palm outstretched to collect money for the last phone call we had made, for the taxi.

During the week we spent in London with the family, before leaving England, we visited Mr Schmelz, my consultant in Sheppey, who had given me my first job.

Mike's mother wanted to visit India, and we invited her to stay with us for as long as she wanted. Mike was leaving his family behind, but seemed genuinely happy about going back to India. As for me, I did not want to return to England again, even for a visit.

Chapter 22

A MONUMENTAL DISAPPOINTMENT

After four and a half years, I was home at last. Ann, Suku and Cheena were at Madras Airport to meet us. As we drove into the drive of Alpha, my mother's house, I could see the servants lined up in front of the house. Some of the older ones, who had known me for years, were crying. Alpha was almost unrecognisable since I had last seen it. The house had been considerably enlarged. There was an elegant new wing with a double storey, verandahs and terraces. But what astonished me was the garden. It was completely unrecognisable. What had been not much more than a field with small plants now had tall cocoanut and palmyra palms, mature clumps of thick-stemmed bamboos, a multitude of fruit trees: pomegranate, papaya, sapota, pomeloe, lemon and guava, all fruiting heavily. Bordering the drive were bougainvillea and largostraemia in full flower. There were beds of orange zinnia, gaillardia and calendula clashing with magenta portulaca. The gardeners and Cheena had made the garden flourish in my mother's six-month absence.

It was a typical Indian homecoming. Friends, neighbours and relatives all turned up without warning, and met the three-year-old they had not seen. Kiran was the centre of attention for days. They hugged and kissed and played with her. Cheena called her a wonderful child and carried her everywhere, and showed her the brightly coloured birds she had never seen. This little extrovert revelled in the attention. Though it was October, the heat was stifling and we slept at nights on the top terrace, coming in early to escape the heavy dew.

We paid a visit to Annie Lodge. Eddie Uncle had retired and returned from Burma. This was now his home, where he lived with his family, including Tom, his second son who had married and had three daughters. Samson Uncle still lived there and was allowed to keep his room. Annie Lodge was not the same without Thatha.

Two weeks later we left for Kolar, a small town forty miles from Bangalore where Mike and I had been at different boarding schools at different times. Its neighbour, Kolar Gold Fields, was more famous and had been developed by the British. A large colony of them, and Eurasians, had lived there for many years. It looked as though the entire staff of the Ellen Thoburn Cowen Hospital (ETCM), the Mission hospital we were to work in, was on the station platform to meet us. The road to the hospital had flags and streamers. In traditional fashion, banana trees with clusters of bananas were placed on either side of the road. Everywhere there were banners and posters that said, 'Welcome to the Cartners'. We cringed with embarrassment. Michael said, 'I don't like this. This is crazy.' We had come to work in a small Mission hospital, because we felt it was the right thing to do, and we were uncomfortable with all this adulation.

The hospital was run by an American missionary doctor, ES, and an Indian administrator. ES had come to Kolar as a young woman and was now in her sixties. Softly spoken, she was made of steel. The administrator, who was not very bright, had gone to a local college and was the son of ES's cook, an illiterate woman. ES had arranged for the administrator to have his training in America. She had also arranged his marriage to the daughter of the matron of the hospital. The matron was a widowed Brahmin, disowned by her community, and had sought refuge, as a young woman, in the Mission hospital. She trained as a nurse, converted to Christianity and was given special status by the missionaries, because she was a Brahmin. Missionaries in India regarded the conversion of Brahmins to Christianity as a triumph, and treated them preferentially, to the annoyance of other Indian Christians.

Despite his protests, Mike was made the Director of the hospital. He was told by ES that he would treat all the male patients in the hospital. There was a middle-aged Indian lady doctor who treated the female patients. Mike refused flatly to go along with this long-held policy. He said he was a surgeon. He would treat all surgical patients, male and female. ES reluctantly agreed. Mike had not bothered to enquire about the terms and conditions of his appointment, including his salary.

'I would like to know how much you are going to earn,' I said to Mike.

'So would I,' he replied.

Salaries were set by ES and the administrator, and though Mike was supposed to be the Director, his salary was considerably less than the administrator's. He accepted this without making an issue of it.

During the next few weeks we tried to meet as many staff as possible. Some said that now we had arrived, they hoped there would be a new culture of justice and fairness. We were perplexed.

There was a very large house called Big Bungalow (BB) very near to the house allocated to us. In the BB, there were four small flats and a communal dining room for the missionaries. Apart from ES, there was the anaesthetist, Dr C, a large jolly American with blue-tinted grey hair, given to enjoying the simple luxuries that life had to offer, during weekend trips to Bangalore. Another one was Miss N, a fiery English public health nurse, who had worked with my sister, Ann, in Vellore. After retirement, she refused to return to Britain as was expected of missionaries. Kolar gave her employment. She found the chaos of outpatients, and her ignorance of the local language, too difficult to handle, and spent much of her time shouting and pushing patients. There was also a young Scottish woman, Jean, a radiographer, who had come to develop the X-ray department and was taken under the wing of Dr C. She was not a missionary, and enjoyed the trips with Dr C to Bangalore for some good eating. Jean was heard to remark to Dr C that she thought it ridiculous that the administrator was paid more than the senior doctors. The missionaries in India had enhanced pay scales, paid for by their Missions. We Indians found this quite acceptable.

It soon became obvious that ES, with her soft gentle voice, ruled the hospital. She was called Doctor-amma by everyone as a mark of respect. Not only did she expect total obedience, but adulation as well, from time to time, when her birthday and other events came along. Her birthday was approaching, and the administrator's wife, with whom I was trying to establish a rapport, asked me what present I proposed to give Doctor-amma.

'Nothing,' I replied. 'I might send Kiran with a few roses from my small garden.'

'She won't like that. I am giving her a gold chain. Doctor-amma likes jewellery.'

I was taken aback, but sent the roses all the same and ES did not seem offended.

෴

At the age of three, Kiran was expected to attend kindergarten at the local Christian school, where the medium of instruction was Canarese. The head teacher told me she would pick up the language in no time. But she did not, and came home every day saying that everyone in school spoke rubbish. She did not like school, and would run and hide under the bed when the school bus came to pick her up.

We decided to keep Kiran at home with Mary, the ayah, who spoke fluent English. She had been ayah to the children of my mother's great friend, Audrey Forret, since Censor's Office days. The Forrets had returned to Britain years earlier, but Mary had remained in touch with my mother. Ayahs who had worked for Europeans regarded themselves as superior to other servants, and Mary regarded herself as even more superior as she had been to Scotland with the Forrets during a year's furlough. She was unmarried and lived with a niece in Madras. Quite old now, she agreed to work for us only because we had come from England. I was Madam and Mike was Sir. She insisted on cooking for us, but what she decided we should eat was quite different from what we wanted, which was some hot curries. She was a poor cook, and lazy as well. The cooking was done on a kerosene stove, and she was too lazy to turn it off when it was not in use. The result was a huge kerosene bill. She was also constantly quarrelling with the young maid who was employed to assist her. But worst of all she started to steal, and though sad when she left after a few months, we were relieved.

Mary's replacement was Philomena, a twenty-five-year-old plump, buxom, low-caste Catholic. We took to each other at once. She had four children, the oldest of whom was nine. She assured me she had someone to look after them. I then discovered she was pregnant. She coped well until the baby's birth. She insisted on returning four weeks after the baby was born. I let her bring the baby to work, and we enjoyed seeing him grow. She asked Kiran what she should call him.

'Peter Rabbit' came the reply. And that is how he was christened. I urged Philomena to get sterilised. It is what she and her husband Anthony, a peon in an office, wanted. But she said she would be in trouble with her Holy Father, the local Catholic priest. I told her he was not to know. These priests had a great hold over their parishioners, and if the women did not get pregnant regularly, they would be interrogated in very threatening ways. I finally persuaded her to have a contraceptive coil fitted and told her to blame me for it. The Catholic church does much for the poor in India, but as far as population control is concerned, they are a menace and blight the lives of millions.

ES urged me to work part-time in the outpatient department. I took on the role of a general practitioner, as there was no system of primary care. There was no appointments system. I did not speak Canarese and had an interpreter who spoke it, as well as Tamil (the latter being my mother tongue, in which I was fluent). I was to call the interpreter 'Ujji', which meant 'grandmother'. She was tiny and in her late sixties, always dressed in a clean white sari. She was not just an interpreter, but a source of all wisdom and advice, often speaking out of turn to comfort, cajole and advise patients. She would advocate birth control, often remonstrating with husbands who would resist it as they felt it would lead their wives to stray. It was an ongoing problem. I once spent an hour speaking to three men who between them had twenty-seven children, trying to persuade them to allow their wives to be sterilised or to have vasectomies themselves. They agreed it would be a splendid thing, but when the time came they changed their minds, to the disgust of their wives.

Though I played a useful role in my part-time work, I felt someone had to get to grips with birth control, not only in the hospital but for Kolar District as a whole.

A few months later, Mike, Kiran and I were driving from Kolar to Vellore to visit Ann and Suku, when we came across a broken-down van. A white man and his driver were under the bonnet. We stopped and offered assistance. They needed a lift to Vellore, and during lunch at Ann's, the Englishman, a Mr Howard, told us he worked for Oxfam in South India. I mentioned my interest in birth control. He became very excited, and said that was just the sort of thing Oxfam would like to be involved in. He asked me if I would like to draw up plans for a joint project with Oxfam and ETCM Hospital. He said it could be fully funded by Oxfam. When I mentioned it to ES, she was very enthusiastic and welcomed collaboration with Oxfam. Michael was very supportive, and suggested we base it on the Roadside and Eye Camp programmes of Vellore. We would go to the people, rather than they come to us. We would go into the villages and set up temporary clinics and camps, preceded by intense publicity. We would offer contraceptive advice and materials, and perform tubal ligations on women and vasectomies on men. We met Mr Howard and outlined these plans. He was ecstatic. Oxfam would supply all the necessary materials, including transport, fully equipped vans, tents and so on. We would supply the staff. In five years we could make a significant reduction to the birth rate in the district. Mike and I involved the administrator at every step, but right from the onset he tried to block every move, making some excuse or other. Mike and I were devastated, and to add to our exasperation, ES started to support him to the point of eventually becoming hostile to all our ideas. Michael and I were totally perplexed and crestfallen, and eventually had to abandon the project. Mr Howard went away a disappointed man. We subsequently heard from members of staff that this was the history of the hospital. Ideas and initiatives were stifled, unless they came from ES or the administrator. Perhaps this explained why it was such a backward hospital.

⁘

I was becoming increasingly worried about Michael. He was swamped with work. Junior doctors were usually short-term locums who moved on, and he relied a lot on nurses. He was promised an assistant before he came to Kolar, but none materialised. ES said a young doctor who was completing his training in Vellore would be joining Mike soon. This turned out to be the administrator's brother-in-law, a personable young man.

Mike was becoming further frustrated as there were no adequate Pathology services to back up his surgery. Biopsies and specimens had to be sent away for analysis and reports, which would take days and sometimes weeks to arrive. The other branches of Pathology were undeveloped. The only solution was for me to go to Vellore to do a one-year intensive course in Pathology, leading to a Diploma in Clinical Pathology, and return. I would take Kiran with me and stay with Ann and Suku. They had a large house on the hospital campus. I could rely on Philomena to take care of Mike and the house, and he would have his meals with the missionaries in the Big Bungalow. Michael agreed with much reluctance. ES thought it a good idea, and encouraged Mike to spend an occasional weekend in Vellore with us. I would of course have to apply and be accepted on the course in Vellore, but I knew both the professors from my student days, and spoke to them. They were very encouraging.

I had become increasingly uneasy about other aspects of life in Kolar. All geared up to use my new tennis racket, I was informed by one of the senior male nurses that women did not play tennis in Kolar. It was not their culture. I said it was time to change that culture, and I knew some female nurses in the hospital who were longing to learn how to play the game. He gave me a disapproving look. I had no support from Mike, who just shrugged his shoulders and said I should accept things the way they were.

A few weeks after we arrived in Kolar, the administrator's wife said that, as the Director's wife, it was demeaning for me to be going to the butcher's to buy meat.

'Send a servant,' she said.

'But I don't have one at that hour of the morning.' The best meat had to be bought early in the day.

'Send a hospital gardener or a peon. They start work early. That's what I do,' she added.

I told her I did not think it was appropriate to use hospital staff for my private needs. She was not offended. She just thought I had strange ideas.

A year after we arrived in Kolar, I started the one-year course in Vellore, leading to a Diploma in Clinical Pathology. It was based on a similar course at the Royal Postgraduate School in Hammersmith, London. Kiran and I were very comfortable in Ann's house. She had an excellent cook, who was also ayah to Kiran. Ann was pregnant and suffering badly from morning sickness, and had gone to Alpha for a month. That she had become pregnant was a great relief to us. She had been married for three years, and her father-in-law had been making uncharitable remarks about her failure to get pregnant, and had been heard to say that 'women who do not have issue, should be put away'. He was given to using biblical language. In India, women are expected to produce an infant nine months after marriage, or at least to get pregnant in the first year of marriage.

I started my course and was very motivated. Unlike in my undergraduate days, I did not allow myself to be distracted or to procrastinate. I worked very hard, going back to the Pathology department after dinner, when Kiran had gone to sleep, and returning home only at midnight. Ann's house was one of many on the hospital campus, and there were many children for Kiran to play with. They all spoke English and went to the local convent in a rickshaw. She was four, and joined them. They were pushed very hard by the nuns and given homework, which we did not let her do. She came home one day and said, 'I have zams next week.' And then, 'What are zams?' The exams were in maths and English and she was ranked fiftieth in her class of sixty. My mother strongly disapproved of this school, and from time to time she and Cheena would drive to Vellore to see us, and take Kiran back to Alpha for a few weeks. She loved these breaks from school, and for the last three months of my course stayed happily with my mother.

⌣

The discipline of Pathology embraced four subjects: Haematology and Blood Transfusion, Biochemistry, Microbiology, and Histology. I spent three months in each section. The training was outstanding. Ann and Suku would return from work in the evenings and remain at home, apart from Suku's night rounds.

Kiran enjoyed being with them. Mike visited twice a month and would occasionally take Kiran back to Kolar for a few days, to be lovingly looked after by Philomena, who was enjoying a long pregnancy-free period, thanks to her coil. She had not as yet been approached by her Holy Father.

Mike was becoming more and more dissatisfied with the set-up in Kolar. Being a fully qualified surgeon, and that from Britain too, he was attracting an abundance of rich patients to the hospital, greatly improving its coffers. The trouble with Indian patients is that they feel they own their doctors, and some of them started visiting Mike at our home, and inviting him to theirs. He resisted the latter, making his busy work an excuse. But in conversation with outsiders, he learned that the hospital had been mired in recent scandals involving very senior staff. When he tried to get at the truth, there was a wall of silence. And then he discovered the surgical assistant ES had been promising him had registered for a three-year postgraduate course in Vellore, and his sponsor for the course was none other than ES herself. And all the while, she had lied to Mike that the surgical assistant would be joining him. Mike was very perplexed.

Ann gave birth to a boy, Mithran, the following March. I was delighted for her that it was a boy, as her father-in-law had been going on and on about how essential it was for the male line to be propagated. Suku's three siblings were girls.

I was due to take my exam in October of the same year. In June, on one of his visits to Vellore, Mike said he had resigned his job in Kolar and intended to return to England in August, a few months later, after Kiran's birthday. I was flabbergasted. He had not discussed his plans with me. He saw my dismay, and said Kiran and I could join him after my exam. We could make our plans for the future, while we worked in England for the next year or two. He had been in touch with Robin Tagart, the Newmarket surgeon, since leaving England. There would be a job for Mike, and with further training, he was certain Mike could get a consultant's post. To me this was pie in the sky. There was tremendous competition among British graduates for consultant posts in general surgery. There was no room for foreign graduates, who could get a look-in only in less popular specialities such as ENT and eye surgery. Orthopaedics was also a less popular speciality. I had no wish to see Mike condemned to a permanent sub-consultant role for the rest of his life. It might have been all right for now. But in twenty years' time, he could find it frustrating, working under a young, inexperienced consultant.

ES accepted Mike's resignation, and did not ask him to reconsider it. She organised a farewell party. The administrator said nothing. Mike's staff were shocked; some wept openly. In the short time he had been in Kolar, he had started the process of improving their salaries and working conditions. More importantly, he involved them in policy decisions.

When news of Mike's resignation got around Kolar, a group of wealthy businessmen approached him to say they would build a private hospital for him in six months, and asked him to stay on and run it. He felt it would be unethical to have another institution in Kolar, competing with ETCM.

But I felt all was not lost. A Tamil friend, Harry Daniel, who had become the first Indian priest to be in charge of St Mark's Cathedral in Bangalore, knew of Mike's situation. Closely connected with the Church of South India (ex-Anglican) Hospital in Bangalore, he asked Mike if he would consider the post of Head of Surgery. Mike agreed. The department was being run by a young, inexperienced Englishman, Dr R, who had no postgraduate surgical qualification. A meeting of the hospital board was hastily convened to ratify Mike's appointment. The matron, an English missionary, said Mike was acceptable, but on condition he agreed to work under Dr R, who should remain Head of Surgery. Harry, who had spent many years in Britain, pointed out that Mike was much more experienced and was an FRCS. She retorted that Mike was only an Indian graduate, whereas Dr R was a British graduate, and therefore superior. Dr R, clearly embarrassed, remarked that this was not so, that Mike should be the head, and he would be happy to work with him. The Bishop of the Diocese, an Englishman, who was chairing the meeting, sat on the fence and remained silent. Harry was disgusted and advised Mike not to take up the appointment. Mike made up his mind to return to England. He was obviously more attached to his family, especially his mother, than I had realised. Our house had to be dismantled. The kitchen sink had yet to be installed. There was no dearth of takers for the things we had brought from England. Anything foreign, often spelt *phoren* by Indians, was much valued. Philomena wept. We found her another employer and promised to keep in touch. Over the decades we helped to educate her children. Two more were born to her, after she confessed to her Holy Father that she was using contraception. Her coil was removed. She had eight children in all. Her mother had sixteen.

Dr ES was as pleasant as ever when she bade us goodbye. I think she was secretly pleased Mike was leaving. She wanted the hospital to stay the way it had been. Besides, she must have been worried we would find out about the scandals, which we finally did, from the Kolar businessmen. We would have left, anyway, because it would not have been possible to work with people for whom we had lost respect.

⌣

I had two more months before I took the exam for a Diploma in Clinical Pathology. The course was exacting but very interesting. The only part I found distasteful was doing autopsies, especially when I was required to do them late at night, or in the early hours, something not done in the West. I was on call for autopsies on only seven days during the three months I was in Histopathology, but for me, that was enough. It was necessary in a hot country like India, with inadequate mortuary facilities, for relatives to take bodies home for cremation or burial as soon as possible after death. Vellore, because it was famous, attracted patients from all over India, and the time it took to take a body home, often hundreds of miles away, was a major consideration. Permission for autopsies was seldom given, and when it was, despite conditions imposed by distressed relatives, the opportunity had to be grabbed, as it was the only way experience and material for research could be obtained.

The night duty mortuary technician would walk from the mortuary to my sister's house on the hospital campus. He would come to my bedroom window, hold up a lantern and call, 'Amaaaah.' I would get up with a start, and see this brown, morose face, lit up by the lantern. I would throw on a few clothes, and be escorted by him to the mortuary, hoping I would not tread on a snake or scorpion on the way. After the autopsy, which could take about two hours, I would inject blood vessels with a preservative, and stuff the body cavity, from which I had removed the organs, with straw or coir soaked in formalin, a powerful preservative. Preservation was an inducement for giving permission for an autopsy. It would delay decomposition.

After Kiran's fifth birthday, Mike had left for England and my mother persuaded me to let her take Kiran to live with her in Alpha. There she roamed around the garden, climbed trees, and made trips to the city and beach and to Buharis roof-top restaurant, where the friendly waiters served her with her favourite foods: tomato soup and baked beans on toast.

I worked hard and accumulated much knowledge quickly, but to no avail, as far as Kolar was concerned. However, engaging with any subject produces more and more interest in that subject, and I decided my career would be in Pathology, but as to which discipline within it, I was not yet sure.

I took my written exams in Madras, in Examination Hall, one of many imposing buildings on the Marina, the second longest sea road in the world. So well prepared was I, that the exams held no fears for me. The two-day practicals were held in Madras Medical College. They were harrowing but uneventful, except that halfway through the autopsy I was required to do on an emaciated unclaimed body, which was thought to be cancerous, I had to abandon it. Never have I seen such an advanced state of tuberculosis. Being an infectious disease, it was too risky to proceed, and the mortuary technicians were hastily summoned by the examiners to take the body away to the incinerator.

I passed.

At the request of Professor Robert Carman, a haematologist, I spent the next two months in Vellore working with him. A young and enthusiastic American, I found him an inspiration during the three months I spent in the Haematology department. Here was a discipline in which I could spend my working life.

Ann and my mother were deeply shocked at Mike's decision to go back to England, but they were neither critical nor judgemental.

My mother reminded me that the problems of Kolar and Bangalore were widespread in Mission hospitals, and finding a satisfactory hospital would not be easy. Working in a Government Hospital had never been an option for us. Jessie Aunty and Samson Uncle, whom we saw often after our return, could not understand why Mike wanted to return to England. My mother hoped I would be happier in England this time. We left the mini-van for her. She enjoyed driving it, and she and it were forever an object of curiosity.

Kiran wanted her father back and said she wanted to stay in India. We told her she would go to a wonderful school in England, where she would not have zams, and have to learn her nine times table.

I wondered how I would manage the flight to London with a small child. Because of air sickness, I needed to drug myself into a comatose state. This was solved by our taking two separate flights on the same day, arranged by an uncle (by marriage) who was manager of Air India at the Madras Office. We both left on Christmas morning, I via Moscow and Kiran later via Western Europe. One air hostess was solely responsible for Kiran. My mother and Ann were allowed on to the aircraft with Kiran. Ann said my mother wept, took off the gold chain she had worn since she was a child, and put it round Kiran's neck. The parting did not affect Kiran, who was consumed with excitement, and distracted that she was travelling alone.

Chapter 23

RACE AND POWELL

My plane landed gently at Heathrow in the late afternoon, just before the winter sun was disappearing below the horizon. London was bathed in a golden glow. Mike and Kiran met me, and we drove straight to Delicia's house for a delayed Christmas lunch. It was a gathering of the entire clan, all fourteen of them to meet us. There was a new member, a flaxen-haired two-year-old Nicola, who was my god-daughter. Her parents were Betty and Geoffrey.

We left for Doddington the same evening as Mike was on call. He had a flat in the hospital grounds, and we arrived on a bitterly cold frosty night. The heating had been switched off for the few days Mike was away, and he had forgotten to ask the maid to switch it on again. It could only be switched on later the next morning. The three of us jumped into the icy-cold bed and huddled together, but we could not get warm. Kiran kept wailing, 'Take me back to my Paati. Take me back to India.' I felt the same way. Mike moved to another room to get some sleep. My spirits sank to an all-time low.

Doddington was a small village near March in Cambridgeshire. It had a small hospital with core specialities. Robin Tagart had arranged for a temporary sub-consultant post to be created to assist Mr C, the full-time consultant approaching retirement. He was a pleasant, frail man, a bachelor, who was pleased to more or less hand over everything to Mike. From what I could see, Mike, who had been in post for four months, was permanently on call, but was not particularly busy. We enrolled Kiran in the local primary school when it opened after the Christmas holidays. She came home ecstatic after the first day, and said it was the best school in the world. She was the only non-white child in the school and was soon being called 'Black face, black face,' which led her, undaunted, to knock on the door of the headmaster's study and go in.

'Headmaster,' she said. 'The children do not know their colours. My face is brown. It is my hair that is black.'

He agreed, and said he would speak to the children. He told us this amusing story when we met him and his wife at dinner in Mr C's house.

If he gave up his first choice, general surgery, to improve his chances of becoming a consultant, the only other speciality Mike was prepared to consider was Orthopaedic Surgery, in which he had some considerable experience. We decided to apply for registrar (mid-career) posts in Orthopaedics and Pathology respectively, wherever these were advertised in the same hospital. We were not going to be separated again. Every week we scoured the job section of the *British Medical Journal*. After a few weeks, two such jobs came up at the newly built Royal Infirmary at Huddersfield in Yorkshire, a northern county. We applied and were shortlisted to appear at interview, both on the same day at the Leeds General Infirmary. What if only one of us was successful? What would the other do? We would cross this hurdle when we came to it. We were both successful. We were offered, to rent, a new two-bedroom house near the hospital, which we accepted. Geoffrey advised us to buy a house as soon as possible, and offered to lend us the deposit.

'What!' said family, friends and colleagues. 'Surely, you are not going up north. There are plenty of jobs in London and the south. They are strangers up there.' We had never been to the north of England. The way the southerners spoke of their northern neighbours, it sounded like another country. We did not change our minds, and never regretted our move to the north.

∽

Mike's mother had lived with Delicia since his father had died eight years previously. The arrangement had not been satisfactory, and she did not have the confidence to live alone. When Geoffrey and Betty had asked her to live with them in Nottingham, two years earlier, she had jumped at it. Now, they were offering her to us.

'You can have Mum,' said Betty. That is what we called her. I agreed. I was happy for her to live with us and it meant I could work full time. Since I married, my relationship with my mother-in-law had been a good one, and earlier fears had not materialised. Mum said she would be delighted to live with us. Things seemed to be working out for us, and I had Mike's assurance that we would be back in India within two years.

We piled our meagre belongings into a newly acquired Volkswagen Beetle, a discounted demonstration model, and set off for Huddersfield in April 1967. We were perplexed to see large numbers of immigrants from the subcontinent, mainly men, wandering about the town. They were shabbily dressed, unable to speak English, and would have been equally out of place in any of the big towns and cities of India and Pakistan. They lived in ghettoes in the poor section of this rather unattractive town. We learned that they were mainly Pakistanis from the Punjab region, and had been recruited to work in the woollen mills. Some had brought their families. They had come to escape a life of unemployment and poverty in their villages, and having earned adequately, intended to return after a few years to their country. Talking to white taxi drivers, we realised they were deeply resented by the local population. I was soon to learn that Yorkshire people were proud and very insular, preferring to keep to themselves. They even resented people from other parts of Britain moving there, referring to them as 'comers in'.

We had to find a school for Kiran. I wanted her to be privately educated but Mike, with socialist leanings at the time, insisted she went to a state school. We took her to the nearest state primary school to be told that, as an immigrant child, she had to attend the Assessment Centre for one month. The next day we were visited by a social worker. She said it was mandatory for Kiran to attend this Centre, to be taught to speak basic English, to learn to use a knife and fork, and to learn to use a Western-style lavatory.

'But English is the only language she speaks, and she can already read it well; she has always used a Western-style lavatory; and she eats her meals with a knife and fork,' we protested. But to no avail. Rules were rules. The social worker was very unsympathetic. She did not seem to believe us. I felt helpless. We left Kiran at the centre the next day. There was an assortment of children, black, brown and white. The latter were Poles and

Ukranians. When she came home that evening, she complained they were all talking rubbish. She was the only one talking English, but she could at least talk to the staff. Next day, she had to go for a medical assessment. We had no objection to this, as Mike and I had always felt that all persons, children and adults, from the subcontinent, where tropical diseases and tuberculosis were prevalent, should have medical check-ups before entering Britain.

We met the Medical Officer of Health, a down-to-earth middle-aged woman, and told her that Kiran was required to attend the Assessment Centre for a month and we felt distressed by this.

'But this is absurd,' she said. 'The Centre is intended for a different kind of immigrant child, certainly not yours. Can't they see the difference?' She picked up the phone and spoke to someone in authority, then turned to us and said Kiran did not have to go back to the Centre. She was also exempt from 'bussing'. This was a system where immigrant children were dispersed to various schools, so that no one school would have a surfeit of them. Michael and I thoroughly approved of this system, which was opposed by white liberals.

Kiran went to a state primary school within walking distance of our house and was very happy. She was in a class of over thirty pupils. Her teacher was pleased to have a brown child who spoke English and could read and write.

I was the only junior doctor in the Pathology department and was required to work in the sections of Histopathology (called Histology in Britain) and Haematology. This pleased me as these were my preferences, though it meant I had to do autopsies. I worked for two consultants: Alan Barlow (AB) and Roda Allison (RA), two splendid people who immediately put me at my ease. AB, a brilliant man, was a Lancastrian, from a working-class background. Through the grammar school system, he had found his way to medical school. He was a haematologist, but liked to dabble in Histology as well. He had a thriving private practice but did not neglect his NHS work. RA was the Histologist and much older, a small, eccentric, grey-haired lady, with her hair in a little bun. She had come late to medicine, having had to overcome opposition from her upper-middle-class parents to attend university. She lived on her own, but not entirely on her own, as she kept twenty-six dogs. Their heated kennels were larger than her unheated bungalow in Brighouse, in Yorkshire. She bred mastiffs and had six of these enormous dogs. She had the passenger seat of her car removed to accommodate one of these beasts, so they could drive around with her. She would sometimes take me with her to visit other hospitals. I would sit in the back seat, terrified of this lion-like creature accompanying us. There was a third consultant, DG, who was near retirement and did very little.

We set about looking for a house to buy. The hospital house was too small. Mum needed a large bedroom to herself, though she did not complain. Mike's secretary told him about a new development in Almondbury, a pleasant suburb, and urged him to buy a house there. We saw these houses advertised in the *Guardian*, our daily newspaper. We had read the *Daily Telegraph* when we lived in Britain before, but now decided it was too right wing. A building firm, C&W, was selling the houses through an estate agent in Huddersfield. We visited the site, liked it and the look of the show house, and told the little man in the hut taking deposits that we would be back the following Sunday if we decided to buy a house. Mum, Kiran and I returned to put down the deposit on a half-built house. Mike was on call. The little man asked to speak to us outside the hut.

'I'm really sorry,' he said. 'The building firm refuses to sell to you because you are coloured.'

I think he was genuinely sorry. I was speechless, as was my lily-white mother-in-law. We went home and told Mike. He was enraged.

'Let's get out of this wretched country as soon as possible,' he said. There was no comment or word of criticism, comfort or encouragement from his mother. I wondered if she was thinking that had her son not married an Indian, he and she would not be in this humiliating situation. It was impractical for us to leave the country at that time. We looked for another house, this time not in a development or through an agent. A very suitable house, nearer the hospital and near a park, was being sold privately. I rang to make an appointment for viewing, and a pleasant middle-class voice answered, a woman. We arranged a mutually convenient time for us to look at the house. Just before I put the phone down I said, 'I want you to know I am Indian.' There was a pause and then she said, 'I'm afraid, I cannot sell to you. I am sorry.'

When I told Mike, he shook his head and said nothing. Neither did his mother, and I thought I saw a smirk on her face.

The next day the phone rang and a man said, 'You spoke to my wife yesterday about a house. I am ashamed at what she said to you, and I am apologising on her behalf. If you are still interested, we would be happy to sell it to you. Would you like to come round this evening?'

We bought the house, a handsome three-bedroom semi-detached, with a black-and-white mock-Tudor façade and a moderate-sized garden.

I was not prepared to let the insult of the Almondbury house rest. Mike told me we should put it behind us and move on. I would have, but for the fact that it was advertised in *The Guardian*, which prided itself as a liberal newspaper. I wrote to its northern editor, Brian Redhead, and asked him why his paper was advertising for a building firm that was racist, and told him of my experience. Back came a reply from him, in his large handwriting, three pages of it. He was appalled, and had contacted Mr Couper of C&W, who himself was a *Guardian* reader. His firm had no idea that racism was involved in the sale of his properties. He threatened to take away the contract from the Huddersfield agent, unless he stopped this unsavoury practice. Mr C asked Brian Redhead to tell me to go to the Almondbury site, and choose whichever available plot or house I wanted. I expressed my deepest gratitude to Brian Redhead, and told him we had already found a house. I remembered what my mother had said to me years ago about the British.

Our neighbours gave us a warm welcome and we did not encounter any problems when buying houses in the future, but the experience left a lasting wariness. I was always apprehensive when buying a house again. The Race Relations Act of 1976 was a great leap forward. It might not have changed attitudes or feelings, but it altered behaviour. My consultants took a keen interest in my welfare and were very distressed at what took place. RA asked us to come and live with her. She tried to console me by telling me how much gender discrimination she had faced. She thought it was the same as racism. But I could not agree with her. Race discrimination does not condemn just the person concerned, but future and unborn generations as well.

We worried about the move to our new house. Mike was required for it, but he had been on call continuously for weeks and thought he might not be available to help. The other registrar he alternated with, a man in his thirties, was struck down with an inoperable cancer, and was on sick leave until he died nine months later. Mike, without complaining, covered for him all this time and his three consultants allowed him to do so. But the weekend we planned to move, the youngest consultant told Mike to take the entire weekend off and covered for him. Junior doctors had a basic salary. No money was paid for being on call.

We settled quickly into our new house. I wanted a cleaner and RA suggested I use hers, a pleasant, reliable, middle-aged woman, called Kathleen. She was delighted to get some extra work.

'Why do you need a cleaning lady?' asked my mother-in law. 'Because I do not want to spend the weekends cleaning the house.' Mum was clearly unhappy about the cleaner, and I could not understand why, as it made her life and mine easier. We had given her a large bedroom, and let her chose her furniture and furnishings, and now once a week her room would be cleaned as well.

Shortly after Kathleen came to work for us, Delicia told Mike that Mum had complained to her that it was not right for a white person to work as a servant for an Indian, and it made her feel uncomfortable. Mike hoped I would dispense with Kathleen. I did not, and she remained with us as long as we were in Huddersfield.

After this, I wondered whether Mum was embarrassed when she sometimes went to pick up her brown grandchild from school, or took her to the local Methodist church with her on Sundays. Mum had been a regular churchgoer all her life. Mike and I had drifted into agnosticism but we wanted Kiran to have belief, and we encouraged her to go to Sunday School, which she enjoyed.

Kiran came into our bedroom one day and asked why Mike's legs were a different colour to hers and mine. I had some explaining to do about her father's race and mine, and she accepted it. But to reduce her confusion, Mike would refer to himself as Indian. This upset his mother, and one day she exclaimed to Kiran, 'Your father is NOT Indian.' Mike could be mistaken for being a Jew, Arab, Italian, Welshman or North Indian. In England, he was often mistaken for a Welshman. Kiran, as she grew up, did not have any hang-ups about being mixed race. From an early age we told her she was the best of East and West.

⌇

My work was very satisfying. Both RA and AB found it hard to believe that I had worked in Pathology for only just over a year, and for only three months in each of its four disciplines. Very soon they allowed me to work unsupervised. AB was pleased he could devote more time to his private practice.

My work required me to report on blood films and bone marrow biopsies. I had one or two of the latter each week, but in Vellore, I was reporting on about fifteen a week. I was also responsible for anticoagulant clinics and helped AB with haematology clinics. There were patients on the ward with blood diseases, including haemophilia. Haematology was a new speciality, an offshoot of General Medicine. Apart from the transfusion of blood and its products, there were very few drugs in use. Chemotherapy was in its infancy and largely experimental. I also reported on tissue biopsies, and anything I was not sure of I referred to AB and RA. The only unpleasant duty I had was to do a few autopsies every week. It was the smell, not the sight, of opened up corpses that I detested. It was not a bad smell, and not the smell of decay, but the sickly-sweet smell of flesh. The mortuary technician was a large, gentle, serious man who kept everything in order. In Vellore, we did detailed examinations, lasting two to three hours. Here, they were generally cursory, lasting barely half an hour. One day, I walked into the mortuary to see RA walking slowly round and round a slab, stopping and starting, and stooping to look closely at the body on it, that of a large, well-built black man.

'Isn't he a splendid specimen,' she exclaimed. 'Just like a gorilla in the Natural History Museum.' From her, that could only be a compliment. She was obsessed with animals. One day, she asked me if I had a dog.

'No,' I replied.

'You must get one. I will find one for you,' she said. And that is how we got Dougal, a highly pedigreed, neurotic, miniature dachshund.

⌇

My office was in the Pathology department, where consultants and medical secretaries also had their offices. There were about thirty laboratory technicians who received and analysed the various specimens. The title of 'technician' has changed over the years to reflect their enhanced status, resulting from the complexity of tests, and the increasing interpretive element. Recruited locally, they were from the working and lower middle classes. They were highly skilled, and very proud of their Yorkshire roots. Aloof at first, once they came to know me they were very friendly and helpful, and lasting friendships were made. They were surprised that I spoke English with scarcely an accent. But they would try to correct the words they thought I did not get quite right. 'Bus,' they said was not to be pronounced 'buss' but 'booz' and 'us' was not 'uss' but 'ooz'. I continued to speak the way I already did.

⌇

In 1968, I had a letter from my mother to say my father had died. A servant had been sent by my father's brother with the news, and to tell her that the funeral was about to take place in a few hours. She did not attend the funeral but was very shaken by the news, although there had been no contact between them for twenty-five years. I felt no sense of personal loss, just enormous regret at what he must have suffered, having not been with his daughters as they grew up, and that we did not get to know him as adults.

⌇

The same year, my general unease about racism in this country was compounded by a speech made by a member of the Shadow

Cabinet, Enoch Powell. Some years earlier when he was Health Minister, I had noticed advertisements in some Indian papers for people with skills to apply to work in the British National Health Service. Four years earlier, he had expressed valid concerns about unchecked immigration, but these went unheeded and were not taken up by the media. The speech in 1968, again expressing grave concern about immigrants and their dependents, was called the 'Rivers of Blood' speech. His intemperate language caused a tremendous row. A brilliant Greek scholar, Powell was alluding in part to a quote from Virgil, but that went over everyone's head. Sacked from the Shadow Cabinet, he spent the rest of his political life in the wilderness. Three quarters of the British population agreed with him, but the whole matter of racism was pushed under the carpet, allowing these feelings and resentments to fester for the next three decades.

This is where Powell and his fellow politicians went wrong. He had no constructive suggestions, and they lost an opportunity to bring the matter out into the open and seek solutions. Any sensible discussion about immigration could never proceed after this, as it was immediately branded racist. Mike and I felt that allowing in large numbers of poor, illiterate people, of a different appearance and culture, and who could not and would not integrate, without restrictions on how long they could remain, was stoking up problems for the future. These people were diligent and hardworking and were grateful to the host country. But it was the next generation we worried about. They would be born and brought up here, and there was bound to be a clash of cultures, each one rubbishing the other. And it would mainly affect the working classes in each race. The speech was a boost for the National Front, an extremist right-wing organisation which demanded repatriation for all immigrants. It was active in Huddersfield. Its members were not confined to the working classes; it also had educated professionals among its members.

That the native population was hostile to immigrants was never in doubt. But it was also a white problem, because of ignorance. The man in the street had a very superficial knowledge of colonialism, Empire and the Raj. No politician, or the history he had been taught, had told him about the enormous riches the colonies had brought to Britain, or that three million Indians died fighting voluntarily for Britain in two world wars, or that Britain had committed some dreadful crimes in India, or that these lands had well-developed civilisations and cultures. As far as they were concerned, coloured people came here to take their jobs and to live on welfare benefits.

Kiran must have heard me and Mike discuss Powell and immigration. One night as I put her to bed, she asked me in a small frightened voice, 'Do you think someone will put a petrol bomb though our letter box?'

I was finding Kiran's Yorkshire accent and intonation becoming more entrenched and unattractive. It did not bother her father. My mother wrote to suggest she have elocution lessons and be sent to a good boarding school.

'Fancy living in a country with schools like Roedean and Cheltenham Ladies' College, and not making use of them.'

So Kiran had elocution lessons. These transformed the way she spoke, and continued to speak, but we could not part with her to boarding school.

We had an unexpected two-week visit in 1968 from my mother on her way to Canada. It was Ann's and Suku's sabbatical year, and they were visiting fellows at McGill University. Suku had been injured in a car crash and had broken his hip. My mother had gone to look after Mithran, now aged two.

It was my mother's first visit to our new house. We took her proudly around it, and the well-stocked garden. She looked puzzled. 'How do you get into the rest of the house?' she asked.

'What "rest"?' I said. 'There isn't any "rest". This is it.'

'You mean you could afford to buy only half a house?' she exclaimed.

We explained about semis and detached houses. She wasn't convinced.

'Next time, buy a whole house,' she said.

Once again, she had left Alpha in the care of Cheena and the servants. But she had acquired a dog: Tony, a handsome Alsation with a fierce temperament. Alfred Uncle, now retired, visited Cheena frequently, and was concerned that he was becoming out of breath easily. He was found to have chronic heart failure, but they decided not to tell my mother.

⌐

Mike and I had to decide when we were going to return to India. Working in state hospitals there was never an option. Michael did not want to do private medicine, so that left only Mission hospitals. My mother advised us against returning, as she was certain the Kolar experience would recur, and Mike's gentle nature would not be able to cope. His brother, Desmond, and family were about to emigrate to Canada, and they urged us to do likewise, but this would mean more examinations for Mike and me.

It became obvious that, unlike me, Mike had no wish to return to India. We did not make a decision about staying in Britain so much as decide that Mike needed to get on with his career in Orthopaedics, which he had started to enjoy. His consultants found he had a great flair for it, and urged him to move to a teaching hospital, from where he would have a greater chance of getting a senior registrar post, the grade below consultant. This was where the bottleneck was, and many doctors gave up at this stage, either going into general practice, emigrating or going back to the country they came from. As usual, being a foreign graduate, he was at a disadvantage, but surprisingly got a registrar post in a teaching hospital in Sheffield quite quickly, probably because of his excellent references.

⌐

Mike's move to Sheffield proved to be a wise one, and his consultants, two fine orthopaedic surgeons, ensured that his experience was as wide as possible.

But for me it was not easy. In Mike's absence, his mother would make snide remarks about Indians, and was often unkind to Kiran, an affectionate child, full of vitality and very biddable. They did not bond. Mum would spend all hours of the day watching television. I was concerned at the influence this would have on Kiran. Left to me, I would not have had a television in the house. I confided my unease to Violet, my eldest sister-in-law. I asked her why she thought Mum continued to live with us, when she felt so uncomfortable under the same roof as me.

'Because she knows no one else wants her,' was the sad reply.

After two years in a state school, we moved Kiran to a private one, where in a class of eighteen she was ranked thirteenth after the first term. She pulled herself up, and then remained within the first five. She had an excellent and inspiring teacher, whose daughter, Rachel Wood, was in the same class. The girls went to each other's homes, which meant we got to know Rachel's parents socially. A charming couple, Pamela and Edward Wood became and remained friends.

I took a half-day off and went to Kiran's first Sports Day. It was nothing like Sports Days in India, and a disappointment. That morning, Dougal the dachshund jumped up at me and ripped the hem of the only presentable coat I had. I had no time to mend it, and felt unable to sit with the well-dressed parents in the marquee. I stood a little distance away on an elevated culvert and watched. Edward Wood saw me, and came and stood with me, and smiled when I told him why I was not with the other parents. Just then, one of these well-groomed ladies, instead of using the facilities provided a little distance away, brought her small son to pee in the bushes, just below us. She did not know we could see them.

'Well, Lindy,' said Edward, looking down and laughing. 'What do you think of the affluent English middle classes?'

'Edward,' I said, 'if it were my child peeing there, people would say, look at those bloody immigrants!'

'How right you are,' he said.

✎

My mother, Ann, Suku, and Mithran returned to India from Canada. My mother was shocked that Cheena's health had deteriorated so sharply. She took him to Vellore, where he was seen by a cardiologist and found to be in severe heart failure. Despite intensive treatment, he did not recover. News of his death filled me with profound sadness. I loved him. He was never a substitute for my father; he was a deeply cherished, loyal and generous 'uncle'. And to my mother, he was a trustworthy and generous friend.

Chapter 24

THE FINEST JOB IN THE WORLD

After Mike's first year in Sheffield, a new post of senior registrar in Orthopaedics was created in his hospital. His consultants urged him to apply for it, and were confident he would get it. One of them was to be on the appointments committee, which consisted of various people, including some from both the teaching hospitals, administrators and representatives from the Royal College of Surgeons. Mike was shortlisted and had a good interview, and was bitterly disappointed when the job was given to an Australian, who had considerably less clinical and research experience. Mike's two consultants were disgusted and said it was blatant racism. They said he was to supervise the newly appointed senior registrar, a thoroughly decent man, who acknowledged that an injustice had been done to Mike, and said he was happy to be supervised by him.

Mike's pain and despondency were also mine. He applied for several other senior registrar posts and was turned down. He decided to opt out of the rat race and apply for an Associate Specialist's post, a sub-consultant grade, mainly occupied by foreign graduates or part-time women. I pleaded with him not to give up just yet. Shortly thereafter, he was shortlisted for a senior registrar post in Sunderland, on the north-east coast of England, and was successful. I had to look up the map to see where Sunderland was. Friends, family and colleagues said this was even worse than Yorkshire, and further away. We did not care. They had been wrong before, and besides, we thought Yorkshire was a delightful and interesting county, full of character. We had also enjoyed Huddersfield's local newspaper, *The Examiner*. And we had made some really good friends.

Apart from a few foreign doctors, there were no brown or black faces to be seen in Sunderland. And the local people sat next to me in the bus, not trying to avoid me, as they did in Huddersfield.

'Why are people smiling at us, Mummy?' asked Kiran. And indeed they were, because we were a rarity.

Once again we rented hospital accommodation, a large red-brick Edwardian house opposite a well-maintained park. There was no central heating. There were unused fireplaces in every room. Sea gulls screeched above us. The sea, with large sandy beaches, was a few minutes away, as was the football stadium. We soon learned that football was very important in the north-east of England.

Mike was required to start his post in Sunderland as soon as possible. It was Kiran's summer holidays. Mike moved to Sunderland with his mother, Kiran and Dougal. I stayed on in Huddersfield to finish my contract and sell the house.

Dr Allison and Dr Barlow had been urging me for some time to take the primary exam for membership of the Royal College of Pathologists. I told them I was not ambitious, and had no inclination to become a consultant. I had hoped to work part-time and perhaps provide a sibling for Kiran. I enjoyed my work so much that it was a hobby. I took the exam to keep the consultants happy; I did not think I would ever take the final exam. I scoured the *British Medical Journal* for suitable jobs in Sunderland and Newcastle. There was nothing, until AB found one for me, at senior registrar level, in Newcastle. I did not want to apply as I was not yet a member of the Royal College of Pathologists, but AB said to go for it. And I did.

I spent the night in Sunderland, and Mike drove me to the interview in Newcastle. He was to come back later, to take me to the station to get the train back to Huddersfield. There was another candidate at interview with me, Anne, a cheerful plump woman, a graduate of the Royal Free Hospital in London, now living with her husband and three small children near Newcastle. We had a long wait before the interview. We laughed and chatted together amicably. She said I should get the job, because I was more experienced and knowledgeable, but she expected to get it, because she was a British graduate. 'You know how it is,' she said, and I nodded. But I got the job and felt bad for Anne, and wished she could be a colleague.

Michael was late, and we rushed to the station. Just as he dropped me off he remembered, and said, 'What happened?'

'I got it,' I said.

'What!' he exclaimed 'It took me twelve attempts. You've done it in one.'

'Orthopaedics is far more competitive.' I hoped that would make him feel better.

Anne rang me a few days later to say a supernumerary post at registrar level had been created for her, and she would be working alongside me. Another lifelong friendship was established.

I worked my notice, put the house up for sale, made arrangements for the rest of the furniture to be moved to Sunderland, and said goodbye to Pamela and Edward Wood, the lab technicians, and my consultants. Dr Allison said she would keep Dougal, the dachshund, anytime, if we went on holiday. Dr Barlow said he would see me at haematology meetings in London. Kiran's headmistress had said she was sorry to see Kiran go. The school had been a better place because she had been there.

The north-east of England, said to be a depressed area, has its own strong identity, just as Yorkshire does. Its way of speaking, too, is quite distinct, and sometimes difficult to comprehend, but easier on the ears. But we found the people more friendly, perhaps because they had not been asked to host people from alien lands. Family ties are very close, and its people do not transplant easily to other parts of the country or the world, and even after decades they tend to return.

I drove every morning, except Sunday, to the Blood Transfusion Centre, sited at Newcastle General Hospital, one of two large teaching hospitals in Newcastle. Michael dropped Kiran off at school on his way to work. Her grandmother picked her up and they came home by bus. Friday was half-day, and they treated themselves to lunch at a nearby department store. These were satisfactory arrangements and I was grateful to Mum for making them possible, but I wished she would show more warmth towards Kiran and me.

Anne, the registrar, had started work a few weeks before me

and primed me on what to expect. This was not a hospital. The Director (SM), a doctor, was a woman, very similar in appearance to Margaret Thatcher, though the latter had not yet appeared on the scene. Immaculately groomed, with a variety of expensive matching shoes and handbags, she ruled supreme. The staff were terrified of her. Though she was cold and aloof, and not given to small chat, Anne and I developed a good relationship with her. Her role was an administrative one. She sat all day in a huge room, at an enormous desk on which was a metal stand with half a dozen buttons. These were connected to bells in the doctors' and senior technicians' offices. Though each of us had individual internal phones, she would summon us by pressing the appropriate button, which would result in an almost continuous piercing ring. We were expected to drop everything, and rush to her room. Any delay would result in a stony stare. I found this unnerving at first, but learned fast.

The main purpose of the Transfusion Service was to collect blood from suitable donors between the ages of eighteen and sixty-five, rigorously check it for safety, group it, make blood products and ensure distribution to hospitals in the northern region. The latter extended from east coast to the west coast, and from the Scottish to North Yorkshire border. Donors were actively recruited and gave blood voluntarily, no more than twice a year. This noble and admirable arrangement is well described in the book *The Gift Relationship* by Fred Titmus.

My job was different from anything I had had before. I did not see a patient, dead or alive. There were donor sessions every day in the Transfusion Centre, but much of the blood was collected throughout the region, in factories, church halls and even in prisons. One pint of blood was collected from every donor, by a doctor inserting a needle into a vein in the arm. The blood ran through the needle into a tube connected to a plastic bag. Nurses, technicians and clerks were also in attendance. The doctors were mostly part-time, and when one of them was absent, Anne or I was required to conduct the session. There were sometimes as many as 120 donors at a session. I could never understand why venesection had to be performed by a doctor. I had no doubt that a nurse or technician could do it just as skilfully. But I could not have my views heard. Donors were sent away with a bag of iron tablets, which quickly found their way into the nearest roadside bin. Iron tablets are notorious for causing abdominal discomfort.

I was surprised to find that none of our blood products which we produced were tested for quality. There was no culture of Quality Control. I decided to look at the effectiveness of Factor VIII, used to treat haemophiliacs, in a concentrate called cryoprecipitate (cryo). To my astonishment, I found it had half the activity that was expected of it. The technical staff, careful and diligent, ensured the production process adhered to strict directions. Probing further, I found that the cryo was made in the morning from blood collected the previous evening. Factor VIII has a half life of eight hours. This meant that by the time the cryo was processed and frozen, it had lost more than half its activity. The Director was horrified when I told her we were sending out a very sub-standard product. From then on we made cryo only from freshly collected blood. It was gratifying to get feedback from users that the new cryo was significantly more effective.

My next project was to make platelet concentrates. Platelets are small cells in the blood which help to form a blood clot. A reduction causes bruising; severe depletion can cause bleeding and death. I had to get the Director to agree, which was not easy. When I told her we were again lagging behind other centres, she told me to go ahead. Soon we were delivering them throughout the region.

These innovations were interesting, but I thought they could be done with some encouragement by competent technical staff. They did not need a doctor. I missed patient contact and the thrill of diagnosis. Diagnosis and treatment is the essence of medicine, and together with patient contact is what makes the long training, anxiety, excessive working hours and exhaustion worthwhile. Transfusion medicine was not for me.

My mother had always been closely interested in my work. She said I was a doctor for people, not for cutting up dead bodies or examining specimens.

'With your easy manner and empathy with people, why are you doing all these other things?' she asked. 'It's time you went back to proper doctoring.'

I was expected to spend the next three years in clinical and laboratory haematology at the two teaching hospitals in Newcastle. But there was no vacancy, and one of the hospitals, the RVI, was not recognised by the Royal College. I went to see Sandy Mackenzie, the consultant haematologist at the Royal Infirmary in Sunderland, which was recognised for training, to see if I could transfer to his department, which had a vacancy, without the post being advertised. He thought it a good idea and obtained agreement from the Northern Regional Health Authority, who were our employers.

When I handed in my resignation to the Director of the Transfusion Service, she erupted. But she was calmed down by Willie Walker, a jovial haematologist/paediatrician who had been asked to unite the fragmented bits of haematology at the RVI. He did this very successfully, and was subsequently awarded a Chair. Anne got my job, and eventually became a consultant and then succeeded the Director. She became very involved in designing the new Transfusion Centre when it was decided to build it at another site. Totally without guile, she was a remarkable woman. She died prematurely from a brain malignancy. I still mourn her.

⌣

Working in Sunderland was a totally new experience. For a start I did not have to battle with the rush-hour traffic, to and back from Newcastle, particularly onerous in the dark evenings during the famous Three-Day Week, when traffic lights were switched off in Newcastle because of strikes, and there was chaos and gridlock. Now I was able to pick up Kiran after school, take her home and return to work or, occasionally, take her to work with me. She sat quietly and did her homework. In Huddersfield, when she was younger, she would ride with the porters on their trolley train, delivering supplies all over the hospital. Those were the days when words such as Health and Safety, Human Resources, mission statements and SWOT analysis were not known. And we were none the worse for it.

I found it very stimulating to work with Sandy Mackenzie, a somewhat manic but likeable Scot. He had great vitality and liked to be confrontational, not just about work but about everything else: the NHS, politics, foreigners, Englishwomen, Scottish women, gardening, whisky, art, men, women—the list was endless. He was a bundle of prejudices, but he was a good man, a kind man. He was not a racist, but once he did call two incompetent Indian doctors 'savages'. I told him the only savages I knew came from north of the border. He laughed. He considered all things Scottish superior, apart from Scottish women. Both his wives—he was divorced—were English roses, gentle and beautiful. He did something I had hitherto only once encountered in a consultant. He swore.

I relished being with patients again. But one thing, I discovered: Sandy did not like patients, preferring to treat haematology patients under the umbrella of general physicians. They gave him a free hand, but I felt it restricted my innovations. Sandy came late to haematology, from general pathology, as did the haematologists of his era. They had not taken postgraduate exams. When the Royal College of Pathologists was founded in 1962, they were elected Fellows. Sandy was to a large extent self-taught in haematology, but was extremely competent and had developed an outstanding laboratory, considered one of the best in the country. Sunderland had a huge catchment area, and about a dozen hospitals to which we provided services. The haematology department was based in the Royal Infirmary in the town centre. Sunderland was awarded city status some years later.

⌣

Michael worked in a hospital in the Monkwearmouth district of Sunderland. It was solely devoted to trauma and orthopaedics. He worked mainly with two consultants who were nearing retirement. A third one, a flamboyant man, was nearer Mike's age. The senior consultant, David Brown, was a reserved, large, heavily built man with great presence. He worked maximum part-time for the NHS and had a thriving private practice. He was also surgeon to the Sunderland Football Club, and quickly involved Mike in their orthopaedic problems. The other consultant, Charles Robb, was a quiet, shy man, a bachelor, and lived in a hotel. He soon came to rely heavily on Mike, and would only operate when Mike was present. The hospital was well staffed with nurses, physiotherapists and junior doctors, the latter being mainly Indian. There was a very happy atmosphere. Mike soon realised that football was the religion of the working classes in the north-east. He started to attend football matches with David Brown most Saturday afternoons. He often took Kiran with him.

Mike went in to work seven days a week and seemed to be eternally on call. When there was a problem, the first port of call was the Senior House officer. If the situation was serious or if he could not cope, he would call the registrar. If the registrar was in difficulty, he would call Mike, who was always covered by a consultant. Such was Mike's competence and confidence that I do not think he ever called a consultant, unless there was a big accident and extra pairs of hands were needed. I was on call every night, but I could deal with most problems on the telephone. The Senior House officer and registrar who worked with me were rarely able to give the appropriate advice. I used to alternate weekends with Sandy. One of us needed to go in on Saturday mornings. For a period, I had to go in every Saturday morning, as Sandy got into a rage and refused to go in, even though it meant that I had to, because there were always problems to be sorted out. He had taken his car into his garage one Saturday morning for a minor repair. The garage refused to do it because it was a Saturday.

'Bloody hell,' said Sandy. 'If they won't work on a Saturday, neither will I.' His fits of irrationality were fortunately rare.

We had six weeks' annual leave every year, but rarely took all of it. We had now been in Britain for five years without returning to India, even for a visit. I longed to see my family and suggested a trip for Christmas. Mike and Kiran shared my enthusiasm. I thought it might make Mike think of returning to India. He was more specialised now, and it would be more difficult to find work in India, unless he did private practice. There were many such clinics with excellent facilities opening up in India, and he was being approached by them. He did not relish the thought of another rat race in England, chasing after a consultant post. The Sheffield experience had left him disillusioned.

It was another splendid homecoming. My mother, Ann and her family, servants and relatives had all assembled at Alpha to greet us. The garden was a haven. Balaraman, the teenage labourer, who had helped to build Alpha was now its caretaker, and presented the ten-year-old Kiran with a newly born kid. She was overwhelmed. I felt Cheena's absence acutely. Ann, now nearly forty, had unexpectedly had a baby in the October. The ten-week-old girl, called Nandini, ten pounds at birth, was exceptionally beautiful. I secretly worried that such a big baby meant Ann had incipient diabetes, the curse of our family. Ann said Nandini was her greatest gift. Kiran, Michael and I were her godparents and she was christened during our visit. An astrologer in Vellore, an acquaintance of Suku's, on hearing of the baby's birth urged Suku to allow him to draw up her horoscope. When it was finished, not bothering to read it, Suku threw the scroll on to the top of a wardrobe. My mother found it and read it. She was filled with rage. It said the child's parents would die when the child was young, before she became an adult, that she would not marry, and if she did, it would be late in life. My mother burnt the scroll and reprimanded Suku for indulging in this superstitious nonsense, and said no one was to know about it. She did not divulge its contents to Ann or Suku, and told me about it some years later.

This was the time of the Indo–Pak war when Bangladesh was created. Kiran and Mithran stripped the garden of all its fruit and vegetables, set up a stall in front of the house and sold the lot for Indira Gandhi's soldiers' fund. We made a trip to our favourite beach, twenty miles away in Mamallapuram, never tiring of seeing the seventh-century shore temples, with their exquisite rock carvings depicting scenes from the ancient epics. Mike and Kiran would sometimes hire cycles and ride to bazaars and villages near Alpha, stopping at cafés to quench their thirst.

But it was soon time to return to England.

'Can't we live here?' cried Kiran. We both realised how much we had missed and were being missed.

᷾

I knew Mike had no intention of returning to India. I felt unable to ask him to do so. He enjoyed his work, and was appreciated by his colleagues and adored by his patients. His two consultants told me that if they or their families broke any bones, they would go to Mike for treatment. He did research, published papers and spent short periods at centres of excellence, to gain expertise in Children's Orthopaedics.

As a senior registrar, I was expected to have a research project, take the final exam of the Royal College of Pathologists and prepare to become a consultant, over a period of four years. I was not interested in any of these. I was not a natural researcher. I preferred to spend my time diagnosing and treating patients, spending long hours talking to them and their relatives, and teaching anyone who wished to be taught, be it medical students, doctors, nurses, lab scientists or even Sandy. However, I thought it would be wise to do some research. Sandy and I were perplexed by three fit, pregnant women with mild anaemia of the iron deficiency type, not uncommon in pregnancy. They did not respond to repeated courses of iron. Further probing showed they were not deficient in iron, but had a mild hereditary anaemia called beta-thalassemia trait, hitherto known to occur in people of Mediterranean or oriental origin. The defect is in the composition of globin, the protein component of haemoglobin, which carries oxygen in the blood. All three women were indigenous British, and all came from Murton, a small village near Durham. As far as they knew, they had no foreign ancestry and were not related to each other. With the help of the local general practitioner who provided the blood samples, I investigated 500 people for beta-thalassemia trait, and found over fifty of them to have the trait. They were all indigenous British with no foreign ancestry. This meant they were heterozygous for the condition, indicating that they had inherited the abnormality from one parent only.

During this research, I came across another haemoglobin abnormality in a young woman. It was also present in her siblings, children and parents, though the latter were not related as far as they knew. Unable to proceed further without very specialised facilities, I wrote to the expert on thalassemia in Britain, Professor David Weatherall, and went to see him to discuss what should be done next. Blood samples were analysed in his lab and the abnormal haemoglobin was found to be a new one, never described before. We called it the British variety of hereditary persistence of foetal haemoglobin, Greek, Negro and Swiss varieties already having been described. We published our findings in the *British Journal of Haematology*. This haemoglobin was later found to be a variant of thalassemia. Professor Weatherall's research into thalassemia and its global implications are unparalleled. He was knighted and elected a Fellow of the Royal Society.

We had started to use chemotherapy for leukaemia and other blood and bone-marrow malignancies, but Sandy was very cautious. Many of our patients had dreadful side effects, which we could not ameliorate. I wondered if homeopathy had anything to offer. I was prepared to explore it with an open mind. Doctors in training in the NHS were given generous study leave and grants, but I funded myself to attend courses at the Royal Homeopathic Hospital in London, so that I was deemed to be competent to practise this form of alternative medicine. Homeopathy is based on the principle that 'like cures like', that the very substance that causes the symptoms of a disease can cure it. The concentrate of the medicine, called the 'mother tincture', is put through a series of dilutions, each dilution being shaken vigorously. Final dilutions have often been found to have nothing of the original substance.

During the first one-week course, I discovered my friend Sunil, married to my eccentric friend Shubha from Lucknow days, was also doing a course, but at the hospital for neurological diseases in Queen's Square, across the way from where I was. We sat on a bench outside, sometimes, and had lunch together. He was astonished that I was studying homeopathy. He did not approve.

'I am seeing patients that homeopaths are hanging on to and treating, instead of referring them to us,' he complained. 'I saw one today with an inoperable brain tumour, initially misdiagnosed at the homeopathic hospital.'

At the end of the first course, I bought a large textbook of homeopathic medicine and a large box of drugs, pills and creams, and took them home. Mike was very sceptical, but did not discourage me. Sandy Mackenzie was less polite.

'Complete waste of time,' he said.

We attended lectures and clinics and saw many patients. We were taken to the Chelsea Physic Garden, where medicinal plants for the mother tincture were grown, and to the Homeopathic Pharmacy near Oxford Street, where pills, potions and creams were made. I was astonished at the way the pills were made. Sugar tablets were placed in small transparent containers. A few drops of a dilution were placed in the container and closed with a cap and inverted a few times. And that was it.

'But how do you know the diluted solution has diffused evenly and penetrated the pill?' I asked our demonstrator.

'It must have,' he replied.

I was not at all convinced. I too was becoming increasingly cynical. On the last day of my final course, any belief I had in homeopathy was laid to rest. My group was shown a boy of about seven. Wrapped in a shawl, he looked very ill. He was the son of a general practitioner, and he and his mother had flown down from Glasgow. We had to ask questions about him, including the usual ones in homeopathy relating to fear of darkness, thunder and lightning and so on. It transpired that the child had been plagued for years with ear infections and had had repeated courses of antibiotics. He had become unwell and, in desperation, the parents wondered if homeopathy was the answer, and had brought him to London. His symptoms of headache, double vision and projectile vomiting suggested to me that he had a lesion in his brain, an abscess or a tumour. I stood up and said he should be admitted urgently to the hospital for neurological diseases across the road. Our tutor was not pleased and said to me, 'You obviously have not grasped the principles of homeopathic practice,' and proceeded with discussion on treatment.

I do not know what happened to this child, but the memory of him has stayed with me.

I was now declared fit to practise homeopathy. After I returned to Sunderland, for several months I had phone calls from members of the public asking if they could consult me, my name having been given to them by the homeopathic hospital. I declined and asked the hospital to erase my name. I binned my textbook and box of drugs, but kept the arnica and burn creams, which sometimes seem to work. Millions of people believe in homeopathy, and when over the years my patients have asked me if they could use it in conjunction with traditional drugs, I have not stopped them, and have said that I did not think it would do them any good, and I did not think it would do them any harm. As for the patients treated for leukaemia who had distressingly painful mouth ulcers, homeopathy had no answers. But we did find a solution.

ᴧ

It took us eighteen months to find a suitable house. It was in East Boldon, a small agricultural village to the north of Sunderland, and on a lonely unmade lane. The large back garden shared a high wire fence with the tennis club, and had views beyond, of the golf course. In front, on the other side of the road, a ditch ran along its length to drain the farmer's fields. Across the fields we could see the sea and ships. It was a spacious, white, four-bedroom semi-detached house called Wren House. We hardly ever saw a wren and renamed it Sandalwood. I wondered if the people occupying the other semi might have objections to us as neighbours. My concern was unjustified. The couple, he a lawyer, and their four young sons were very cordial and welcoming.

A few months after moving in, Mike's mother announced that she wanted to leave to live alone, nearer her other children on the outskirts of London. For the past five years we had included her in our activities, outings and short holidays. But looking back, I don't think she felt really comfortable with us. The subtle racist barbs continued. I ignored them. My mother said to be tolerant and understanding, as Mrs Cartner could not help her upbringing. I expressed my gratitude to Mum, and said we would help her to find a flat and would furnish it for her. At the same time the cleaning lady retired, and I advertised for another one. I struck gold in Vivienne Smith. A seamstress who taught at a further education college in Surrey, she had moved to be near her son. Plump, cheerful and a widow in her sixties, she responded to my advertisement, and turned up in a bright red car with her terrier, Punchy. She spoke the Queen's English. I thought she was too posh for us and told her so.

'Don't you clean your own house sometimes?' she asked. 'Of course,' I said.

'Then why can't I?' So that was settled. We called her 'Mrs Smith'. Not only was she at Sandalwood two afternoons a week, to combine house work and being there for Kiran when she came home on the bus, but she also painted and decorated for us, made our furnishings, shopped for us and took us to and collected us from Newcastle Airport when necessary. When my mother came for a visit, they struck up a friendship and had several outings together.

⁃

Charles Robb, one of Mike's consultants, decided to take early retirement. Mike had been a senior registrar for under three years. The post was usually for four years, though this was not mandatory. David Brown told Mike that competition would be stiff, and there was no certainty he would be successful, but insisted Mike apply for the vacant consultant post. Mike was not sure he was ready, but what was really worrying him was that he felt he was sure to be rejected, and it would be a repeat of the Sheffield experience.

Mike and I spent hours putting together his curriculum vitae, looked over by David Brown. He was shortlisted for interview at Newcastle with five other suitable candidates. The committee of about twelve included David Brown. Mike and I rehearsed the questions he was likely to be asked. He was unassuming and highly articulate, and I hoped his sense of humour would shine through.

Mike was offered the job, accepted it and was appointed. The elation was not as great as the anguish which preceded it. It never is. My hope of returning to India was completely extinguished, but I was not unhappy. We would be able to afford to see my family at least twice a year. And to crown it all, Sunderland had won the Football Association Cup in the summer. The last time had been in 1937.

⁃

I remember hearing one of my professors in medical school in Vellore say that a consultant working in the NHS in Britain had the best job in the world. He had had experience of working for several years in Britain. What he said was true. There was autonomy, adequate salary, excellent support staff in the form of junior doctors, nurses, scientists, technicians and administrators, uniform standard of health care throughout the country, excellent facilities, no financial restrictions on treatment, permanent security of tenure, permission to do private practice and, most importantly, no payment whatever by the patient at the point of delivery of health care. We might have worked ludicrous hours, junior and senior doctors, but we were happy and fulfilled. We felt a sense of ownership of our hospitals and were intensely loyal to them. These were the golden years of the National Health Service. How privileged we were to be part of it.

But times were beginning to change, politicians were starting to meddle and needless changes were being discussed. All institutions have to keep evolving, but change for the sake of change is an ominous sign. Egos and ideology were at play. Mike wrote and had published a series of anonymous articles about the NHS for the *Sunderland Echo*, the local paper. He ended the last article with the words: 'Better still, give it to Marks and Spencer.' He was referring to the National Health Service.

Chapter 25

THE END OF A HOPE

Mike promised to spend more time at home and switched from cigarettes to a pipe, smoking a fragrant tobacco called Clan. But I did not see much more of him. We were like ships passing in the night. And I noticed he was inhaling the pipe tobacco. He would come home late from work, sink into his armchair and watch comedies on television, laughing out loudly from time to time. All domestic chores, the garden, Kiran's schooling, the buying and servicing of cars, insurances, the buying of his clothes, visits to and from his family, were left to me to organise. I told him this was not my idea of marriage. He laughed, gave me a hug and said, 'Don't you know doctors, drunkards and clergymen make the worst husbands.'

A few months after Mike became a consultant, David Brown retired from the NHS. He made sure that Mike became the official orthopaedic consultant to the Sunderland Football Club. Mike had already come to know the manager, Bob Stokoe, and the players. David also asked Mike to take over his private practice. Mike wanted to work full time for the NHS for the first nine months, after which he would drop one of his sessions to enable him to do private practice, which he intended to start on 15 August 1974, an auspicious day he said jokingly, Indian Independence Day. He said he still felt more Indian than Anglo, and perhaps that was because he was married to me, but he had a genuine love for India.

Now that Mike was a consultant, I told Sandy I wished to work part-time, and had sufficient experience to become a Clinical Assistant or Associate Specialist. I did not wish to do any more exams. He refused to accept this, and said he expected me to do the final exam as soon as possible. I decided to have one attempt at it only, six months later. The only time I had to study was late evening, after dinner. Over the years, I had, once a year, attended a Haematology course at the Royal Postgraduate School in Hammersmith, London. It was very intensive, and we used to be like wet rags at the end of the day, after which we were invited to examine nearly a hundred exhibits related to everyday practice. Most of the doctors had no energy to do this and went home, but I dragged myself around the vast hall every day. By the end of the week I had seen all of them. It was to pay off. I took the written papers in London in the June and, having passed, was called for the three-day practicals, clinicals and viva voce in Leeds, one of the exam centres in Britain.

On a sunny summer Sunday in 1974, Mike drove me to Leeds and left me in a hotel near the General Infirmary where the exam was to take place. The first day consisted of lab procedures. I could never understand why we had to do these, as in hospital practice they were carried out by medical laboratory scientific officers, which is what technicians were now called. Haematologists interpreted the results and then took action accordingly. I sat up till the early hours learning the procedures, hardly slept, and could not eat breakfast because of nervousness. I arrived at the exam hall bleary eyed, and wondering why I had ever embarked on this. The stress was unbearable. There were three of us candidates and three examiners; the latter were three middle-aged men. One was small and grumpy. The other two were very pleasant.

On arrival, we were told that the programme had been altered. Clinicals—that is, seeing patients—would be on the first day and lab procedures on the second. This threw me, as there was a lot of last-minute looking up I needed to do for the clinicals, such as memorising lab test norms and drug doses. The so-called long case took all morning and in the afternoon we were presented with six more patients. I got into an argument with the grumpy examiner who started to raise his voice. When he was out of the room briefly, the other two examiners came to me and gently advised me not to disagree with him. At the end of the day we were thoroughly exhausted, and I wondered whether to give up and go home as I had offended one of the examiners, and he had probably failed me. I rang Mike, and he said I was to finish the exam.

The practicals were a nightmare. Starting at 8.30 in the morning, we were given symptoms and signs of an imaginary patient, a twenty-four-year-old pilot with severe bruising. On the lab bench, each of us was provided with samples of his blood, together with numerous reagents, test tubes, slides, samples from blood donors and apparatus. Each of us had a microscope. At the end of the day, we would be questioned on treatment and management of the patient. There were also ten exhibits we had to identify. We felt overwhelmed and did not know where to start. I looked across to the other candidates. One was on the verge of tears. The other shrugged his shoulders, rolled his eyes and looked heavenwards.

At seven that night I was still in the lab, the other two candidates having left. I had deduced that the patient had acute leukaemia with a severe anaemia, and a bleeding and a clotting problem as well. It was obvious to me that I had to match the patient's blood against the donor samples as he required a blood transfusion. One of the four samples was incompatible. The examiner stayed with me until I finished and handed in my reports. I went back to my hotel and slept, too spent to go down for dinner.

I had the viva the next day. The grumpy examiner had left early for a meeting in Glasgow. The other two seemed quite laid back, and I was able to answer all their questions. Then one pulled out an electron microscope photograph from his briefcase, showed it to me and asked me what the diagnosis was. I told him.

'What!' he exclaimed in astonishment. 'Have you ever seen a case?'

'No.' I said. It was very, very rare.

'Do you know anyone who has?' asked the other.

'No.'

'How do you know it is that?'

I explained to them the abnormal, but typical, characteristics of the single cell in the photograph. They looked at each other and said they had nothing else to ask me. I had seen this photograph on display when I had gone to the course in Hammersmith. That is how I knew.

I took the train back to Sunderland, struggling with my microscope. I really did not know what the outcome would be, nor did I care. I told Mike I would never take the exam again.

'Fair enough,' he said.

Ten days later, a thin envelope arrived from the Royal College of Pathologists, and I knew I had passed. Thick envelopes contained application forms to repeat the exam. I was now eligible to apply for a consultant's post, this being an exit exam, unlike exams of the other Royal Colleges, which were taken early in the training period. I told Sandy again that I wanted a part-time post in a sub-consultant grade in Sunderland or Newcastle.

'Don't be silly,' he said in his usual blunt way. 'Sunderland badly needs a second consultant in Haematology and you are going to be it. Sunderland General Hospital (SGH) is to be expanded substantially and will become the main hospital. The lab is to transfer there, and there will be a purpose-built Haematology unit with its own beds. I want you to be in charge of commissioning for all aspects of Haematology. Michael will be here till he retires. You belong to Sunderland. Anyway, the exam is behind you. It is time you and Michael started enjoying yourselves.'

Three weeks later, it was a morning like any other. Mike dropped Kiran off at school and went to Grindon, to one of the nearby rehabilitation hospitals, to do a short ward round, before he went to his main hospital. I went to my main hospital: The Royal Infirmary. A couple of hours later, my phone rang. An unfamiliar voice said not to be alarmed, but Mike had been admitted to the coronary care unit (CCU) at the SGH. His electrocardiogram was normal and results of blood tests were pending. He was fine. They would keep him till the evening, when he could go home. The registrar who was on the phone said he would explain everything when I came to the hospital. I let Sandy know, and I drove the half-mile to SGH.

Mike was sitting on his bed, smiling and looking sheepish. He said the silly ward sister at Grindon Hospital had called for an ambulance to take him to the CCU. He had developed chest pain during his ward round, and had asked the sister if he could lie down for a few minutes in a side room. She had become alarmed, but the pain had subsided by the time the ambulance arrived. He had decided to drive on to his main hospital, but the sister had hidden his shoes. He said he felt embarrassed to be in the CCU. He was wired up to monitors. There were two consultants, one a cardiologist, as well as the registrar with him. They reassured me he was quite well, but it was policy that once a patient was admitted to the CCU he was kept a few hours for observation. Mike asked me to go home and get a book and newspaper, and some tobacco. I refused to bring the latter, as he was wired up, and no one was going to disconnect him so that he could smoke. Smokers always have a sense of entitlement. I drove back to my office to finish some microscope work, and as I entered the room the phone was ringing. It was a CCU nurse.

'The doctors want you back straight away,' she said.

'But I was there only half an hour ago,' I exclaimed. 'What's the matter?'

'Please come at once.' And she put the phone down. I was convinced that, wanting a smoke, Mike had disconnected himself and insisted on taking his own discharge against medical advice. I was beginning to feel annoyed with him.

When I arrived at the CCU, the curtains were pulled around Mike's cubicle and people were running in and out.

'What's happened?' I asked, but no one answered. I went in. The cubicle was full of people. Mike lay semi-comatose on his bed wired to his monitors, with intravenous drips running into both arms. Apparently, shortly after I had left him, he was sitting on his bed, talking to the registrar, when he gave a gasp and fell back. He had had a cardiac arrest. The crash team were on site, but defibrillation did not work. The registrar then thumped Mike's chest hard with his fist, and his heart started again. He was pumped full of drugs and appeared stable. Later in the day his electrocardiogram and blood tests would became grossly abnormal, confirming he had had a massive heart attack. The cardiologist said the outcome was uncertain, but the situation was stable at the moment. I could see it was bad. Mike was muttering, 'So sorry. Sorry to be a nuisance.' Kiran was brought from school by a friend.

'Will he be all right?' she asked. 'I think so,' I replied.

We went home in the evening for a few hours and came back. Mike was more awake.

'I haven't made a will. Get Ian,' he said. It did not matter. There was little to leave.

Ian—a lawyer and our neighbour—came and took a few notes and told Mike not to worry. I was told to go home and to contact the ward a few times during the night. Mike remained stable, and there was no change in the morning. Kiran went to school. I went to work.

Over the next few weeks, Mike improved slowly. He told me one day he was coughing up blood, but had not told anyone. He had developed a blood clot in his lung. Three weeks later he was discharged. He was gaunt and grey, and breathless with the slightest exertion. I drove him home. A few minutes later he had disappeared. He was not in the garden. I went out into our lane, and there he was at the other end, smoking a cigarette. He had not smoked for three weeks and I remonstrated with him.

'I have to smoke,' he said. I did not bring up the subject again. I did not know where he got his cigarettes from. He no longer smoked a pipe.

Mike was told by the cardiologist that he would not be able to work for at least three months and probably for longer. His recovery was slow. He remained in heart failure and was on several drugs. He was becoming bored and losing hope. There was a string of visitors, but he became breathless when he spoke. I remembered that some years previously I discovered he had a talent for drawing. I was convinced he had the making of an artist but he refused to follow it up. I bought him some Daler boards and oil paints and brushes, but he shrugged his shoulders. I also bought him a new wardrobe, the excuse being that he had lost weight, but really because I wanted him to know that I believed he would get back to work. We both desperately needed hope.

After two months he had improved a little, but not enough to get back to work. He received a phone call from a consultant colleague, DH, to say he was in Edinburgh and had broken his hip while horse riding. An ambulance was bringing him to Sunderland, so Mike could operate and fix his hip. He knew about Mike's illness. Mike said he was on sick leave, and would not be well enough to work for at least another four weeks. DH, a fussy, obsessive man, who had been a missionary surgeon at Vellore when

I was a student there, said Mike could come and do his operation, and then go back to his sick leave. Mike had two colleagues who offered to do the operation, but DH declined. I knew that once Mike did even one procedure, he would be deemed fit to go back to full time work, and this would hinder his recovery. I urged him not to give in to DH, but he finally did. That was the end of his sick leave. His cardiologist was furious, but the administrator and his colleagues now expected him back, and required him to do on call again. Fortunately, his senior registrar was an old friend and tried to relieve him as much as possible. He also had a very able Senior House Officer from Bangalore. Mike did not spend endless hours working, as he used to. He started work very early, came home early, and rested upstairs in bed until dinner. He rested at weekends as well. But he did attend the Saturday home football matches, and his return was greeted with great joy. They referred to him as the 'wee genius'. He got injured players back on to their feet very quickly. Any hope of his ever doing private practice was abandoned.

Mike played down his symptoms. He never complained. He would tell everyone he was fine. But he was not. Left to himself, he would forget to take his drugs, or take them at the wrong time. He spoke to his family on the phone, and told them there was nothing to worry about. They believed him and did not come to visit. Suku, my sister's husband, was a cardiologist who knew the gravity of the situation, and he made Ann and my mother aware of it.

Mike had not referred to his prognosis or future, so it surprised me when a few months later he said to me that he was living on borrowed time, and had been thinking about my future. He realised I was eligible to apply for a consultant's post, but hated the thought of my facing probable discrimination, and thought Kiran and I should return to India.

'And when you marry again, make sure he is ten years younger than you,' he said. I said my only priority was his health, and he seemed to be getting stronger, day by day. But he had started to get sudden bouts, in the evening, of pulmonary oedema—that is, congestion of the lungs. I would give him an intravenous injection of a diuretic (similar to water tablets), which would give him almost instant relief.

Mike's illness had sharpened our sensitivities. We no longer bothered about trivialities, and when spring arrived and the garden started to stir, the grass was greener and the flowers brighter. I felt indebted to the ward sister at Grindon Hospital for sending Mike to the CCU, and to Sandy for pressurising me into doing the exam.

That summer Mike got the idea that we should spend a month over Christmas and New Year with my family in Southern India, in Madras and in Vellore. But that was not all. He wanted to show me and Kiran the Taj Mahal in Agra. He had seen it but we had not. I showed no enthusiasm whatever, and told him it was a crazy idea. His cardiologist agreed with me, and suggested he postpone the idea for a year, when his heart might have recovered a little.

Michael's response was: 'What guarantee is there that I will not be worse in twelve months' time?'

'None,' said the cardiologist.

So Mike decided we had to go that year. He had also been invited to do the first hip replacement in Vellore, as well as in Manipal, in Karnataka State. The more I heard about all this, the more panic-stricken I became. The thought of wandering around India with Mike in this fragile state filled me with horror. But he would not be deterred. He set about buying not only the artificial hips, but also the various materials and tools that he would need. They filled a large suitcase. I collected the drugs and syringes that he would require for himself, and this filled another suitcase. And what with our clothes and gifts for everyone, not to mention cheese, fresh celery, Harris paint brushes, and Spear and Jackson tools for my mother, we were well and truly laden. We arrived in Delhi early in the morning. By the time we had collected our luggage, which was scattered everywhere, overcome Indian bureaucracy and reached our hotel, Mike was grey and out of breath. Though he had eaten and drunk fluids on the plane, he had not passed urine for nearly twenty-four hours. I gave him an intravenous injection. There was not the usual response, where he would cease to be breathless and pass copious amounts of urine. Two hours later I gave him another injection, and again, there was no response. I tried to get in touch with a Parsi classmate, a well-known physician in Delhi, but he was at a Christmas function, and not due home before midnight. Mobile phones had not been invented. We had booked, from England, to go to a performance that evening of *Son et Lumière* at Delhi Fort. Michael was determined to get to it, despite the fact that his kidneys were not functioning. Obviously, his heart was not pumping enough blood to them. I suggested we miss the performance and stay in the hotel.

An hour before the performance, Mike said, 'Let's go. But first, give me another shot of Lasix.' Reluctantly I did so. Again, there was no response.

The taxi dropped us off at the entrance to the Red Fort. We had a little distance to walk. Mike was very out of breath. Kiran and I supported him on either side, and we walked very slowly, and took seats near the exit. The performance started. I was only aware of Mike breathing heavily next to me. After what seemed an eternity, he whispered, 'I need a pee. What shall we do?' My relief was enormous.

'Come on.' I said. 'There are some bushes nearby, and I don't care who sees us.' We took Kiran with us. It was the loudest and longest pee ever. There were some men standing close by, smiling. This was India, where nobody cares what strangers are up to. Mike immediately felt better. We took a taxi to the Moti Mahal, famous for its tandoori chicken. It was a disappointment. The legs and thighs were scrawny, and those we had eaten in the restaurant of the same name in Newcastle were much tastier.

After two days, we left by train for Agra and stayed in a comfortable hotel, from which we could see the Taj Mahal in the distance. We went to see it mid-afternoon. It was not the vast gleaming white marble structure I had imagined. It was much smaller and off-white, a softer, gentler white, delicately carved all over. It looked so vulnerable, I had a lump in my throat. I remembered what the journalist Bernard Levin had said when he first saw it, that it made him aware of the secret harmonies of the universe. The three of us just stood and looked and looked. We saw it again at daybreak the following day, when the mist was rising from the river behind.

That same night we arrived at Agra station to get the train to Madras, a journey of two nights and a day. Michael would have an enforced rest on the train. Stations on the way would be few and far between. Waiting on the platform for the train, chatting to the coolies, Mike suddenly became out of breath. I quickly filled a syringe. The platform was so badly lit I could not see a vein on Mike's arm, but Mike had large veins, which I was able to feel, and I found one and emptied the syringe into it. The improvement was dramatic. Passengers were staring at us. They must have thought we were a pair of junkies. The train arrived. Our names were on a board on the outside of the first-class compartment, with four berths. The fourth occupant was an educated man, fluent in English. We had many interesting conversations. Our bearer brought us our meals and made up our beds. Mike got into his pyjamas and stayed in them. Rail travel had not changed since the days when I went to Lucknow, nearly twenty-five years before. Kiran and Mike got down at major stations and delighted in the chaos and colour and confusion. Crossing the great Godavari River, glistening in the gibbous moon, was an awesome sight. It was the time of Indira Gandhi's Emergency, when all of India was functioning to time and order, so it was not surprising that the train arrived early into Madras Central station. The family, including Samson Uncle, were there to meet us. On seeing them, like Christian in *The Pilgrim's Progress*, I felt a great burden fall from me. It was the burden of the responsibility for Mike. This was now shared, especially with Suku, who was by this time a cardiologist of international repute.

The hip replacements were a success.

We could not return without spending a few nights at the beach at Mamallapuram. There were eight of us, including my mother and the Sukumars. Four-year-old Nandini, highly articulate and extrovert, took a great liking to Mike. He kept her entertained with a string of silly jokes. On the last evening, as usual, we sat on the sand, watching the setting sun colouring the sky with every shade of pink, orange and red. And later a huge moon arose. We were all affected by the beauty and sadness of the occasion. No one spoke, not even Nandini, sitting on Mike's lap. We were all thinking the same thing, that it was the last time for Michael.

Spending time with my mother was always precious, and I savoured the last few days at Alpha. Jessie Aunty and uncles Samson and Alfred commented on how youthful and healthy Mike looked. Jessie Aunty wept when she hugged Mike goodbye.

We arrived at Heathrow and had to clear immigration before getting the connecting flight to Newcastle. There was not much time. We were confronted by an immigration officer who did not look much more than sixteen. He started to question us in great depth. We had Indian passports and had never had any difficulty going in and out of Britain during the past fifteen years. We told him we had a connection to make. He was unimpressed. He asked for all our old passports. We looked blank. Who carries their old passports? We told him Mike was a hospital consultant in Sunderland. He continued to be unimpressed. And then I blurted out.

'My husband has been orthopaedic surgeon to the Sunderland Football Club for some years, and when they won the FA Cup in 1973.'

The immigration officer's eyes lit up. Now, he was impressed. He stamped our passports and told us to go. We made the connection. Mrs Smith met us. My relief was enormous, that we were home and had made the trip without any catastrophes.

Spring arrived. There was an increased intensity to our feelings. No longer did we take the small pleasures of life for granted. Nothing was said, but we could sense what was obvious. Mike was getting worse and now had bouts of irregular heart rhythm, called arrhythmias. He was referred to the Professor of Cardiology at Newcastle. Kindly, but a man of few words and no bedside manners, he carried out an angiogram to determine the state of Mike's coronary vessels, which supplied his heart. We heard nothing from the hospital for weeks. I arranged to go to see the professor. He matter-of-factly said that all the blood vessels were blocked, and the heart muscle severely damaged. He said nothing else. He just remained silent. I thanked him and left. I later heard that he had suffered deep personal tragedy. I told Mike that he did not need any adjustment to his treatment. He did not ask me anything about the angiogram. His only salvation was a heart transplant, but these had been suspended in Britain after the first few that were done were unsuccessful.

Mike had started to find relaxation in oil painting. Some mornings I would come downstairs and find a finished or partly done painting on the dining room table. They were superb and were usually of the South Indian countryside. That summer, there was to be an exhibition of paintings by local artists at the Light Infantry Museum in Durham. Submissions, of no more than three works per artist, were invited. Mike did not think his paintings were good enough, but Kiran and I found three of the best, and took them to Durham. There were thousands of entries, and two weeks later the best would be exhibited. Mike refused to come with us when we returned a fortnight later to scan the walls. Kiran let out a whoop of delight, when she spotted one of her father's. We rushed back to tell Mike of his success. He continued to paint, giving away many of the better paintings to friends.

At about this time, one of Mike's colleagues, AB, the flamboyant one, about the same age as Mike, became unwell. He had a split appointment, working in Sunderland as well as in the district general hospital, Dryburn Hospital, in Durham. He was found to have bowel cancer with secondary spread. Staff of both hospitals were very shaken by the news.

I was concerned that Mike was not being regularly followed up. Perhaps his cardiologist was embarrassed that he could not do any more for him. It is always difficult for a doctor to have a colleague as a patient, but Mike was very undemanding. It has always been my belief that, even if there is no further treatment available for a patient, it is extremely important to continue to see the patient and relatives regularly. This ensures that the patient does not feel neglected or abandoned. The relatives feel supported. Questions and fears can be addressed, and adjustments can be made to treatment. It is wrong to say to the patient that no more can be done. The complexity of medicine is such that this cannot always be left to the family doctor. During a troublesome episode of arrhythmia, I tried to contact Mike's cardiologist. He was on holiday. I rang the on-call physician for advice. He turned out to be Tony Martin, the renal (kidney) physician. He was also a general physician whom I knew well; we both worked in the Royal Infirmary. He gave me some advice about drug dosage. But within half an hour, he was ringing our door bell. That was the sort of person Tony was. By now Mike's symptoms had abated. Tony spent an hour chatting with Mike and admiring his paintings. He said he would call again; and he did, frequently, after that. The cardiologist did not mind Tony taking care of Mike. He said the important thing was that someone kept an eye on him.

⌇

Out of the blue, an advertisement appeared in the *British Medical Journal* for a Consultant Haematologist at Dryburn Hospital in Durham, a jewel of a medieval city, sixteen miles south-west of Sunderland. We had visited the city a few times to see its famous 1,000-year-old cathedral and to go on riverside walks. For years, Mike had said this was where he had wanted to live, and to go by boat to Sunderland. It was only a dream, as the river Wear was not navigable, and anyway he was required to live ten road miles from his place of work, as were all consultants.

Sandy and I were surprised by this development at Dryburn. We used to regularly attend regional meetings held in Newcastle, for haematologists to present interesting and difficult cases. No one had mentioned this new job. With Mike's health in such a parlous state, I decided I needed a substantive post, and I could not wait to get something in Sunderland. Sandy immediately requested the Regional Health Authority to sanction a second haematologist's post for Sunderland, but he encouraged me to apply for the Durham job, as it would take at least six months for the one in Sunderland to materialise. And then there was never any guarantee that I would get the post.

On a visit to AB, his seriously ill colleague, Mike mentioned that I was going to apply for a consultant's post in Durham. AB perked up and said, 'They will not touch Lindy with a bargepole. Dryburn Hospital has always had a strict "whites only" policy.'

'You are not to apply there and be humiliated,' said Michael. 'I'll show them,' I said.

I knew that the NHS suffered every prejudice known to man. But I was still taken aback by AB's comment. Mike would have preferred me to work in Sunderland, which was closer to his work and home. I reminded him that Durham was only half an hour away.

For the first time, Mike was prepared to discuss early retirement. 'But what will I do?' he said.

'Paint and read,' I said.

A builder friend drew up plans for an extension to the rear of the house, overlooking the garden. It would be Mike's studio.

Mike was forty-seven on 7 October 1976. Nine days later it was my birthday. I came home in the evening to find flowers everywhere—in vases, in jugs, in mugs, even in buckets. He and Kiran were excited, as it was a surprise.

'I've always meant to give you flowers on your birthday, but I've always been too busy.' He went on to say that if he had his time again, he would have lived differently. It had been work, work and more work, and there was so much he had neglected, particularly his family.

'I always thought of it as the pursuit of excellence, when all the time it was the pursuit of ego,' Mike said.

I knew he had made a big difference to people's lives, but I did not contradict him. I had seen it over and over again in male doctors, working all hours, never at home, not taking domestic responsibilities, not taking their allotted leave, and hardly ever seeing their wives and children. It often had to be this way for them as junior doctors, but was not necessary to the same extent for most consultants, though the latter carried ultimate responsibility. They all thought the same, that it was the pursuit of excellence, when a lot of the time it was an ego trip. Our good friend Benty Karat, also a Vellore graduate and an outstanding physician in Sunderland, bemoaned the fact that there were only twenty-four hours in the day. He worked such long hours that he required three secretaries. When he lay dying from cancer at the age of fifty, he quoted to me from *Ecclesiastes*: 'Vanity, vanity, all is vanity'. He too wondered why he had worked so much, and not seen more of his family.

✓

I contacted the senior physician, Robert Mowbray (RM), at Dryburn Hospital, and told him I was a prospective candidate for the Consultant Haematologist post, and asked if I could meet him and look around the hospital. He said he knew about me from the

Professor of Haematology at Newcastle and wished to meet me. We fixed a date: the morning of 21 October. Mike had sat up till the early hours typing my application, which had to be in within the next two days. He was better at typing than I was.

I drove to Durham with some trepidation, and was met by RM, a portly, grey-haired man in is sixties with tremendous presence. I could see that he could be intimidating. He was very influential in the Northern Region Health Authority, and sat on appointment committees for consultants throughout the region. He ran Dryburn Hospital as he thought fit, and was responsible for attracting medical students from the Newcastle teaching hospitals, who later came back as junior doctors, something that other district general hospitals in the region were not able to do so successfully. The haematology post was a new one, and RM asked me what ideas I had to develop a new department. He knew about Mike's ill health, and spoke about it with some feeling. I sensed that he was sincere. After the two hours I was with RM, I felt I had established a rapport with him. But what he thought about me, I had no idea. He gave nothing away.

Instead of going back to work, I stopped off at Sandalwood and was surprised to see Mike walking around the house, inspecting the recent building work outside. I thought to myself how young and fit he looked. His health had improved significantly since Tony Martin had taken over his care and adjusted his drugs. He had not required intravenous injections from me for some weeks. I was sure Tony could keep him going until heart transplants were being done in Britain again. Mike suggested we have a light lunch before we went back to work. He told me he would be operating all afternoon. I told him about my visit to Durham. After lunch, we got into our respective cars, waved to each other and drove off.

I had asked Kiran to come to my hospital after school. We did some shopping after I had finished work, buying some veal at the local delicatessen. We then went home and did what we always did, Kiran her homework, and I, getting the supper ready, while Mike rested upstairs. The veal was a treat for him. A couple of hours later, I asked Kiran to go upstairs to wake him up. I heard her scream. I knew the worst had happened. Mike lay dead on the bedroom floor. I closed his eyes, and took Kiran downstairs. We sat in silence for a while, and then I rang Mike's friend Sandy Dow, a consultant colleague, who had gone out of his way to befriend us when we first arrived in Sunderland six years earlier. He and Michael shared an interest in oil painting and often viewed each other's efforts, each heaping praise on the other.

Sandy Dow arrived, and telephoned Michael's family and others who needed to know. Mike's senior registrar spoke to my family in India. Sandy did all the formalities.

'You will be all right, Lindy,' was all my mother said.

Sleep did not come that night. It is not that I was completely unprepared. A hundred times I had thought of this moment, and how it might happen. But what I had not anticipated was this overwhelming sense of finality. The shutters had come down forever. My thoughts were mainly about Kiran. When Mike had his heart attack two years earlier, I decided that whatever happened to him, I would not let it blight her life. And now, I felt the same. I would do everything possible to allow her to flourish. I remember my mother telling us, when Ann and I were in our teens, that one good parent was enough for a child to grow up satisfactorily. Mike and I had drifted into agnosticism after the Kolar fiasco. Belief came and went. We encouraged Kiran to go to church with Mike's mother, who was a regular churchgoer. Neither Kiran nor I had any sense of Mike's presence after his death, but he would live on in our thoughts and memories and we often talked about him.

It was intended that the funeral service at the Methodist church at the end of our road be private. This was ignored. The church was packed. Members of the Sunderland football team carried Mike's coffin. The entire team and the manager, Bob Stokoe, were there. The memorial service was held a few weeks later. Sandy Dow spoke movingly about Mike, and at his insistence several of Mike's paintings were displayed at the entrance to the church. Several very elderly patients came up to me to say Mike had got them back on to their feet, and had given them back their lives. I remember Mike telling me a few years earlier, before his heart attack, that some of his anaesthetists had asked him why he was operating on eighty-year-old patients, and he had replied, 'So that they can throw away their wheelchairs. And who knows, some of them might even outlive me.'

All of Mike's four siblings and their families were at the funeral. They were devastated by his death, not having realised how ill he was. I had told them repeatedly of the seriousness of his illness, and asked them to come to visit us. But because he kept on working, and he looked so well when he visited them, they did not give it much thought. Mike's mother did not attend the funeral. She had had a minor stroke two years earlier, and this was the reason she gave, but I think it was more because she was so deeply upset. She was now living with Owen, her youngest son, and his Irish wife. Mike's mother wrote me a long letter and apologised for her attitude towards me and Kiran, and said how wrong she had been. She thought Mike was very fortunate to have married me. I felt sorry for her, that she had outlived one of her children, a grief not to be surpassed.

I was relieved when our friends Benty and Shaku Karat insisted that after the funeral we spend a week with them in Hoylake, near Liverpool. The clocks had gone back, and I did not relish the thought of long dark evenings at home, in our unlit road, Bridle Path. A few years earlier, the bodies of two eleven-year-old girls had been dumped in the ditch running along opposite our house, and we relied on Mike to make us feel safe.

Kiran and I returned to Sandalwood to the routine of our lives. Various friends came to spend evenings with us. One of them, an accountant, on whom Mike had done a tricky operation, insisted on looking after probate and my financial affairs. Sandy Mackenzie gave the lawn its last cut for the season. There was no end to people's kindnesses and the letters of condolence we received. Esther Shoemaker of Kolar, now retired in America, said she had deeply regretted the way she had treated Mike, and had realised her mistake in letting him leave Kolar.

Michael's ashes were immersed in the sea off north-west Scotland by Tony Martin, when he was on one of his naval exercises. He was a Surgeon Commander in the Royal Navy Reserve.

Almost immediately, a letter arrived from my mother to say she was arriving to spend the next six months with us. I was concerned that she was leaving Alpha and Tony, the Alsation, for such a length of time. They were devoted to each other. But Alfred Uncle and the servants reassured her that all would be well. As always, I felt a great sense of relief when she arrived. And she was such excellent company. She took over the running of the house, and was obviously delighted to be back in England. She renewed her friendship with Mrs Smith, who was no longer our cleaner. She had always wanted to work in a shop and as she was developing arthritis, we encouraged her to move on. Her replacement was nothing like her. Very talkative, she took to invading the drinks cupboard. I did not remonstrate with her as I needed her services.

Chapter 26

LIFE RENEWED

I received a letter to say I had been shortlisted for the interview for the Haematology consultant's post, but if the given date was not convenient, in view of my recent bereavement, the interview would be held at a later date. I wrote back to say this was not necessary. Sandy was very encouraging as I set off for Newcastle for the interview. I was not as well prepared as I would have liked to have been. The other candidate was a pleasant man from one of the London hospitals. My interview lasted about forty-five minutes. There were no awkward questions or silences. At the end of it, I felt I could have done a lot better. The other candidate and I chatted while we waited for the decision. He was younger and considerably less experienced than I was. After a short wait I was called back, and offered the post by the Chairman. I accepted it, of course. A letter of confirmation would arrive later. The Chairman was Master of University College, one of the Durham University colleges, situated in the ancient Durham Castle. During the interview, he showed interest at my having been born in Rangoon. It transpired that he had been a young lecturer in Judson College in Rangoon, at the time my mother was there as an undergraduate. Had I a crystal ball, I could have told him that in ten years' time I would be one of the first women in his male-only College to be invited to become a member of the Senior Common Room.

Robert Mowbray congratulated me warmly and said they would waive the rule which required consultants to live within ten road miles of the base hospital. If I wished, I could continue to live in Sunderland, sixteen miles from Durham. As this was a new post, I could start at any time. My contract stated that I was to provide and develop haematological services in Durham. It was for thirty-seven and a half hours a week, which was the standard period for full-time consultants. Every consultant knew this was a farce. I would work fifty to sixty hours a week and be permanently on call. If I wanted to be away at any time, consultants in Newcastle and Sunderland would cover me. Locums would be provided for me during my holidays.

When I returned home from the interview, my mother did not ask me about the outcome. After a little while, I said, 'I got the job.'

'I knew you would,' she said. Her confidence in me never wavered.

∫

I decided to make a clean break with Sunderland. I would live in Durham. I would not apply for the Sunderland consultant post, which Sandy assured me would be advertised within six months. Kiran, who was due to sit her O-level exams that year, would then leave her present school, and go to a different school in Newcastle for the next two years and take the A-level exams. I had always regretted that when she passed the 11+ test, we did not send her to the outstanding Grammar School in Sunderland. At her headmistress's insistence, we kept her on in the private school she was attending.

∫

I had to sell Sandalwood and find a house in Durham. Several months earlier, Mike had shown me an advertisement in our local paper for a new development of townhouses in Durham. They had views of Durham cathedral and castle from almost every room. If I worked in Durham and he retired, that was where he wanted to live.

I went to have a look at these houses in Briardene, but the five that were nearing completion had already been reserved. The next phase would not be ready for a year, and I could not wait. I was told there was a house available on a parallel street, the most desirable street in Durham, cobbled and overlooking the cathedral. The owner wanted a quick sale. The estate agent took me to see it on a bitterly cold day in December. The steep street was covered with a sheet of ice. I refused to get out of the car. That street was not for me. A few days later, the retired Archbishop of Canterbury, Michael Ramsey, who lived on this street, slipped on the ice and appeared on local television with two black eyes. A few days later, I was driving past Briardene when I saw a 'For Sale' notice on one of the reserved houses. The potential buyer had withdrawn that very morning. I quickly put a deposit on it to reserve it, and hoped my mother and Kiran would approve. Cleverly built on a slope, the four-bedroom town house was on four half floors, with magnificent views of Durham cathedral and castle from nearly every room and from the small walled garden, which had a wrought iron gate. Kiran was delighted with it, but my mother was not so sure, as it was not detached. But she agreed that because of my distaste for being alone at night, it was right for me. Sandalwood was sold to a family doctor in the village.

My time at Sunderland was coming to an end. My successor had been appointed. When I said goodbye to Sandy, he said, 'Honey, I will miss you dreadfully. You have taught me so much haematology. Don't forget, I expect you back.'

I started my job in Durham at the beginning of March, but our move to Durham would not be till the summer. I was greeted warmly by Robert Mowbray (RM) and the older of the two pathologists. The latter was an old-style pathologist who had dabbled in all four disciplines. The younger one, who had been appointed recently, could be abrasive but was exceptionally competent and already beginning to make a significant difference to the quality of work being put out by his department. The chief lab scientific officer (MLSO) in Haematology was in her fifties and had a reputation for being cantankerous. I trod carefully and kept my head down, and we soon became good friends. There were about eight other MLSO's, some of them extraordinarily able. If only they had had proper guidance and encouragement in their early years, some of them could have become doctors. The overall standard of the lab was poor. It was so different from the excellence I had been used to in Sunderland.

I shared two wards with other physicians. There were two other woman consultants, one of them newly appointed. The sister in charge of the male ward, Sister Pat as she was called, was abrupt and certainly not polite. She sat most of the time in her office, in a haze of cigarette smoke, chain-smoking from the time she arrived to the time she left. She gave short, crisp directions to her nursing and domestic staff. Junior doctors were scared of her. When I first arrived on her ward, there was a brief, hard handshake.

'We managed all these years with two consultants,' she remarked. 'Now, we suddenly have four. I cannot understand why. I'm afraid I'm much too busy to accompany you on your ward rounds.'

'That's all right, sister,' I replied. 'Just give me a junior staff nurse. I can manage with her, and the two junior doctors. I don't need you.' She glared at me.

I always believed that ward rounds were not only for a face-to-face exchange of information for all concerned, but were for education and entertainment as well. All of us, patients included, often had a good laugh together. More and more nurses joined my round, and one day I saw Sister Pat's head bobbing up and down at the back of the group. She was laughing. After that, she came regularly on my round, and we developed a warm relationship. She did, however, gently reprimand me from time to time. I regularly went on to the wards for a few hours at weekends. The first Sunday, I disconnected a patient's intravenous drip so that he could go home for Sunday lunch.

She said, 'Just what do you think you are doing? Can't you see the patient is on intravenous antibiotics?'

'Sister,' I said, 'does it really matter whether his antibiotics are delayed for a few hours? You and I know he is not going to be around in six months' time. Let his family have some good memories.' She became an advocate of 'Sunday lunch leave'.

I took my lunch in the doctors' dining room. Consultants had their own tables, and it was a good opportunity to get to know everyone. The conversation could be interesting. Medical problems were discussed and often resolved. The background of consultants was varied, and I realised that in subtle ways class was alive and well. My colleagues were friendly and very helpful. Robert Mowbray would often come to my office in the evening for a chat and to find out how I was getting on. We had a common interest in gardening. He would describe the magnificent Magnolia soulangeana in his large south-facing garden. I told him I was intending to plant the smaller stellata variety in mine, as I had read it was more suited to northern climes. He was also a collector of books of medical history, and had a large room in his seventeenth-century Georgian house that he used as a library. Neither he nor I could have imagined then that decades later I would live in this beautiful house in the heart of the city.

⌒

It was spring once more and time for renewal and hope. We felt Mike's absence acutely. My mother was peering into all corners of the garden, looking for new shoots and buds. She was in her element, and looking forward to another visit to the Chelsea Flower Show in May. Kiran was preparing for her O-level exams. For the past three months my mother had made her read *The Times* leaders and précis them. This was to improve her written English. It paid off as she passed with an A grade in the subject.

My mother was constantly encouraging me to do things I had not done before. Michael was an expert D-I-Y man, with the result that I was the opposite. So I was learning to put in light bulbs, run up ladders and mend fuses, as was Kiran. I was not a natural driver, and had never driven anything other than very small cars, but my mother insisted that I sell my mini and start using Mike's Peugeot shooting brake. Furthermore, she said it was a disgrace that we had never visited the Lake District, and set about planning a trip in the Peugeot for the three of us and Dougal. And we were to go through the Kirkstone Pass as well, which I did manage with some trepidation. For my mother, going to Wordsworth's grave was a special moment.

On 27 July, my mother's seventieth birthday, we left Sandalwood and moved to Briardene. I was determined never to take for granted the inspiring view from our house of Durham cathedral and castle, floodlit every night. The river Wear enters and leaves Durham in a loop, forming a peninsula high above the city. The cathedral and castle sit in this peninsula and are separated by a turfed expanse known as Palace Green.

I wondered what our immediate neighbours would be like, and how they would feel about us as neighbours. Durham was very much a white city. There was hardly a brown or black face to be seen, and when there was, it belonged to a doctor or a member of the university staff. I need not have worried. Ed and Maureen Potter were splendid people, both school teachers, with a young son. From a mining background, they were ambitious and assertive and had reached the top of their professions. Constantly asking if they could do anything for us, they carried out endless tasks, making our move painless. Ed relished my mother's cooking, and dishes of curry were frequently passed across the back garden's fence. Neighbours were tolerant of Dougal's intrusions into their open-plan front garden. Our garden was little more than a builder's yard, but with Ed Potter's help my mother and I laid a lawn, dug flower beds and stocked them with plants from the local nursery.

Kiran started at a new school in Newcastle. Now sixteen, she was a slim, attractive young girl with wavy shoulder-length hair. Every morning, she walked to Durham station and joined a group of girls and boys on the fifteen-minute train ride to Newcastle. The journey there and back seemed to be the highlight of their day.

At about this time, Sandy Mackenzie informed me that the Haematology consultant's post was about to be advertised. I told him my reasons for wanting to remain in Durham. And then I received a letter from the Director of my medical school and hospital in Vellore, inviting me to join another haematologist, already there, to set up a new department of clinical haematology. I was sorely tempted to accept. I had not lost my desire to return to India. Kiran's schooling would be disrupted, but there were excellent boarding schools in India. My mother had no hesitation in advising me against such thoughts.

'As a widow, your life will be easier in the West,' she said. 'Even among educated Indians, single women and widows have a diminished status. You will have a far more fulfilling life in England. It is such a wonderful country, not just its natural beauty, but its liberal attitudes, tolerance, sense of discipline, justice and humour. And they queue. Where else will you find all this?'

What my mother said was true. In the months after Mike's death, I was offered much hospitality by my British friends and colleagues, which I readily accepted. I was grateful that they were often prepared to have their table seating plans disrupted. It led to some unwelcome remarks from some Indian friends and colleagues. 'What! You are already going out?' But I knew that in England, too, widows had their problems. A recently widowed English friend told me her social life had collapsed. This was a very couple-orientated society, and some considered widows predatory. In the months and years to follow my social circle would expand considerably, not least when I was offered membership of Senior Common Rooms of two colleges in Durham University. I had lived ten years in England, and had come to know the ins and outs of middle-class living. I even knew all about U and non-U. But it would be a few more years before, while on a visit to see my mother in India, I had a sudden pang of homesickness for England. I had turned the corner. No longer would I yearn to return to India. Mike would have been pleased.

⁓

We were approaching the first anniversary of Mike's death. The pain of remembering him had not abated. One morning, there was a phone call from his sister, Delicia, to say that Desmond, their older brother, a pilot in Canada, had died suddenly. He was fifty-two and, like Mike, a heavy smoker.

My mother's stay, extended to twelve months, was coming to an end. Frequent letters from Alfred Uncle and Ann had assured her that all was well in Alpha. A date in early December was set for her departure. Undaunted by strict Indian customs regulations, which prohibited plants and creatures from entering the country, she had decided what she was going to take with her. There was a tiny live terrapin for six-year-old Nandini, her granddaughter. For herself, there were green houseplants which would quadruple in size in her tropical garden, white gerberas and two rose plants: Peace and Queen Elizabeth. When I remonstrated with her she said, 'Every known pest and disease exists in India. What do they think I can possibly bring in from Britain?' She had a point.

Before we left Durham, she said, 'I hope you will not marry again. You have a rewarding job, a good salary, a lovely daughter and several wonderful friends. If you marry, you will end up washing his socks, cooking his dinner and doing as he wants.'

We took a train named the Flying Scotsman from Newcastle to London. My mother, with her zest for life, wanted the thrill of travelling in this particular train, even though it was not the most convenient, and not the original Flying Scotsman. Next morning, Delicia drove Kiran, my mother and me to Heathrow Airport.

'You will come back to England soon?' we begged.

'Of course,' she said. 'Many more times.'

And as she disappeared through immigration, I remembered the last few lines from her favourite author:

> But the effect of her being on those around her was incalculably diffuse: for the growing good of the world is partly dependent on unhistoric acts; and that things are not so ill with you and me as they might have been, is half owing to the number who lived faithfully a hidden life and rest in hidden tombs.

George Eliot

She never returned.

Durham
December 2011

POSTSCRIPT

When I showed the unpublished text of this book to a few friends, they were curious as to what happened to the main characters. Decades have elapsed since the book ends in 1977.

My mother, Alice Rajan, died unexpectedly in her sleep in December 1988, at the age of eighty-one, just a few hours before my plane from London was due to touch down in Madras, for my annual visit. She was active, fit, and well until the end.

Ann, my sister, died in 1990, at the age of fifty-one, from a rare lung disease. Her husband, Suku, had died five years earlier, unexpectedly, while at a conference in Australia. Their children, aged twenty-three and eighteen, became part of my family. Mithran is now a professor of thoracic surgery in Portland, Oregon. His wife Shirin, like him, is also a Vellore graduate. Their daughters are Anika and Rhea. His sister, Nandini, graduated from Edinburgh University and works in the world of finance.

Samson Uncle and Jessie Aunty lived into their eighties. He was devotedly cared for by nuns in a Catholic nursing home and she, by her daughters.

Kiran did a degree in business and married Richard Gommo, an Englishman and an investment banker. Their three children—triplets—were born in November 1997, a week after I retired. Kiran, eventually like her Indian grandmother, qualified as a teacher.

In 1989, thirteen years after I was widowed and seven months after my mother's death, I married Alan Piper, a medieval historian at Durham University. My mother knew of my friendship with him. His mother had been my patient, and he liked to say that ours was an arranged marriage.

March 2014

ACKNOWLEDGEMENTS

I would like to thank the following friends for generously providing me with help, advice and encouragement: Sheila and Vir Narain; Narayani Ganesh; Vrinda Narain; and Ann Lloyd-Taylor. For technical help, I thank Simon Higgins, Maurice Landsberger, and my grandson Seb. My daughter Kiran has given unstintingly of her time and advice; my granddaughter India's enthusiasm and interest during this writing journey has helped me persevere.

I would also like to thank Aienla Ozukum and Vidisha Ghosh at Aleph Book Company for getting this book ready for publication.

Finally, but not least, I want to thank Santhosh Matthew Paul, son of Amy Chaly, my late friend and room-mate at medical college. He encouraged me to approach Aleph Book Company. He has shown endless patience in going through the text and suggesting corrections and enhancements.

TRIBUTE TO ALAN PIPER

But for Alan Piper, my husband of twenty-three years, this book would not have been finished. During the fourteen years it took to write, he coaxed, cajoled, and bullied me to get back to it when my enthusiasm and effort waned, and this was a frequent occurrence. A medieval historian and archivist, he had already been published extensively, his most notable work being *Medieval Manuscripts in British Libraries, Volume IV*.

Younger than me, he died suddenly and unexpectedly, while I was on a short visit to Delhi with my daughter and granddaughter, two months after I had finished the book in long hand. He did not read it in its entirety, but knew every story in it, and particularly enjoyed those about India, a country to which I introduced him and which he loved. On a visit to China, I pointed out to him the cleanliness, orderliness, and discipline of their cities, and wished India could emulate some of this, to which he replied, 'But India has a soul'.

On our visits to India, he showed me places and wonders I did not know existed, as he did on our trips to Europe and Turkey.

Wise, witty, warm, and charming, he did not suffer fools gladly. Probably the cleverest and rudest man in Durham, he enriched my life immeasurably.

DRAMATIS PERSONAE

Mr Adrian Bain: consultant orthopaedic surgeon, Sunderland

Dr Alan Barlow: consultant haematologist, Huddersfield

Dr Alan Gibbs: senior house officer, Stoke Mandeville

Alfred Wason: Alice's younger brother

Alice Wason: Lindy's mother

Ann Cartner: Mike's mother

Ann(e) Rajan: Lindy's older sister

Dr Anne Collins: registrar, Blood Transfusion Service, Newcastle upon Tyne

Dr Asirvatham: professor of medical jurisprudence and toxicology, Vellore

Miss Beavers: headmistress, Kimmins School, Panchgani

Dr Bertie Pereira: general practitioner, S.E. London

Charlene Chitambar: Lindy's friend at IT

Mr Charles Robb: consultant orthopaedic surgeon, Sunderland

Cheena aka P. R. Stanislaus: family friend

Daniel Rajan: Lindy's father

Mr David Brown: consultant orthopaedic surgeon, Sunderland

Davis Wason: Alice's older brother

Dawn Antram: Lindy's friend and classmate at Vellore

Delicia Cartner: Mike's younger sister

Desmond Cartner: Mike's brother

Dorothea Graham: professor of anatomy, Vellore

Dougal: Kiran's miniature dachshund

Edward Wason: Alice's older brother

Edwin Wason: Edward and Violet Wason's son

Eldon Walker (Don): Delicia's husband

Elizabeth (Betty) Josephs: Lindy's friend at Bishop Cottons

Ernest Wason: Edward and Violet Wason's son

Miss Falloon: Lindy's headmistress, Doveton Corrie School, Madras, India

Geoffrey Cartner: Mike's brother

Miss Hardy: Lindy's headmistress, Bishop Cotton Girls' School, Bangalore, India

Dr I. P. Sukumar (Suku): Vellore graduate. Married Ann Rajan in 1963

Ian Harrison: neighbour in Sunderland

Dr Ida S. Scudder: founder of Christian Medical College and Hospital (CMC and CMCH), Vellore, South India

Dr J. C. David: professor of pharmacology, Principal, CMC, Vellore

James Cartner: Mike's father

Jessie Wason: Alice's younger sister

Dr John Lloyd-Hart: consultant physician, Stoke Mandeville

John Webb: professor of paediatrics, Vellore

Kiran Cartner: Lindy and Mike's daughter

Leela Singh: Lindy's friend at IT and in Bombay

Leonie Whitlock: Lindy's friend at Bishop Cottons

Lindy Cartner aka Rosalind Rajan: the author

Margot Harrison: neighbour in Sunderland

Maureen Bowell: Lindy's friend at Bishop Cottons

Dr Michael (Mike) Cartner: graduate of CMC Vellore; married Lindy in 1960

Mithran Sukumar: Ann and Suku's son, born 1966

Nandini Sukumar: Ann and Suku's daughter, born 1971

Owen Cartner: Mike's brother

Paati aka Annie Wason: Lindy's maternal grandmother

Paul Brand: hand surgeon and professor of surgery, Vellore

Miss Pharaoh: Lindy's form mistress, Doveton Corrie

Rabindranath Azariah: final-year student and Lindy's stage partner at CMC

Rahat Ahmad: Lindy's friend at IT

Dr Robert Mowbray: consultant physician, Durham

Mr Robin Tagart: consultant surgeon, Newmarket, UK

Dr Roda Allison: consultant pathologist, Huddersfield

Rosalind Wason aka Biggy: Alice's Wason's older sister

S. R.: Lindy's friend, pilot, and engineer in the Indian Air Force

Samson Wason: Alice's older brother

Dr Sandy Dow: consultant, casualty department, Sunderland

Dr Sandy Mackenzie: consultant haematologist, Sunderland

Sarah Chakko: principal at Isabella Thoburn College (IT), Lucknow

Mr Schmelz: consultant obstetrician and gynecologist, Isle of Sheppey

Selwyn Baker: professor of medicine, Vellore

Sheila Soota: Lindy's friend at IT

Shubha Divekar: Lindy's friend at IT

Sucie Amritaraj: Lindy's paternal first cousin. Married Alfred Wason

Thatha aka E. G. Wason: Lindy's maternal grandfather

Thomas Wason: Alice's younger brother

Tom Wason: Edward and Violet Wason's son

Velu: deputy cook and relative

Violet Wason: Edward Wason's wife

Miss Yelland: headmistress, Kimmins School, Panchgani

INDEX